IMAGINE

Using mental imagery to reach
your full potential

IMAGINE

Using mental imagery to reach your full potential

Lydia Ievleva PhD

BIG SKY PUBLISHING
www.bigskypublishing.com.au

Big Sky Publishing Pty Ltd

PO Box 303, Newport, NSW 2106, Australia

Phone: 1300 364 611

Fax: (61 2) 9918 2396

Email: info@bigskypublishing.com.au

Web: www.bigskypublishing.com.au

Cover design and typesetting: Think Productions
Printed in China by Asia Pacific Offset Ltd.

National Library of Australia Cataloguing-in-Publication entry (pbk)

Author: Ievleva, Lydia, author.

Title: Imagine : using mental imagery to reach your full potential / Dr Lydia Ievleva.

ISBN: 9781922132420 (paperback)

Subjects: Active imagination.
            Imagination.
            Positive psychology.
            Self-actualization (Psychology)

Dewey Number: 158.1

National Library of Australia Cataloguing-in-Publication entry (ebook)

Author: Ievleva, Lydia, author.

Title: Imagine : using mental imagery to reach your full potential / Dr Lydia Ievleva.

ISBN: 9781922132437 (ebook)

Subjects: Active imagination.
            Imagination.
            Positive psychology.
            Self-actualization (Psychology)

Dewey Number: 158.1

Imagine elegantly and eloquently expresses in words what is beyond language - the brain thinks in pictures. It provides easy-to-understand scientific validation from neuroscience and quantum physics that your history is not your destiny. It encourages the reader to take full creative control and provides **practical** steps to do so. This book is a must read for my clients.

Dominique Beck, PhD, ICF, Neuroscience-Based Coach,
Corporate Trainer and Keynote Speaker.

At the heart of many strategies from positive psychology, sport psychology and personal development, lies the ability to use imagery - at last a resource that actually teaches us the nuts and bolts of how to develop the skills of mental imagery! This book is an important contribution and a valuable tool for anyone working towards becoming their 'best self'.

Susy Reading, B Psych (Hons), M Psych,
Psychology, Yoga, Health & Fitness Training.

In *Imagine*, Lydia applies her strength of integrating information across various fields, and links neuroscience with positive psychology and the psychology of health and human performance. In doing so, she presents up to date research and practical information that positions mental imagery as a key ingredient for enhancing wellbeing and success.

Prof Marc Cohen, Professor of Health Sciences and
Program Leader for the Master of Wellness at RMIT University, Board
Member and Past President of the Australasian Integrative Medicine
Association and Board member of the Global Spa and Wellness Summit.

CONTENTS

Acknowledgements

I am ever so grateful to everyone who supported and shared in bringing *Imagine* to life. Special thanks to:

My Mum – Zina Ijewliw for believing in me and supporting me when I needed it most – and without asking; and for being a wonderful example of forgiveness and transcendence. And to my father Dmytro Kyslycia-Ijewliw – who resembles who most? for your unconditional love and acceptance, not to mention heritage of your writing genes. Was a privilege to share in your journey onward.

To my big sister Olga Ijewliw (Olya) who provided valuable feedback on early drafts of the book; and for finally seeing me in the image of an adult with something worth listening to.

To Ludmilla Temertey, my virtual couzinka (and beloved Godmother Raia's daughter) – for your consistently enthusiastic encouragement and advice – you're a soul sister to me. Your support has meant so much to me.

To my boy Zenko – who was conceived at same time as this book – one of life's magical coincidences, and who has been essential for maintaining my levity and equanimity.

To my darling Phaedre – who trained me to communicate via images with her (aka dog whispering).

Acknowledgements

To my mentors, colleagues and promoters along the way – beginning with my university training and practice: John Partington (who supervised my Honours thesis about mental imagery) without whose recommendation I'd never have made it into grad school! And who ignited belief in my potential; to Terry Orlick who taught me so much about reaching my target/s, and for providing the opportunities to develop my craft, to *embrace my potential*. To Cal Botterill who enabled reaching the pinnacle forum for my material on mental skills applied to injury rehabilitation in a medical textbook; To David Pargman who allowed me to cultivate my free spirit to further develop my knowledge and skills whose praise I'll always cherish.

To Peter Terry – my colleague at the helm of the APS College of Sport and Exercise Psychologists who's jovial collegiality is matched by seriousness of purpose and commitment to excellence. Your humour always hits the mark and buoys my spirit.

To Eugene Aidman (Zhenia) – my co-editor at *The Sporting Mind* newsletter – with whom it was a joy to collaborate and hone my editing skill.

To Vicki de Prazer – for challenging my perspectives and re-igniting my interest in promoting mental imagery beyond the sport and performance domain. Our collaboration has certainly raised the bar and been rewarding accordingly.

To Jane Henderson – who's friendship I've counted on to keep me on track both professionally and personally. Where's the next conference rendezvous?

To Suzanne Murphy whose friendship and support was integral to embarking on becoming a professional writer.

To Rebecca Long, editor of *Women's Health & Fitness* magazine – who introduced me to her readers as a monthly columnist. I'm in awe of your skill and flare in distilling massively technical information into sumptuous bite-size morsels.

To Carmen Nicotra of *PDP Seminars* – for providing a platform for sharing my material amongst other professionals that has enabled a ripple effect far and wide.

To Sera Nelson of *The Channel Group* – who gave me my first shot at infiltrating the corporate world with my mental imagery material and video blog.

To Liz Cook of ZHUCHI – who has provided the opportunity to take my mental imagery workshop material farther and wider across Australia.

To my colleagues in the Masters of Wellness program at RMIT University (especially our leader Marc Cohen) – where I've finally found my teaching home, that affords and enables me to continue my professional growth and expansion in alignment with my highest principles; not to mention providing an ideal forum for integrating and sharing my knowledge and experience with the most enlightened group of students I could ever hope for.

To my clients and workshop participants -- without whom this book would be meaningless, not to mention non-existent – who have courageously experimented with my mental imagery advice. I cannot imagine a greater honour and privilege than to have been a part of your inspiring journeys!

To my students who have gamely undertaken my experiments disguised as assignments incorporating the practice of mental imagery. I appreciate the insights you've shared.

To Suzy Reading – for her consistently enthusiastic and positive vibe. You are such a treasure!

To DG, for being my super tonic as I finally brought this baby home! Who has long captured my imagination not to mention my heart. Here's to youthing!

To many others who've taken interest in this project who've come and gone, but who's presence, support and influence in my life will be cherished always – if only for getting this classic writer/recluse out of the house to play!

Acknowledgements

Last and foremost – to the team at Big Sky Publishing, especially Diane Evans, Sharon Evans and Denny Neave -- for taking a chance on me and nurturing my book – may it facilitate all of us reaching our full potential!

Introduction

Welcome, readers! Welcome to unleashing your imagination on this journey to discovering and creating your best self.

Thank you for joining me on a journey that will show you how you can use the power of your imagination to discover and create your best self. This book is not about thinking of riches and rewards and having them magically appear — it shows you proven and scientifically based techniques that will help you use mental imagery to achieve change and results in your life. Whether you are seeking to improve your health, performance in sports, business or on stage, how you react to challenges, or any number of lifestyle changes, this book is for you.

Being and Doing Better

This book isn't about becoming the best, but about being the best you can be and reaching your potential. But becoming your best self possible is a process. As the saying goes: It's more about the journey than the destination. And there's no telling if and when we'll ever get there, as we are all projects in progress. As long as we're alive and kicking there's growth and development, and greater potential in store for us. The best we can hope for is staying on track for longer stretches, catching ourselves sooner when veering off, recovering efficiently and getting back on our best course quickly. The best we can hope for is just getter better at it.

While most of how we know that we're on track is based on our actions — on our doing; much of it really depends on how we're feeling — on our being. However, our being (and wellbeing) often gets neglected when we get caught up in all we're doing in our race to achieving. It is said that we ought to be called human doings rather than human beings, based on how we tend to define ourselves more by what we do.

What You See Is What You Get! (WYSIWYG)

Your imagination is one of the most powerful inner mental resources for self-development. It is especially effective for facilitating and accelerating change — whether adapting to change, or changing how you think, act (and react) and feel. Change of any kind doesn't come easy. As they say, old habits die hard; and the best predictor of future behaviour is past behaviour. But history need not be your destiny. You can harness the power of imagination to increase your chances of success, or you can leave success to chance.

You can think of imagery like a screenplay — you can allow life to play you (by reacting according to old and sometimes faulty programming and conditioning); or you can take a more active role in your destiny (by creating new programming and evolving). Actively and consciously creating your inner scripts, bolstered by engaging in positive mental imagery will enhance your chances of reaching your full potential, overcoming obstacles, and flourishing. You will become more adept at getting on track with real confidence towards reaching your destination. You will also enhance your capacity for recovering from setbacks, transcending negative patterns, and transforming lessons from your past.

Best to take creative control of your images,
lest they get the best of you.

Much of how we are and what we do is dictated by images of our mind. We tend to think, feel, and behave consistently with whatever self-image is most dominant at the time. We tend to re-create outer conditions to match our inner conditions. This explains how most lotto winners are in worse debt than ever within one year of their big win.

> *Imagination is more important than knowledge.*
> – Albert Einstein

The advantage of practising mental imagery[1] is that it affords us the opportunity to practise that which we have little experience with. In doing so, we are actually boosting our inner repertoire as the brain cannot tell the difference between what is perceived to be real or imagined (based on fMRI studies). Therefore whatever you imagine registers as actual experience and the information data base of your reality. Of course, there are natural limitations, and this must be tested in real situations.

So, if you would prefer to be more in control over your destiny, and less victim to your (unconscious) fears, then you need to take better control over the images of your mind. Such that, rather than reacting to situations and events, you are in stronger position of creating according to the script you'd prefer to operate from.

> *Everything you can imagine is real.* – Pablo Picasso

Neuroscience has demonstrated that mental imagery is a far more powerful technique than standard cognitive behavioural techniques (CBT) that involve self-talk and affirmations. The reach of mental imagery extends far beyond words, and is the major portal of your brain for transformation and quantum leaping.

Technically, according to the science, applying mental imagery is virtually applied neuroplasticity.

A Guide to Reading This Book

As the purpose of this book is to provide a practical guide, it is organised into three parts to make it easy to follow and obtain the information you need. While there is logic and reason to the order in which the chapters appear they don't have to be read in that order.

And you don't have to read every chapter to benefit and maximise personal results. Many of you will find that some material suits your particular needs and aims better than others. You will, however, gain a better understanding of the mental imagery process, as well as best practice, by taking in all the information contained in this book. Each chapter is best understood in context of the whole.

You might also notice a bit of repetition as key points do bear repeating and integrating into other components of this book. And there's no telling whether you'll have missed it the first time round. There is also quite a bit of cross-referencing to indicate where similar information is covered within a different context.

Part 1: is about building the case for practising mental imagery, by first explaining the concept of mental imagery and its relationship to other mental processes. This part then goes on to explain mental imagery within the context of positive psychology — a field that has exploded in the self-development arena. Finally I have provided an overview of the scientific support of mental imagery for those interested in the evidence base for the practice.

Part 2: provides guidelines for building a sound foundation for your mental imagery practice, beginning with goal setting that is essential for determining your best course; followed by plenty of general advice for optimising your mental imagery practice and developing your imagery skill; and concluding with how to practise mental imagery in groups to gain synergistic value and benefit.

Part 3: is the more practical section of the book, and outlines specific mental imagery techniques and objectives, beginning with the best place to start by reconnecting to previous best experiences; then connecting with your potential; followed by how to undo old habits and hardwiring (emotional reactivity) to developing better ways of being and responding to challenges; concluding with a final chapter that puts it altogether covering how to apply mental imagery across a wide spectrum of personal and professional endeavours and pursuits. This is the part that will guide you to practising mental imagery and reaping the benefits immediately.

The *Appendices* is a compilation of all the guided imagery scripts referred to within the chapters in one place for your convenience; as well as other related activities also mentioned (e.g. positive psychology in practice).

CD and *MP3 recordings* of the guided imagery scripts are also available (from www.bigskypublishing.com.au), the better for allowing your imagination to roam free, rather than having to stop and read each line as you go about your practice. Available recordings are listed the the *Appendices*.

Here's to going where you've never been before … Happy travels!

PART 1

About Mental Imagery

Chapter 1
Defining Mental Imagery

Imagination is more important than knowledge.– Albert Einstein

Your imagination is one of the most powerful inner mental resources for self-development and change. This first chapter introduces you to the concept and practice of mental imagery. You will:

- Be encouraged to be more in charge of your life script and influences
- Become more aware of how your competing inner agendas and scripts affect you
- Understand how mental imagery relates to other mental processes
- Learn what mental imagery is and is not; what it can and cannot do for you
- Learn what interferes with mental imagery, and what approaches are conducive to mental imagery practice

Congratulations on taking this step to becoming more in charge of your destiny! You can liken it to writing the screenplay of your life — you can allow life to play you (by reacting according to old and sometimes faulty programming and conditioning), or you can take a more active role in determining your destiny (by creating new programming and evolving). Actively and consciously creating your inner scripts, bolstered by engaging in positive mental imagery, will enhance your chances of reaching your full potential and flourishing. You will become more adept at getting on track and reaching your destination. You will also enhance your capacity for recovering from setbacks, transcending negative patterns, and transforming lessons from your past.

Mental imagery provides the tool and the vehicle by which you can become more consciously in control, and accelerate reaching your potential. This is why it is such a popular mental skill practised by top athletes and performers. It is equally well applicable to any life goals or pursuits, to address any long-term or recurring issues you'd like to get better at or change, such as communication and relationship issues, weight loss, and substance abuse.

Learn to think like a champion to champion your dreams.

Mental imagery is a method of tapping into your best inner self and more consistently manifesting into your reality. It brings you closer to becoming all that you can be, and letting go of, or overcoming, what is in the way.

The mission isn't to get more people like you to practise mental imagery. The fact is, you already are. What is key is to be more conscious of the images already playing in your head, and make them work better for you (rather than against you) — to be more in control over the images, and create more of what you prefer. What you see is what you get. So, it is best to take control of your images, lest they get the best of you. By more consciously generating and practising positive imagery, you can take greater control over your destiny.

Being the Scriptwriter of Your Dreams

Calvin and Hobbes

Source: Watterson, William, 'Calvin and Hobbes', Cartoon, 1995, Andrews McMeel Publishing, Kansas City.

Have you ever caught yourself wishing your life was more like what you see in your favourite sit-com like depicted in the *Calvin and Hobbes* comic strip above, or that you could be more like a character you admire? For example, to have caring and witty friends such as people seem to have on certain popular television programs? Or maybe, you would like to be more like a character who is more courageous and outgoing than you? On the other hand, maybe there are some characters who you relate all too well to, but who you pity, such as a soap opera starlet who is always losing in love, or like the hapless George on *Seinfeld*?

Keep in mind that those characters all had writers who may have been working on a single line for hours, or are based on collaboration of up to a dozen writers to develop a story or plot. What you see is based on well-developed scripts with clear purpose and agenda in mind, e.g. to make the audience laugh or cry, and more often to terrify. The actors are also usually well rehearsed. They may have practised their lines dozens of times in different ways until they got it just right, and for the desired impact. They also get lots of advice from directors who guide them how to feel and express themselves — how to act.

The fact is, you are acting out a script, albeit unconsciously. You are the one pulling the strings at every moment of your life, even though it might not always seem like it. You are the scriptwriter, director, dresser, hero or villain, victim or aggressor, etc. I like to insert the word

'NEW' in the final panel of the *Calvin and Hobbes* comic strip above when showing it to clients — to read: 'I gotta get my life some *NEW* writers' — to highlight a more pro-active approach to counteracting or improving on old scripts that no longer serve you well. While it may often seem that there are many external forces in control over your destiny, in effect your destiny is in your hands much more than you might think and actively take advantage of and exploit.

Positive psychology researchers have concluded that our circumstances (e.g. how much money we have, where we live, etc.) contribute only 10% to our happiness and wellbeing. Genetics and upbringing make up 50%, while a whopping 40% is up to intentional behaviour and cultivating inner mental resources. This led one of the leading positive psychology authors, Sonja Lyubormirsky, to originally name her popular book *The How of Happiness*, 'The 40% Solution'. Developing and utilising your mental imagery skill serves as one such major *solution*.

Becoming more conscious and aware of the internal forces you own within empowers you to be more in alignment with your best self and acting more consistently towards fulfilling your potential. The good news is that this will lead to manifesting your goals and dreams in a more conscious and efficient way, rather than leaving all to chance or fate. By improving the inner conditions of your mind, you can improve the outer conditions of your life.

The bad news is (depending on your point of view), it also involves taking responsibility for all the consequences — both positive and negative — which explains why many avoid taking full creative control of their life. Perhaps this is why many people choose to relinquish their role, and remain unconscious. They prefer to have their role prescribed for them. And then have someone else to blame.

Keep this in mind: *That which you avoid ultimately controls you.* You might as well take the reins!

The process of empowerment comes hand in hand with the process of self-examination and increased self-awareness that can sometimes seem too painful, but is ultimately releasing. It is only by such a process that we can become unstuck from habits and patterns locked in our brains that are a result of old programming, i.e. as images that you might now wish to delete the impact of.

Consider the following motto: *Trace, Face, Erase, Embrace* — it is only by tracing the origins of our condition/s, facing up to our role in it, and drawing out our emergent strengths, that we are then freer to erase the hold of any past programming that hinders us along our way, and better *embrace* our potential best self going forward.

Sometimes, it is only by breaking down that we can break through, as suggested by Brene Brown, in her popular presentation on TED.com about vulnerability. She equates breakdown with a spiritual awakening that can be liberating. As Socrates famously declared: 'An unexamined life is not worth living.' (More about this in *Chapter 8* on rewriting history.)

> *We can harness the power of imagination to increase our chances of success, or we can leave our success more to chance.*

Practising mental imagery is about enhancing your personal inner mental resources — about controlling the controllables:

1. To be more in control over that which is within control (e.g. how you are thinking, feeling and acting)

2. To let go of control over that which is not within control (e.g. the past and the future, certain conditions and people), and

3. To know where to draw the line. Too often we spend far too much time and emotional energy fussing over what is not within our control, while neglecting what is! This is very much akin to the Serenity Prayer that is well known to AA members: 'Grant me the serenity to accept the things I cannot change, the courage to change the things I can, and the wisdom to know the difference.'

Competing agendas and scripts

The thing is, you are far more complicated than characters in television shows. You have been around longer than any TV series or character, and you also have up to dozens of scripts that you have been adhering to, often without even realising it. These scripts are learned and developed over your entire history of experiences.

Most people also have competing agendas and scripts. If your scripts contain mostly worries and fears, then these will tend to supersede any optimistic ones, and lead to dominant images that will direct your decisions and actions accordingly. On the other hand, if your scripts contain mostly wishful thinking and fantasy, then there will be a major disconnect between your inner world and what is real and within your control, which will lead to continual frustration and dismay.

The aim is to create and develop positive images that are in your best interests and within your capacity to achieve. Generating such images will ultimately lead to more fulfilling results.

Mental imagery practice can help make you more aware of these competing agendas and scripts. You can then choose to integrate the best of them, and override and/or discard the rest. This will enable you to more consciously create more solid images in the directions you prefer to go.

History isn't destiny

Without being conscious and aware of the inner images that direct you, you are destined to repeat the same patterns (and mistakes) over and over (e.g. overreacting to emotional triggers, and missing opportunities).

Old habits die hard.

The best predictor of future behaviour is past behaviour. If you choose to learn from your past experience (and mistakes), however, and change your characteristic patterns of being and behaving, then you have a shot at changing your destiny to something more desirable. In short:

History need not be your destiny.

The choice is up to you. You can choose to continue going in circles (continue the revolving pattern), or to move on and evolving. You can choose to evolve rather than revolve.

Examining the Role of Self-Image

Pay attention to characters you admire or pity, love or hate, as these may reflect the script you have already been following. There's a good chance that what you admire in others are traits you have within yourself. They may only be dormant and underdeveloped traits that you wish to awaken and manifest more fully or consistently. Same goes for the traits you find pathetic or irritating in others. Chances are, you also embody these traits on some level, and maybe would like to change? Or perhaps need to become more (self) accepting of? Or become better at responding to in others?

As Ekhardt Tolle writes in his bestseller *A New Earth:* 'That which you react to in another, you create in yourself.'

It is crucial to be more aware of the dominant self-image that is driving you in order to adjust towards a more positive and effective one if necessary. You need to have a good grasp of what you're dealing with before you can change it. In short, you cannot change what you are not aware of, and you cannot change what you do not accept. When you deny a part of yourself, you are signing up for blinders (limitations), which prevent you from seeing the whole picture, and will tend to hold you back (an inner saboteur).

Exploring behaviour — image consistency

People tend to behave consistently with whatever self-image is dominant at the time. Even when external circumstance may change or improve, they will tend to revert back to their old and familiar ways. As mentioned above, old habits die hard, and the best predictor of future behaviour is past behaviour. But history need not be your destiny. You can adjust the images to be more in accordance with the changes you desire; rather than repeating old patterns of thinking, feeling and acting.

For example, receiving a compliment may not register with people with a poor self-image. They may either miss it entirely, or fail to respond graciously, or worse react dismissively. In contrast, they would likely be super sensitive to criticism — real or misinterpreted. They will be hyper-aware and over-reactive. This pattern is often based on early experiences and perceptions that have become hard-wired in the brain, which become a dominant point of reference, unless counterbalanced with abundant positive experiences. Mental imagery is a useful tool for dislodging such faulty patterns, and replacing with more effective response patterns that are more conducive to optimal functioning.

Too good to be true?

A classic example of this is when things may be going great in your life, but a nagging underlying belief that this may be 'too good to be true' interferes with fully embracing the good. People will often also self-sabotage if the good fortune they are experiencing does not match their self-image.

An example of this is how many who win a lottery find themselves in worse debt within one year after the win than previously. Not only that, their families are often destroyed over money conflicts. This is because the instant wealth does not match up to a life-long self-image of lacking wealth, or a poverty mentality. If this old image is not actively and consciously adjusted, then it will continue to direct the thoughts and feelings of the winner, and they will behave accordingly. People are subconsciously driven to behave consistently with the dominant image they have of themselves and their lives.

Being more receptive to good fortune

People who have grown up with an experience of luxury and plenty find it easier to expect and accept more of the same in adulthood than those who have not. They would be more comfortable with wealth than someone who grew up under different circumstances. Someone who grew up in poverty may not be as comfortable and gracious in the lap of luxury. Mental imagery can help you to become more receptive to good fortune, whatever that may be, in love, money, health, or career.

A classic sport example is when an athlete is beating someone for the first time. Let's say you are in a race where you are ahead of everyone for the first time. All the other competitors have receded from your peripheral vision. If you have never experienced this before, the image may not *compute*. Your mind will ask: 'What's wrong with this picture?' It might be barely perceptible to an observer, but such a thought process often leads to a slight adjustment to bring the situation back in line with the more familiar image. The athlete may slow down or otherwise lose concentration that allows the opponent/s back into the picture. 'Ah, that's better' — as it resonates with the more familiar image.

I cannot tell you how many an athletes have kicked themselves afterwards for having blown such a precious opportunity! This is why we train athletes to practise such scenarios in their mental imagery, so that when they do finally reach such an opportunity they will be ready to rise to the occasion, rather than falter. This relates to the definition of luck that Oprah has declared as her favourite, and that is: *Luck = Preparation meeting Opportunity.* When mentally prepared, not only are we better and quicker at recognising our opportunities as they arise (rather than after the fact), we also have the wherewithal to seize the opportunity (rather than freeze for example).

Think about how this might play out in your life. Could you be better at noticing and capitalising on your opportunities? At receiving help, praise, compliments, encouragement, generosity, love and affection, money? Could you second guess yourself less, and embrace good fortune more, when getting ahead in life?

For example, if you grew up accustomed to being criticised and put down by family, then you would not be as open and receptive to praise and encouragement as an adult, although you would probably deeply crave it. You might discount it, or even miss it entirely. Your own inner critic would tend to drown out any positive feedback. It is said that people will often prefer to cross the street rather than encounter a person who recently paid them a compliment. What is that about?

Taking Compliments Gracefully

The ability to receive a compliment or good fortune with consummate grace is a virtue that many of us fall short of. In fact, it often competes with another highly lauded virtue of humbleness and humility. However, it is false humility when in fact covering for lack of sufficient self-regard; not to mention lack of regard for the giver. I will never forget a potent lesson delivered by the master talk-show host Johnny Carson of the famed *Tonight Show* (now hosted by Jay Leno). He had just complimented an ingénue starlet, to which she responded by downplaying it along the lines of: 'Oh, this old thing!' (with a tinge of embarrassment). Johnny proceeded to lecture her on how to receive compliments more graciously, and how this was also more respectful of the person who paid the compliment. He went as far as to say that he felt insulted when his compliment was brushed off, suggesting he had bad taste. That even if she wasn't able to muster up the confidence to believe the compliment, then she could at least muster up the good manners for a more gracious response. I have to admit that this example hit me like a ton of bricks — as I sat bolt upright in recognition that I am guilty of the same offence as that guest. I had not realised the impact of my own lack of ability in receiving compliments and praise (and still get admonished by a dear friend who is prolific in dishing them out — to 'just take the compliment, Lydia!'). So instead of: 'This old thing!' say: 'Thank you! It's an old favourite of mine' plus perhaps: 'Thank you for noticing' or 'How lovely of you to notice.'

It helps to start observing how others react to your compliments to them, and how it makes you feel when they fail to acknowledge your gesture of good will. This might then flow on to enable you to better respond as well.[2]

If you would truly like to change your experiences, you need to change your inner images to become more receptive to positive experiences. This is why the practice of gratitude that is discussed in *Chapter 2* can be so powerful, as it causes a shift from resistance (and whatever self-image and beliefs are contributing to it) to more gracious acceptance and appreciation, which generates a much more positive mood and self-image.

Cherokee Parable of Two Wolves

This famous parable of two wolves below reflects the concept of competing inner images; while also pointing to being in the position of choice. Not unlike the Henry Ford quote: 'If you think you can — you are right; if you think you can't — you are still right'. It is up to you to decide which it's going to be.

An old Cherokee chief was teaching his grandson about life...

'A fight is going on inside me,' he said to the boy. 'It is a terrible fight and it is between two wolves.

'One is evil — he is anger, envy, sorrow, regret, greed, arrogance, self-pity, guilt, resentment, inferiority, lies, false pride, superiority, self-doubt, and ego.

'The other is good — he is joy, peace, love, hope, serenity, humility, kindness, benevolence, empathy, generosity, truth, compassion, and faith.

'This same fight is going on inside you — and inside every other person, too.'

The grandson thought about it for a minute and then asked his grandfather, 'Which wolf will win?'

The old chief simply replied, 'The one you feed.'

Self-fulfilling prophecy

The concept of self-fulfilling prophecy is mental imagery in action. It is based on the concept that we tend to create what we expect, whether or not the expectation has any objective basis in fact. How this works is that we will tend to behave consistently with the expectation (i.e. image) that will increase the likelihood of that expectation manifesting. This concept is alternatively known as the Pygmalion Effect or Rosenthal Effect after the research psychologist Robert Rosenthal, who found that when teachers or managers are led to expect enhanced performance of students or employees, then the children or people would indeed show that enhancement regardless of initial and objectively determined aptitude. Thus confirming that reality can be influenced by the expectations of others. This phenomenon is also referred to as the observer-expectancy effect — when the observer (teacher or manager) begins to unconsciously behave in ways that facilitate and encourage progress, perpetuating what has been termed a 'reign of error.'[3]

Our expectations change our behaviour in ways that we will not consciously be aware of, and therefore cannot adjust unless and until we become more aware.

You cannot change what you are not aware of.

By becoming more aware of what is influencing your beliefs, expectations, and therefore behaviour, you are in a better position to disable faulty/ maladaptive patterns, and enable the creation of a new and improved program of change that practising mental imagery facilitates.

Creating versus Reacting

If you take a close look at the two words reacting and creating, you will notice that they are identical. Take the 'c' out from the middle of the word *reactor* and put it out in front, and you get *creator*. 'C' for taking charge. Or Control? Which would you rather be? A reactor who is at the whim of outside influences? Of whatever life throws at you? Or creator, who is more self-determined?

Mental imagery is about taking the helm and creating your life course, and navigating outside influences to your advantage, rather than merely reacting to outer life forces. Taking the time to clearly identify and imagine achieving your goals will give you a much greater sense of control and confidence (see *Chapter 4* about charting your course with goal setting).

Counteracting negative programming

Positive mental images can be used to counteract old and negative programming that may have been absorbed in childhood. Such negative programming is often hard-wired in the brain and manifests in reflexive negativity, which overrides the facility to be more positive. Most of us have a pretty good handle on being negative. There is no need to practise it any more. Besides which it is not conducive to achieving our goals. It's time to shift the balance to greater positivity, which is something that most of us could use a much bigger dose of. It is also proving to have beneficial flow-on effects for our wellbeing, creativity and productivity. Practising positive imagery helps to consolidate a positive mindset. (Find out more about this in *Chapter 8* about rewriting history.)

If you find yourself persisting in negative worries you are actually generating negative images. If you allow such images to dominate your inner landscape, then you can expect to continue getting negative results. For example, if you continually worry about running out of money, you will tend to behave consistently with that image and potentially waste and squander money. Use the worry or negative thoughts as a cue to shift to a more desirable image instead, e.g. having plenty and being mindful of your spending habits, or whatever else will enable you to be back in control in the direction you prefer.

What Mental Imagery Is and Isn't

Mental imagery is a basic form of cognition that is frequently referred to as 'seeing with the mind's eye'. Technically, it is the mental (perceptual) representation of events and objects stored in memory, and affects how we process and use information, which can either be to our benefit or detriment (depending on the content). Given the central function of mental imagery in cognition, which is generally below conscious awareness — top researchers in the area contend that by developing greater awareness and positive utilisation of this function (aka 'tool'), will lead the way for the study of consciousness and evolution.[4]

Mental imagery refers to how an event or experience is played out in your imagination. It can involve reviewing a real event from your past (from memory), or previewing one for the future. Mental images are constantly playing out in our minds whether we are consciously bidding them or not, and are based, not on what actually happened or may happen, but on what you *perceived* happened and believe will happen. There is an element of illusion and delusion that remains largely outside of conscious awareness, though nevertheless influences our experiences.

By playing out preferred scenarios in your mind, you may actually expand and enrich the 'database' of your experiences from which to draw — to create a more flourishing future.

Terminology and misnomers

The term *mental imagery* is often used interchangeably with other terms such as *visualisation* and *mental rehearsal.* Visualisation is actually a misnomer, however, because mental imagery involves use of all of your senses — visual being only one. In fact, the visual component isn't always even necessary for best results, but an ability to incorporate all of your senses in your imagery practice certainly does add value.

Mental rehearsal shares much in common with mental imagery, but imagery has a much broader focus. As the term 'rehearsal' suggests, it applies to practising a set routine, whereas mental imagery can be applied to a much wider spectrum. (See *Chapters 7, 8* and *9* for more about mental imagery applications.)

Mental imagery as self-hypnosis

The process of mental imagery is equivalent to hypnosis. While the hypnotic state can be induced by a trusted practitioner, it is also a natural state that you drift in and out of daily. At such times, your critical faculties are quieted, leaving your mind more open and receptive to suggestions, as well as more susceptible to influence. A session with a hypnotist typically begins with a hypnotic induction that is simply a technique designed to relax the mind in order to become more passively receptive to the planting of suggestions. You can harness the power of hypnosis by learning to relax your mind and practising mental imagery — as a more active process of self-hypnosis. This involves beginning with a relaxation or meditation technique, followed by generating the suggestions and images you prefer to follow. Such self-hypnosis practice is ultimately more empowering than passively relying on someone else. This is explained in further detail in *Chapter 5*.

To be more actively in charge of your destiny, you need to be more aware of your state of mind, and what images you are letting in, as well as what images you are generating.

Praying as imagining

When you are engaged in worrying, you are imagining what you do not want to happen happening. You are focusing on all the things that can go wrong, instead of what can go right. You are actually preparing yourself to fail rather than succeed! Like the famous line from the iconic American author Mark Twain: 'I've lived a long life and seen a lot of hard times ... most of which never happened.'

On the other hand, prayer involves imagining what you do want to happen, except when you are giving a prayer of thanks, which also involves an image (as discussed in the section on gratitude in *Chapter 2*). In this case, you are actually preparing yourself for success. The process of praying and imagery are very similar. Think about it: when you pray for good fortune, are you not actually imagining what you would do with that good fortune? How you might attain it? Or how you will celebrate? And with whom? Some prayers involve asking for strength, health, forgiveness — and as you do so, are you not imagining what it would be like to be stronger, healthier, and more at peace with yourself or others? The effectiveness of prayer may very well be attributed to the power of mental imagery.

The Power of Prayer

In his New York Times bestseller, *Healing Words,* Dr Dossey uncovered one of the best-kept secrets in medical science: the enormous body of data showing that the act of prayer can greatly affect the practice of medicine. He examines the evidence of prayer's efficacy, the role of the unconscious in prayer, how prayer manifests through dreams, the relationship between methods of prayer and one's personality, and the negative side of prayer. He addresses the complex relationship between spiritual understanding and physical health. The primary function of prayer, Dr Dossey asserts, is not only to help eradicate illness or increase longevity, but to simultaneously remind us of our essential nature. Ignored for much too long, this information is changing the way medicine is practised and revolutionising our ideas about healing.[5]

So, next time you catch yourself worrying, ask yourself the question: 'Am I worrying, or am I praying?' or alternatively for more secular types: 'Am I worrying, or am I planning/imagining?' ... and then turn your attention to practising positive mental imagery instead.

The key ingredient to the power of prayer (in addition to the mental imagery process), however, is that it relies on a belief in a deity with the omnipotence with which to grant us our request. Such belief enables conjuring up the desired image more readily (not unlike suspension of belief in the process of hypnosis discussed above, and the placebo effect discussed in *Chapter 3*). Those of us without such a belief, may find it more challenging to believe in the desired image and our capacity or deservedness to achieve it. Ironically, turning over our will to a higher power, enables greater belief (and thereby strength) in the capacity for manifesting, than if we were to rely solely on our own power to manifest our images. Nevertheless, the actual process in effect is essentially the same.

Teaming up with others can also be viewed as a secular substitute for the benefits accrued through the combination of fellowship and prayer that occurs in church services, temples and the like. We know that those of faith (regardless of religious affiliation) tend to be happier and healthier. This can be attributed to many factors included in religious practice that others miss out on, e.g. the fellowship (aka social support), prayer rituals (aka mental imagery), etc. The vision buddy exercise suggested in *Chapter 6* provides an alternative for secular types — to benefit from the same process without having to be part of a religious movement, organisation or institution. Coincidently, there is a movement afoot for doing something similar in providing venues for the secular population espoused in *Religion for Atheists* by Alain de Botton.[6]

Interestingly, research in Canada has found that those practising a religion appear to have stronger imaginations as well as capacity for empathy than those who profess to be atheists. An explanation for this goes two ways: that belief in a deity requires imagination (as famous atheists fondly proclaim that to believe in a 'God' is merely to believe in an *imaginary friend*); and belief in an all-powerful deity imbues greater *credibility* to our images. Therefore, does it require faith in a god to have our prayers (images) answered? Or, as is more likely the case, can both the religious and secular alike equally benefit from the process of prayer/imagery as is the mission of this book?

Faith and imagery

What is faith but a belief one imagines to be true? A belief one takes comfort in, and that instils confidence. Alain de Botton (2012) contends that although many in the more secular West have little interest and time for organised religion, they still yearn for the 'consoling, subtle or just charming rituals'. We are not immune to being drawn in by the entrancing rituals and awe-inspiring beauty of religious art, music and architecture, yet we remain bereft of access and benefits to such experiences except as tourists. De Botton refers to this as a false choice between faith and scepticism. 'Either you have to accept lots of beliefs that are unbelievable or you end up in a spiritual and aesthetic wasteland,' he says. 'But maybe the choice doesn't have to be that stark.'

To bridge this divide, de Botton has embarked on an ambitious project called 'Temples for Atheists'. These buildings will provide spaces for (secular) contemplation, starting with one in London, but then spreading across the country. I would suggest that it would only be fitting to include the practice of mental imagery alongside contemplation in such spaces, and thereby afford secular types the same value and benefits that believers gain from religious practice and institutions.

Putting it in perspective

Tapping into your imagination can be a powerful resource, but you need to keep it all in perspective. It's about controlling what is in your control. There's no point in imagining things that are either completely out of your control (e.g. other people, nature, time), or wildly unrealistic (e.g. becoming a world class athlete or virtuoso pianist at 50; or winning a lottery), or out of this world (e.g. flying or walking on air).

What mental imagery is best suited to is helping you to think, feel and act in greater alignment with your values, in accordance with your best possible self, developing your skills, abilities and talents, towards fulfilling your potential. Sometimes, it is simply a matter of getting out of your own way. Not unlike how Michelangelo approached his great sculptures: 'I saw the angel in the marble and carved until I set him free.' It is, therefore, sometimes simply a matter of chipping away at the obstacles in our way, which are often merely imaginary.

While the purpose of mental imagery practice may be to stretch your limits, and to surmount all obstacles, it can sometimes be best to start with where you are at now — to be in touch with who you are now before trying to imagine change. This is based on the principle that you cannot change what you are not aware of, and you cannot change what you do not accept. The first part of the above statement means you need to be aware of all the facts as they are now, in order to more accurately and successfully change and create the best image for the future. The second part refers to the tendency to be too desperate to be somewhere or someone else, and lacking self-acceptance, and/or overreach which ultimately leads to increased frustration rather than gratification.

Without self-acceptance, you will tend to not be willing to see what needs to be seen, and therefore miss important data. If you cannot look clearly in the mirror, how can you improve what you don't see, or don't want to see? Alternatively, without self-acceptance, you also risk being stuck on the focus of what you don't like and accept about yourself, which only serves to perpetuate it.

What mental imagery is not

Mental imagery can be a powerful tool for creating positive results, but mental imagery is not a magic bullet. Interestingly, the word *imagine* includes the root for the word magic, but mental imagery is not magic, although the process can seem quite magical. There are limitations to how effective imagery can be. It cannot make you a pop star, an Olympic athlete, business leader, etc., unless you have the requisite skills, talent and commitment.

Not a magic wand

Mental imagery is not about wishful thinking, but about manifesting your best self within the bounds of reality. Mental imagery cannot make you six feet tall if you are only five feet and six inches, it cannot make you a gourmet chef if you've no culinary skills. Mental imagery can only work within the domain of your talent, skills and capacities. What mental imagery can do is facilitate and accelerate reaching your potential.

Does not replace action

Just as mental imagery is not magical and wishful thinking, neither does it replace taking action to achieve your goals. It won't work to just sit back and imagine becoming fitter. Imagining participating in the actions that will lead to your goal, however, will tend to propel you towards behaving more consistent with the image.

Like the famous line from the movie *Auntie Mame:* 'Life is a banquet, and most poor suckers are starving to death', you need to step up to the table to serve yourself. If you wait to be served, then you will starve.

Not fantasy and daydreaming

Mental imagery is not about fantasising and daydreaming, although a related process and state of mind.

Fantasy and daydreams are similar to mental imagery in that they engage the imagination, and emerge more spontaneously when the mind is allowed to roam free. They're a good start for the practice of mental imagery, and also fertile mindset for effective imagery. Mental imagery, however, is a more active, prescriptive and determinative process.

When you catch yourself daydreaming use it as a cue to practise more definitive imagery before snapping back to reality and any tasks at hand. Take advantage of your state of mind at the time, which is conducive to harnessing your imagination and the practice of mental imagery. (More about imagery guidelines in *Chapter 5*.)

A Picture is worth a thousand words.

Positive thinking ≠ positive images.

The capacity of mental images to change how we feel and act goes well beyond where words can reach.

While positive self-talk and affirmations are helpful — to the extent that they at least disrupt and neutralise any negative thinking and fears — they have limited effect in eliciting the desired feeling behaviour and change unless evoking an effective image. Talking to oneself too much is also a known impediment to wellbeing and success known in the sports domain to be associated with poor performance and choking (e.g. thinking too much). In fact, the best way to psych someone else out is to get them to think about what they're doing.

It is also now known that using our verbal capacity is not nearly as connected to our emotions as are images in the structure and function of our brains. This is why overcoming old fears and phobias and conditions like post traumatic stress disorder can be hard to achieve with talk therapy, unless negative associations locked in the mental images can be recalibrated (see the section in *Chapter 7* on rewriting history for more on how mental imagery is effective in reversing such conditions).

There is a direct link between an image triggering a feeling that completely bypasses the section of our brain in control of language. This is why simply labelling a negative emotion can provide some distance and relief, as it requires accessing and shifting away from the part of the brain that is most involved.

George Vaillant poignantly makes this point in his book *Spiritual Evolution: A Scientific Defense of Faith* on words not being enough to evoke positive emotion:[7]

When Friedrich von Schiller wrote in his 'Ode to Joy' the words 'Brothers, beyond the stars surely dwells a loving father,' his mere words do little for us. … When Beethoven put Schiller's words to soaring, triumphant, oceanic music, we finally (get) it.

…..

Go and experience it for yourself! Put this book down and listen to the last movement of Beethoven's Ninth Symphony. Perhaps then you will hear what cannot be put into words.

I wholeheartedly concur, as singing this masterpiece in a choir at the Sydney Opera House is one of my all-time peak experiences and a dream come true; it always sends my spirits soaring upon recollection.

By all means continue to practise your affirmations and positively encouraging self-talk, but ensure that you are engaging your imaginal mind as much as possible as you do so. And/or use your self-talk as a cue to a positive image — appropriate to what it is you are keen to achieve.

There is no point repeating the famous affirmation: 'I am loving and lovable' if this does not evoke an image that resonates with the feeling. This is why the loving kindness meditations common to Buddhist practice begin by connecting with the genuine love you feel for someone close and dear to you, and then extending inwardly towards yourself, before then extending outwards towards others. For you cannot extend what you cannot feel or imagine initially. (See *Chapter 9* for more about loving kindness meditations, and *Appendix A* for two variations on the theme.)

Emerging Tool Across the Spectrum of Human Endeavour

Mental imagery is an inner mental resource that you can draw upon to enhance your capacity to fulfil your potential in any endeavour — at work, home or play. Out of the many self-help techniques promoted in the marketplace it is one that is relatively underutilised, yet probably one of the most powerful. Mental imagery puts you in the driver's seat (rather than the passenger side) — to getting and staying on track —to leaving less to chance, and increasing your chances of success.

Some of you may be interested in mental imagery to enhance your performance — on the playing field, stage or boardroom. Some of you may be more concerned with changing your behaviour in social situations or in relation to your lifestyle. You might wish to change or break bad habits, e.g. biting nails, overeating, smoking. Or you may simply want to create new healthier and more adaptive behaviours, such as speaking up more at meetings, getting along better with your in-laws; or overcoming fears, such as flying, driving, public speaking, etc.

Mental imagery can be applied to any challenges that you seek to overcome, to achieve any changes you seek to embrace and effect, and to get more on track with your life. Your goals provide the road map.

Basically, the mental imagery skill can be applied towards achieving any goal and to fulfil your innate potential. Mental imagery works best on those goals that are within your control, which are directly and immediately within your capacity to achieve or perform. Like all skills, mental and otherwise, the more you practise, the better you get. Use it or lose it!

Like all talents and skills, some people are better at it than others. But like all skills, everyone can get better, Children seem to be most receptive and adept at it. Even the blind experience images. After all, sight is only one of the five senses we have access to.

No Order of Difficulty in Miracles

It is said that *there is no order of difficulty in miracles*. The power of miracles does not discriminate between minor and major goals. You may know someone who boasts of always finding the best parking spot in the most crowded places. Maybe that person is you? To what do you attribute this ability? Many will report that they visualised a car space, and that this belief created the spot. Or perhaps their image of a free spot helped to tune them into divine cosmic good timing, so that they approached a spot just as someone else was leaving? You may have tried this out yourself already? And when you get the spot, you think, AHA! Aren't you clever? And if you don't, it's no big drama. You just keep looking until eventually you find one.

For some reason, some people are really good at seeing and creating such trivial opportunities, but when it comes to the big important stuff of life they either don't believe enough in their capacity, or if they do, they have so much attachment to the outcome that the goal eludes them. This has to do with extent of what is emotionally at stake.

Emotional Stakes in Outcomes

What interferes with the process of mental imagery is the degree of emotional attachment you ascribe to the desired outcome. For example, imagining finding a good parking spot does not have as much at stake as some other goals might. It does not elicit the same degree of desire (or desperation?) and emotional consequence for success or failure as losing weight, securing a major business deal, attracting a potential life partner, recovering from a major illness, performing at the Olympics, etc.

The anxiety associated with the more serious goals tends to evoke negative images related to worries about what could go wrong, and how awful that would be (aka *awfulising* or *catastrophising*). So, you might think that the imagery didn't work. However, it could be that you were engaging in competing negative imagery at the same time albeit unconsciously, but nonetheless powerfully.

In addition, because of the anxiety you might even miss recognising a positive opportunity, such as an attractive individual showing interest or complimenting you. You might even miss a parking spot if you are in too much of a hurry and anxious about what will happen if you are late.

When we cling too desperately to the desired outcome it tends to elude us. If we aren't tenacious enough, however, we might also miss out. It can be likened to holding on to a bar of soap. If you hold on too tight what happens? You drop it. If you do not hold on enough what happens? You drop it. Finding the right touch is key. (More on this in *Chapter 4* on charting your course with goal setting.)

If you are having trouble shaking off the emotional attachment and fears associated with the goal image, then try a lead-up image. For example, if losing weight is your goal (and this is a healthy and realistic goal for you), then instead of focusing on achieving being slimmer and fitter try picturing achieving the little things that will get you there, e.g. going for a walk, choosing fruit for desert instead of cake, eating more mindfully, drinking more water. Get the picture?

Destiny Versus Imagery

There is some question as to what comes first — destiny or imagery; whether following our destiny leads to clear and effective imagery that hastens associated goal attainment, or whether mental imagery can create and/or alter pre-ordained fate or destiny (if there is such a thing). It may be easier to imagine what is already predestined to be within our reach. Or can practising our imagery create a destiny that previously seemed out of reach? How much of goal attainment can we attribute to effective imagery practice? And how much did the practice of mental imagery actually change our course? These are all deeply philosophical and metaphysical questions that await definitive answers.

It has further been suggested (e.g. by Shakti Gawain in her groundbreaking book *Creative Visualization*) that if a certain goal is not predestined and/ or not in your best interests, then no amount of mental imagery will work. In fact, it is suggested that the opposite may occur.

In any case, mental imagery remains an important tool for creating and guiding you on your life's journey. It might very well be that by cultivating your imagination in pursuit of your goals you will gain greater self-awareness, insight and capacity to eventually attain what is ultimately in your best interests — to create your best self, and your best life.

Summary

This chapter began by highlighting your role in developing your life script, and how you can better take charge of this process with mental imagery. It covered how mental imagery relates and is distinguished from other mental processes, in particular as a form of secular prayer, and in contrast to positive thinking strategies. And finally, it clarified how best to approach the practice with the 'right touch' and to beware of staking too much on any results.

Remember: What you see is what you get! Best to take creative control over your images, lest they get the best of you.

Chapter 2

Mental Imagery Links to Positive Psychology Coaching

The past decade since the advent of the field of positive psychology (aka study of psychological wellbeing) has seen an explosion of literature on the topic. More and more research is being conducted to test strategies that are designed to promote sustainable boosts to wellbeing, leading to building resilience and more flourishing lives. Positive psychology in practice is about being (feeling) and doing (acting) better. Despite leading researchers claiming they have yet to determine the mechanisms for the success of strategies, it is my contention that mental imagery is likely the key.[8]

Many of the interventions associated with positive psychology to enhance Psychological Wellbeing (aka Happiness), involve or trigger a mental image upon which efficacy of the intervention may rely. Many of the most popularly touted positive psychology interventions therefore depend on the link to mental images for efficacy.

This chapter will provide an overview of positive psychology in practice, highlighting the links to mental imagery. The strategies to be covered include:

- Experiencing flow (versus fight or flight or freeze)
- Focusing on signature strengths
- Writing your eulogy
- Designing 'A Beautiful Day'
- Mindfulness
- Savouring (versus dwelling)
- Reflecting (versus ruminating)
- Cultivating gratitude and appreciation (versus complaining)
- Acts of kindness
- Hope and optimism
- Positivity
- Boosting self-efficacy/confidence

You might like to try out some of the activities and see for yourself. See how you go with the practices, and be alert to any images you become aware of, and how they make you feel. Are you feeling and acting better?

Positive Psychology Overview

Before launching in to the links to mental imagery, here is a bit of an overview of positive psychology. Over the past decade since the emergence of positive psychology, interventions and coaching have been increasingly embraced across wide spectrum of society, including in education systems and business, as well as in personal wellbeing and development. The movement was spearheaded by Martin Seligman in 1998 in his presidential address to the American Psychological Association. This was followed by the seminal article in *American Psychologist*[9], and by his book *Authentic Happiness: Using the new positive psychology to realise your potential for lasting fulfillment*[10], and more recently by *Flourish: A visionary new understanding of happiness and well-being*[11].

The movement has rapidly grown and is now rich with publications, university courses, journals, conferences and applications to the classrooms and boardrooms as well as in psychological and coaching practice.

The main driver of the positive psychology movement is to redress the imbalance that has dominated the field of traditional psychology, which has largely focused on the study of what is wrong with people and how to fix them (i.e. going from–10 to 0). In contrast, the focus of positive psychology is studying the nature of wellbeing and happiness and how it may be taught and developed (i.e. going from 0 to 10+). In short, it is the study of mental health (rather than mental illness). It is about understanding and creating more of what leads to flourishing in the optimal range of human functioning, rather than merely providing relief from languishing at the lower range of functioning.

This paradigm shift of focusing more on what is right with us rather than wrong has resonated far and wide. The vast ripple effect of the positive psychology movement has spawned great interest in the media as well as many bestsellers. It has led to the transformation of education and even public policy.

The rest of this chapter will focus on the intersection of major positive psychology interventions and mental imagery.

Experiencing Flow (versus *Fight* or *Flight* or *Freeze*)

Peak or optimal experiences are often referred to as being in a state of *flow* — a term coined by Mihaly Csikszentmihalyi (pronounced Chicks-sent-me-high; aka CZ Flow in sport psychology circles). Flow describes the state of body and mind that can seem magical and mystical, but is characterised by being fully conscious, alert and in the moment, totally engrossed in the task at hand, without a worry or care about the result or consequences, even though much may be riding on the outcome.

The experience of 'flow' is rapidly becoming the penultimate state of being to reach in much of the happiness and positive psychology literature, and is associated with optimal psychological wellbeing and functioning. It is far from a new concept, however, as is has long been the focus and aim of sport and performance psychology in practice to create and develop the mental conditions and practices conducive to reaching the state of flow more consistently and readily — to being in the *zone*. There is now increasing interest in extending this practice towards boosting psychological wellbeing and achievement, which is being applied in the workplace and other meaningful pursuits.

The state of flow is characterised as being totally immersed and absorbed in what one is doing to the exclusion of everything else (notice all the water metaphors?). It is when the mind and body are as one, and working in concert, producing an experience of pure joy and fulfilment. For example, a pianist has described not noticing the room, his hands, the keys, the score, but rather being conscious of only 'being one with the music and expressing emotion'. Fears and concerns seem to fall by the wayside, and hope and optimism reign supreme.

Csikzentmihayl's interest in the concept of flow and optimal experience began with his study of 'how to live life as a work of art, rather than as a chaotic response to external events'[12]. He sought to better understand how to create the good life, versus merely reacting to life and life's conditions. His early research involved a survey of creative people, such as artists, writers, and musicians, who reported being in an ecstatic state of mind during a peak performance. Csikzentmihalyi noted that the word ecstasy means to 'stand aside' in Latin, suggesting that the experience occurs when we get out of our own way.

'We have all experienced times when, instead of being buffeted by anonymous forces, we do feel in control of our actions, masters of our own fate. On the rare occasions that it happens, we feel a sense of exhilaration, a deep sense of enjoyment that is long cherished and that becomes a landmark in memory for what life should be like. This is what we mean by optimal experience... moments like these, the best moments in our lives, are not the passive, receptive, relaxing times... The best moments usually occur when a person's body or mind is stretched to its limits in a voluntary effort to accomplish something difficult and worthwhile. Optimal experience is thus something we make happen.'[13]

The first place to start in generating more experiences of flow is by reviewing a previous peak experience or performance. You are your own best teacher, and drawing from previous optimal experiences (aka flow experiences) will point you towards creating more in the future. The peak experience and peak performance recall guided imagery exercises in *Chapter 7* are designed to facilitate tuning in to your flow process — the better to create more in future.

Caveat about flow: It's about being in the flow, and not about going with the flow, unless it's in the right direction according to the course you've set for yourself. The way towards your best self and best interest.

Even dead fish go with the flow

The concept and experience of flow is also in direct contrast with feeling stress and pressure. Flow is blocked when you let your focus drift beyond the here and now; when you're focused on the past or concerned with the future, both out of your control in the present. It is also blocked when you are overly concerned with results or overly critical. For example, in a social situation, if you are worried about whether you are interesting enough to the other person, then your attention to the conversation will be lacking, which will then interfere with the quality of the exchange.

Blocking the flow will often involve imagining the negative consequences of doing or saying something wrong. If, on the other hand, you keep your focus on being fully present and engaged in the moment, task, or conversation then it is more likely to go well. Imagining yourself being in your best mindset is conducive to being and staying in the flow.

See *Chapter 7* for more about flow and how to create more opportunities for engaging in flow in your life.

Focusing on Signature Strengths

You might say that the signature intervention of applied positive psychology is applying the concept of signature strengths. Identifying and capitalising on strengths has always been a hallmark of sport and performance psychology, but the concept within the positive psychology arena has more to do with identifying strengths as virtues that lead to a virtuous life, and thereby a 'good life' — one of the major tenets of the positive psychology movement.

Peterson and Seligman have developed a classification system published in their landmark tome *Character Strengths and Virtues: A handbook and classification* (aka 'Manual of the Sanities'). They have identified 24 character strengths and virtues (see sidebar on the following page), which they found to be ubiquitous across every culture, philosophy and religion. It is an attempt to identify positive attributes that relate to good 'character', and reflect a person of good 'values', which in practice (values in action) would lead to a good life and flourishing. The online survey has, therefore, been called the VIA (as per values in action) *Survey of Character Strengths and Virtues*.[14]

Classification of Strengths

The classification of strengths is grouped according to six core virtues. The individual strengths within each core are listed below.

WISDOM: Cognitive strengths that entail the acquisition and use of knowledge.

Creativity (originality, ingenuity): Thinking of novel and productive ways to conceptualise and do things; includes artistic achievement but is not limited to it.

Curiosity (interest, novelty-seeking, openness to experience): Taking an interest in ongoing experience for its own sake; finding subjects and topics fascinating; exploring and discovering.

Open-mindedness (judgment, critical thinking): Thinking things through and examining them from all sides; not jumping to conclusions; being able to change one's mind in light of evidence; weighing all evidence fairly.

Love of learning: Mastering new skills, topics, and bodies of knowledge, whether on one's own or formally; obviously related to the strength of curiosity but goes beyond it to describe the tendency to add systematically to what one knows.

Perspective (wisdom): Being able to provide wise counsel to others; having ways of looking at the world that make sense to oneself and to other people.

COURAGE: Emotional strengths that involve the exercise of will to accomplish goals in the face of opposition, external or internal

Bravery (valor): Not shrinking from threat, challenge, difficulty, or pain; speaking up for what is right even if there is opposition; acting on convictions even if unpopular; includes physical bravery but is not limited to it.

Persistence (perseverance, industriousness): Finishing what one starts; persisting in a course of action in spite of obstacles; 'getting it out the door'; taking pleasure in completing tasks.

Integrity (authenticity, honesty): Speaking the truth but more broadly presenting oneself in a genuine way and acting in a sincere way; being without pretense; taking responsibility for one's feelings and actions.

Vitality (zest, enthusiasm, vigour, energy): Approaching life with excitement and energy; not doing things halfway or halfheartedly; living life as an adventure; feeling alive and activated.

HUMANITY: Interpersonal strengths that involve tending and befriending others.

Love: Valuing close relations with others, in particular those in which sharing and caring are reciprocated; being close to people.

Kindness (generosity, nurturance, care, compassion, altruistic love, 'niceness'): Doing favors and good deeds for others; helping them; taking care of them.

Social intelligence (emotional intelligence, personal intelligence): Being aware of the motives and feelings of other people and oneself; knowing what to do to fit into different social situations; knowing what makes other people tick.

JUSTICE: Civic strengths that underlie healthy community life.

Citizenship (social responsibility, loyalty, teamwork): Working well as a member of a group or team; being loyal to the group; doing one's share.

Fairness: Treating all people the same according to notions of fairness and justice; not letting personal feelings bias decisions about others; giving everyone a fair chance.

Leadership: Encouraging a group of which one is a member to get things done and at the time maintain time good relations within the group; organising group activities and seeing that they happen.

TEMPERANCE: Strengths that protect against excess.

Forgiveness and mercy: Forgiving those who have done wrong; accepting the shortcomings of others; giving people a second chance; not being vengeful.

Humility/Modesty: Letting one's accomplishments speak for themselves; not regarding oneself as more special than one is.

Prudence: Being careful about one's choices; not taking undue risks; not saying or doing things that might later be regretted.

Self-regulation (self-control): Regulating what one feels and does; being disciplined; controlling one's appetites and emotions.

TRANSCENDENCE: Strengths that forge connections to larger universe & provide meaning.

Appreciation of beauty and excellence (awe, wonder, elevation): Noticing and appreciating beauty, excellence, and/or skilled performance in various domains of life, from nature to art to mathematics to science to everyday experience.

Gratitude: Being aware of and thankful for the good things that happen; taking time to express thanks.

Hope (optimism, future-mindedness, future orientation): Expecting the best in the future and working to achieve it; believing that a good future is something that can be brought about.

Humor (playfulness): Liking to laugh and tease; bringing smiles to other people; seeing the light side; making (not necessarily telling) jokes.

Spirituality (religiousness, faith, purpose): Having coherent beliefs about the higher purpose and meaning of the universe; knowing where one fits within the larger scheme; having beliefs about the meaning of life that shape conduct and provide comfort.

Identifying your top five strengths (= signature strengths) according to the VIA or other means (e.g. by asking loved ones, co-workers, etc.) provides a positive look at ourselves, which eventually, by applying the strengths based exercises will supersede and/or override any negative self-images that haunt us — that cause us to shoot ourselves in the foot. Imagining how we have used these strengths, as well as how we might use them in new ways, provides a new positive image template that lifts our spirit as well as leads to greater chance of success in related endeavours. See *Appendix A* for more specific instructions and suggestions for how to identify and utilise your signature strengths.

By recognising our strengths and running with them (rather than focusing on fixing our so-called weaknesses and flaws, and allowing them to dictate our self-image and thereby behaviours), we begin to see ourselves in a completely new light. The implications for boosting self-image are enormous.

Writing Your Eulogy

Writing your own eulogy is a powerful exercise commonly promoted in personal development programs, and featured in the popular ABC series *Making Australia Happy*. Writing your own eulogy is intended to foster connection with your core values and aspirations. It is very similar to goal setting, but goes deeper in identifying what drives your goals.

While the exercise might be entitled 'writing your eulogy' the process is very much linked to mental imagery considering that the basic instructions repeatedly refer to the word 'imagine', e.g. ' ... imagine you've lived your life, and are now — sadly — at your funeral. Allow yourself to get in touch with what it feels like to be there. *Imagine* yourself standing at the back where no one can see you, but you can see and hear everything. Close your eyes and put yourself in that place. To get into the mood, you might like to *imagine* you can hear their voices, see their faces, get a sense of the colours or the warmth or coldness of the place. Take your mind there — imagine.'[15]

By starting with such an end in mind, involves the process of taking stock of your current position and clarifies directions towards being better aligned with your future best self. The stronger your image of your best future self (BFS) the more consistent you will be inclined to think, feel and act accordingly.

It is also important to remind you that while it might be important to hold your ultimate goals in mind, success relies on taking the steps towards reaching those goal/s, and ultimately to daily goals. You know the old adages: You don't need to do it all today, just begin it today; and: A journey of a thousand miles begins with a single step.

For more about writing your eulogy see *Appendix A*.

Designing 'A Beautiful Day'

This exercise is about creating a best day possible — what Martin Seligman calls *'A Beautiful Day'* (see *Appendix A* for full instructions). The idea is to basically design what you would consider a beautiful day considering what is within your control. Too often too many of us go through our days being reactive to circumstance, rather than creatively and proactively determining our experiences — letting our days and hence our lives get away from us.

It is about taking control over what is within control, which can be very empowering, not to mention increase our chances of enjoying ourselves, rather than leaving our enjoyment to chance. It certainly falls under the rubric creating versus reacting as I like to say.

A caveat: It is not about creating a perfect day (which is impossible to achieve), but about creating a day that is full of beautiful experiences. It is not just about pleasure, and can frequently include enjoying accomplishing a cherished task or project — whatever brings the greatest combination/balance of activities and pursuits that bring greatest satisfaction.

For many, it would involve including elements of Seligman's PERMA model of wellbeing that includes: P = Positive emotions and Pleasure; E = Engaging activities, such as those that are associated with flow;

R = for Relationships — thriving interpersonal connections and with whom we share our beautiful experiences; M = Meaning — those experiences that are meaningful and purposeful and aligned with our deepest values; and A = Accomplishment/Achievement.[16]

The next component of the exercise is, of course, to then implement the plan. It is unlikely to happen if not planned, and more likely to occur if the plan has been well imagined being executed. Too often people will design the plan, but not implement. It can seem too hard to believe, especially with competing priorities, even if those priorities may not have been well articulated and often arise from external pressures, versus being self-generated.

Your priorities are revealed by how you spend your time and money. It comes back to making a conscious decision — to be more in *c*harge of your life (remember the 'c' in 'create' can refer to being in *c*harge and in *c*ontrol as much as creating ...). It would help to recruit a partner to increase your commitment, and one with whom you can share, savour and debrief with, and later reminisce with.

Too often we wait until we have enough time or for the perfect time rather than seizing the opportunities and taking charge of our lives. If not now, then when? If not by you then by whom? The more we can imagine such a day (or elements of) taking place, the more likely it is going to actually occur, and potentially override any interfering concerns. May I suggest A Beautiful Day merits weekly practice. Not unlike the traditional weekly observance of the Sabbath in religious practice; setting aside one day per week minimum to connect with the divine, and for sacred contemplation in fellowship with like-minded people.

Of course, A Beautiful Day is unlikely to unfold exactly to plan; however, the more you can imagine the plan the more likely it will flow naturally and spontaneously, allowing for life's usual diversions and distractions. It might also lead to wonderful surprises along the way, which would otherwise have been missed if not for embarking on the plan and being open to beautiful experiences.

Mindfulness

Although mindfulness has only recently been integrated into Western psychology, it is an ancient practice found in a wide range of Eastern philosophies, including Buddhism, Taoism and Yoga.

Mindfulness involves consciously bringing awareness to your here-and-now experience with openness, interest and receptivity. It is about waking up, connecting with ourselves, and appreciating the fullness of each moment of life. Jon Kabat-Zinn (who is credited with popularising the practice with his Mindfulness Based Stress Reduction program covered in his book *Full Catastrophe Living*), calls it, 'The art of conscious living'. It is a profound way to enhance psychological flexibility and resilience, and increase life satisfaction. Kabat-Zinn defines mindfulness as *'Paying attention in a particular way: on purpose, in the present moment, and non-judgmentally'*.[17]

Mindfulness relates to selective attention that is a critical component of perception and memory, and therefore relates to the process of what gets stored in one's imagery bank. It also enhances the level of awareness that fosters psychological flexibility and awareness of options. Mindfulness can be viewed as providing the blank canvas onto which you can more freely project what is in your best interests, rather than be unduly influenced by past conditioning and external considerations.

Focus of attention is an essential component of the mental imagery skill for which the practice of mindfulness is foundational. See *Chapter 5* for more about this.

What you focus on grows.

Ellen Langer is another proponent of mindfulness benefits, contending that what we attend to and perceive has a profound impact on our wellbeing and health. She set out to prove this in her landmark study[18] in which she organised for elderly participants to experience a week-long retreat that virtually took them back in time to their youth. Everything in the environment was reconstructed to recreate conditions identical to this previous era. The participants were also instructed to live 'as if …' they were back in 1959, which included conversations about events current to that time (and to avoid any discussion about events beyond that time). The results indicated a profound youthing effect based on measures taken before and afterwards. The experiment virtually did turn back the clock as far as health and wellbeing indicators were concerned. It would appear that their bodies cooperated with the images of their minds.

You may have experienced similar results whenever you joyfully reminisce with others from your youth. It energises you and brings a bounce back into your step.

Savouring (versus Dwelling)

The practice of mindfulness then leads naturally and organically to becoming more aware of simple pleasures in life (rather than preoccupations typical of the 'monkey brain' indiscriminately jumping from limb to limb). As I constantly advise my clients: Catch yourself feeling good! The best way to bring up a positive image later is by fully tuning in to an experience in the present. If you would like to have more consistently good feelings then you need to practise becoming more aware of them when they occur. We are often more acutely aware of when we feel bad than when we feel good.

As Rick Hanson and Richard Mendius put it in their book *Buddha's Brain: The Practical Neuroscience of Happiness, Love and Wisdom* our brains are like Velcro to negative emotions, and Teflon to positive emotions. This has become our *human nature*.[19] The brain has been wired to get our attention when feeling bad in order to mobilise action for the better. This was critical to our survival historically. However, this process is now killing us (i.e. stress kills). Our evolution now depends on turning down the fight or flight or freeze mechanism and turning on more flow. To be happier, we need to tune in more to when feeling good in order to have more of the same in the future.

You are your own best teacher. If you catch yourself feeling good more often, you will then have a stronger and more readily available reference point and image with which to project into the future. Or even to change a present experience by calling up an appropriate image that is stored for this purpose. Without consciously savouring you limit the extent to which such an image will take hold and be filed away for future reference.

Because of our human nature it appears more natural to spend more time dwelling on regrets and mistakes, rather than savouring positive experiences and successes along the way. This is especially the case with high achievers and perfectionists, who tend to dwell on the gap of usually small imperfections rather than acknowledging if not celebrating the enormity of what they have achieved, which seems so unnatural for them.

For example, many golfers (professional and recreational) report how they keep replaying a bad shot between holes along with kicking themselves along the way, and then they wonder why the next shot doesn't go well. If the last shot went well, however, it's over and done with. Whereas it ought to be the reverse. While it is important to draw lessons from our mistakes, we are far better off replaying a corrected version rather than dwelling on the bad one as is the tendency.

High achievers need to be coached into allowing themselves to savour the little successes along the way. In the case of golf again — if the last shot went well, take a moment to savour and celebrate it for a moment, before rushing into moving on. To store better in memory what it is you would like to repeat.

Savouring has become such an important component in the positive psychology and wellness arenas that entire books have been written about it (e.g. *Savoring: A new model of positive experience* by Fred Bryant and Joseph Veroff and *Savor: Mindful Eating. Mindful Life* by Thich Nhat Hanh).

Savouring involves focusing on positive associations that deepen positive experience and generate positive emotions. This then serves to consolidate the image in your memory/imagery bank as frame of reference for future experiences. This process is augmented by focusing on your breathing, as the same part of your brain that controls respiration also controls emotions, and are inextricably linked.

While this connection largely functions below conscious awareness, we can use it to our advantage. By bringing more conscious attention to the process you are in a better position to lay down a preferred pattern in your brain. Focusing on breath can function as a bridge between your conscious and unconscious mind, and thereby optimise better control over your emotional experiences.

Reflecting (versus Ruminating) Over Negative Experiences

Reflecting versus ruminating is similar to the above about savouring versus dwelling. While it can be important to review incidents that did not go well, it is far more productive to reflect on what happened rather than ruminate over it. Quality reflection involves a process of drawing out the lessons from an experience or performance. Rumination, on the other hand, is characterised by replaying a negative incident and negative judgements about oneself or others in the process. Replaying a mistake or negative experience over and over again, however, only serves to increase the likelihood of a repeat performance.

A common feature of anxiety is to ruminate over past negative experiences and to worry about upcoming catastrophes. It is also well known that the tendency to ruminate over negative experiences leads to poor mood, which is no wonder, considering that the process of ruminating involves replaying things that have gone wrong over and over again. This only serves to make a bad situation worse, and increase levels of anxiety or depression.

Rumination is gratuitous self-flagellation — gratifying only to the extent that you punish yourself, but it is well known that punishing does not beget new behaviour. It actually ingrains that for which you are punishing yourself by amping up the negative emotions associated with the image, which serves to further embed the very image of what you do not wish to repeat, leading to more rumination and self-flagellation. It's a vicious cycle.

We all know how distressing it can be to have regrets and misgivings. The problem is that you do not have control over the past. You do, however, have control over drawing the lesson from an event, and then applying it to a future situation. This ultimately allows you to regain a sense of control, and to break the cycle of negativity. Focusing on the lessons and replaying corrections in mental imagery brings a surge of positivity in focusing on how you can be and do better; and might even relish such an opportunity to do so — thus improving self-confidence and wellbeing in the process. As I like to say: No mistakes; only valuable lessons.

It also pays to reflect on what went well, so you can repeat it!

Cultivating Gratitude and Appreciation (versus Complaining)

Savouring and reflecting set the stage for feelings of gratitude and appreciation. They seem to naturally and organically lead to what I like to call a *flow-on effect*. Noticing and savouring what there is to appreciate and being grateful further consolidates the focus and hence image to file away. It increases the well of positive memories from where you can draw at any future time when needed.

Practising gratitude is a major positive psychology intervention (e.g. *Thanks! How the new science of gratitude can make you happier* and *Gratitude Works!* Both by Robert Emmons).[20] It can take various forms, such as keeping a daily gratitude journal to list the highlights of your day and what you are most thankful for; and paying a gratitude visit to someone who has played a positively pivotal role in your life. All involve appreciation of a thing, event or person, which is in direct contrast to complaining. Both involve imagining that thing or person in action. Just like worrying versus praying, when you practise gratitude you are replaying the positive experience in your imagination, which tends to generate more of the same, if only in heightening perception.

In his latest book, *Flourish*, Seligman begins a chapter featuring gratitude interventions with a brief imagery exercise (memory) … 'Close your eyes. Call up the face of someone still alive who years ago did something or said something that changed your life for the better. Someone who you never properly thanked; someone you could meet face-to-face next week. Got a face? Gratitude can make your life happier and more satisfying.'[21]

Actively expressing gratitude directly to the person in question, called the Gratitude Visit, has also been shown to have lasting effects.

Whether a gratitude intervention involves reviewing the highlights of the day, counting blessings, or keeping a gratitude journal (that Oprah was fond of promoting on her show), it clearly involves remembering and thereby imagining that for which you are being grateful for. This is akin to the concept of that which you focus on grows. The wellbeing effects are clearly a result of imagining that for which you are grateful for. Even if it involves merely remembering, imagining the event evokes the same feelings as if it had just happened

In addition, keeping a gratitude journal tends to lead to looking out for and even generating opportunities to be grateful for (to fill up your journal). This causes you to keep in mind the attitude of gratitude, which becomes your focus and thereby mood throughout your day. See *Appendix A* for a more detailed guide for gratitude exercises.

What is important is not the semantics of gratitude and thanks, but the element of appreciation. Simply acknowledging that you love a rainbow, sunset, kindness, or even material goods, such as a certain car or shoes generates a sense of wellbeing that is consistent with the benefits of gratitude.

This can be applied when you become aware of something you want, but do not or cannot have (under current circumstances). This can quickly devolve in to feelings of frustration or worse, as your focus turns to a sense of lack — whether material or otherwise (and that leads to the suffering caused by envy, yearning and craving that Buddhist teachings warn against).

You can choose to refocus instead on simply noticing and appreciating — what a fabulous car, gorgeous body, wonderful relationship, deserved success (being zealous rather than jealous). This alters the negative association and transforms into a more positive one. This moves you away from the negative emotion that brings you down, replacing it with a more positive frame of reference and imagery which is more conducive to wellbeing and potentially achieving goals.

Acts of Kindness

Kindness is one of the virtues among the 24 identified by the VIA Survey of Character Strengths. As a positive psychology intervention, the practice of random acts of kindness (RAK) is considered responsible for the biggest (and most sustainable) boosts to wellbeing according to Seligman.[22] Kindness can take many forms, such as altruism, generosity, being considerate, compassion, caring and nurturing. It is also evident in helping behaviours, volunteerism and charity.

RAK is defined as: 'a selfless act performed by a person or persons wishing to either assist or cheer up an individual or in some cases an animal. There will generally be no reason other than to make people smile, or be happier. Either spontaneous or planned in advance, random acts of kindness are often encourage by various communities such as commercial or community organizations.'[23]

How kind are you? How able are you to give unconditionally? Consider past (unconditional) acts of kindness that you participated in — giving and receiving. Why not more often? Interestingly, it appears that our evolution may have depended on being kind given how our wiring seems to generate a boost in our immune system, even upon simply witnessing acts of compassion, such as in the case of the research featuring films of Mother Teresa in action (in contrast to watching violent films that caused immunosuppression). The effect of observing role models engaged in RAK causes a ripple effect, such as is commonly observed following natural disasters. Witnessing so many showing up to help strangers tends to generate a wellspring of good will that can be a joy to behold.

Studies comparing giving and receiving have actually found that those who do the giving seem to benefit most from the transaction than those on receiving end of any largesse;[24] and much of this can be attributed to the effects on one's self-image that feels good. Given the fact that we benefit personally while engaging in an act of kindness, the question is often raised whether there truly is such a thing as genuine altruism. Or is it merely self-serving to serve others?

Researchers have surmised that the key mechanisms for 'helper's high' — how helping and volunteering makes people feel good about themselves — is primarily about boosting self-image. For example:

1. Being kind and generous changes your perceptions (i.e. images) of others — to view them more positively, charitably ... and fosters a sense of interconnectedness (i.e. image of belonging).

2. Often relieves sense of guilt (for own good fortune) and discomfort at plight of others' misfortune. And shifts the focus to more positive actions and images.

3. Increases sense of appreciation for own good fortune in contrast to another's misfortune, thereby making you more aware of your advantages, and therefore more thankful; changing your image of your circumstances to be more positive.

4. Shifts focus of what is wrong with your life (and what you perceive not in your control) and providing help to others (gaining a sense of control) — providing a welcome diversion/distraction and therefore image.

5. Creates a positive change in how you perceive yourself — your self-image. When you engage in acts of kindness you can gain a better view of yourself as a 'good' person, someone who is compassionate and caring. It highlights more of what you can do (rather than cannot do), which increases your sense of control, of being useful and making a positive difference to another. Such an improved identity engenders a greater sense of confidence and optimism.

Research has also shown how circular the process from gratitude to kindness and back to gratitude can be. Feeling gratitude begets an increased urge for acts of kindness which feels good and increases awareness for what there is to appreciate.[25] This can largely be attributed to the imagery generated about the acts, which does not discriminate between the giver and receiver, but simply evokes an image of the acts of kindness.

The loving kindness meditation (LKM) that is common to Buddhist practice has been found to also lead to wellbeing benefits, and relies entirely on generating images of being loved then extending outwards to being loving to a wider and wider circle.[26] See *Appendix A* for variations on the LKM.

Optimism and Hope

Focusing on optimism is one of the major hallmarks of positive psychology. Being optimistic involves focusing on what can go right versus wrong. It can be such an important quality in order to persevere when the going gets tough. When you can see the positive possibilities rather than the limitations and obstacles, then you are more likely to persist in the pursuit of a challenging goal, and not give up. Being optimistic has been linked to

- Positive mood and good morale
- Perseverance towards meaningful goals
- Effective problem solving
- Success — athletic, academic, military, occupational and political success
- Popularity
- Good health and even long life

Pessimism, on the other hand, has been found to lead to depression, passivity, failure, social estrangement, morbidity and mortality.[27] While hope and optimism share conceptual features, there are also differences according to theory and research that is beyond the scope of this book. They nevertheless both feature mental representations of a positive future outcome which is the very definition of mental imagery.

Both hope and optimism are opposite of fear and pessimism. When you are afraid or pessimistic you are actually imagining the very thing you wish to avoid. By being hopeful and optimistic you will be more engaged in the positive image of what you hope for. This is a more uplifting mindset to be in, as well as more conducive to positivity. Fear, however, is a potent motivator, and usually only to the extent it drives us to avoid and prevent that which we fear, but rarely is it conducive to facing challenge and fulfilling our potential.

It is human nature, however, to be more motivated to avoid that which we fear than to approach that which makes us happy; the consequence of not listening to our fears in our evolution used to be death. Hence fear is far more intense a motivator as our survival has depended on it. This risk of not being more positive, however, is merely that we don't become as happy and successful as we might like — not a life and death proposition such as fear presents.

While positive thinking is implicated in being hopeful and optimistic, such thinking is only effective to the extent it evokes positive images (as discussed in *Chapter 1*, and explained in *Chapter 3*).

Positivity Ratio

One of the most well established and researched theory in positive psychology is on the broaden and build theory of positive emotions (as depicted in the book *Positivity* by Barbara Frederickson, which is based on research from her lab). The theory basically postulates that when positive emotions are generated we are more flexible in our thinking, which is reflected in the capacity to consider more options and possibilities, as well as being more creative when faced with a challenge or problem. This then leads to better results and outcomes, and therefore building of personal resources for coping and achieving, which in turn further increases our potential for personal growth and transformation, and produces upward spirals of wellbeing.

In contrast, negative emotions tend to have the effect of narrowing attention; thinking becomes more rigid thus limiting capacity for achieving best results, and leads to downwards spirals of wellbeing.

One of the most reliable methods of generating positive emotions in the lab has been by imagining or viewing a positive or amusing scene, e.g. puppies playing with a ball of wool.

Experiencing positive emotions such as joy leads us to be more playful, to be more explorative and courageous, to savour, and to integrate, which according to Frederickson[28], has the potential to lead to greater personal growth and fulfilling potential. This takes us far beyond being adaptive and functional to being fully creative and productive beings. This further extends to building resilience, and to increasing our capacity to ride out the storms of life; to not only bounce back well, but to bounce forward — now referred to as post traumatic growth (PTG). Increasing our positivity ratio (of positive emotions to negative emotions) is thought to be the difference.[29]

Positive emotions carry the capacity to transform individuals for the better, making them healthier and more socially integrated, knowledgeable, effective and resilient. In short, the (broaden-and-build) theory suggests that positive emotions fuel human flourishing.

Positivity in Action

Going for a walk with my puppy causes me to feel joy as well as receive the benefits of physical exercise and being outdoors. I begin to feel positive, to become friendlier and more aware of my surroundings. I engage in interesting conversations with others in the dog park, make new friends, or learn new, valuable information. I return home feeling refreshed and in better condition to work on a creative project. This, in turn, produces positive emotions of self-confidence as well as a sense of meaning and purpose when the outcome is well received and/or helps others. I then feel more optimistic about problem areas in my life and may see them more as opportunities. This strengthens my self-image and belief in capacity to take on more challenges and projects which leads to a more fulfilling career which results in a steady upward spiral of wellbeing.

One of the quickest and easiest ways to generate positivity is to recall a previous happy experience. That is to draw an image from your memory bank, which will then link to the positive emotions associated with that experience. As the brain cannot tell the difference between what is real or imagined, simply recalling a pleasant experience is enough to do the job. This process is akin to the peak experience recall exercise that is covered in *Chapter 7*.

Boosting Self-Efficacy/Confidence

I'll see it when I believe it.

Boosting self-efficacy (aka self-confidence) fits well within the positive psychology mandate, and is integral to coaching as well. Self-confidence is the key to being successful in any endeavour whether in the personal or professional domain (e.g. whether to approach an attractive person for a date; or to ask for a raise at work). How do you know when you are feeling confident? When you can imagine performing successfully, you already feel successful. This boosts confidence, and lowers anxiety about an upcoming event or opportunity, as confidence and anxiety tend to be mutually exclusive.

Self-efficacy is the more technical term that is often used interchangeably with the concept of self-confidence, and pertains to beliefs about specific capabilities. How confident you are to perform a specific task. Self-confidence, however, may apply to a broader spectrum of capacities than a single specific task. Both are not, however, the same as self-esteem. Self-esteem pertains to belief about oneself, and about how one feels about one's self-worth in general.

Having healthy self-esteem is clearly a critical element of psychological health and wellbeing. However, the concept is rife with controversy, though more so for how best to develop it. Artificially boosting self-esteem tends to actually undermine it whereas genuine self-esteem stems from meeting real challenges.

There is a clear link between self-efficacy/confidence and the concept of self-esteem, although they're not necessarily related. For example, a person can have high self-efficacy and perform well in a task that they take no pride in, e.g. being a bank foreclosure officer. Alternatively, an individual could feel 'hopeless' at a task without this affecting their self-esteem, if they do not care about the outcome. For example, you might not feel very confident about your ability to surf, but this does not shake your sense of value about yourself in any way.

In addition, it takes more than high self-esteem to do well. It is true, however, that people do tend to pursue activities they are good at, and that enhance their sense of self-worth. You might assume that it would follow that high achievers have high self-esteem, but you'd be wrong. Many high achievers are very hard on themselves and demand (impossibly) high standards of themselves, and may therefore lack self-efficacy. In fact, they can often be plagued with self-doubt, which is what drives them so hard to succeed. Others with high self-esteem may not necessarily strive so high, and therefore are unaffected by lack of self-efficacy on a particular endeavour.

Sources of self-efficacy

Bandura has outlined five basic sources for self-efficacy, which are summarised below.[30] The first three of those sources are clearly linked to mental imagery as covered in this book.

Performance experience: This is obviously the most powerful source of self-efficacy as it provides actual evidence for one's capacity beyond just belief. That not only 'yes you can', but 'yes you did'. Replaying previous successes can boost one's self-efficacy for an upcoming similar challenge. For example, recalling a previous peak performance will instil greater feelings of self-efficacy and confidence for an upcoming similar event.

Vicarious experience: Observing someone like yourself performing a particular behaviour also boosts self-efficacy that you can do it too. 'If they can do it, so can I'. This is why role models can be effective in changing the behaviour in others. For example, observing how someone else has overcome an illness fosters belief in one's capacity to also face such a similar illness.

Imaginal experience: Being able to imagine executing a task boosts one's self-efficacy. For example, if you can picture yourself looking and feeling confident as you step up to a podium to deliver a speech, then you are more likely to actually be confident.

Verbal persuasion: Often our belief in ourselves begins with someone else believing in our abilities, i.e. someone who can imagine us delivering on a task, helps us to imagine the same. Being encouraged by someone we know and trust instils the belief that we can try something new and challenging, e.g. go to a networking function and strike up conversations with strangers. This can also take the form of positive self-talk as one internalises the encouragement (e.g. 'Go on. I can do this.' 'I am friendly and outgoing…'). Keeping in mind that such self-talk is most effective when it evokes the appropriate and desired imagery.

Physiological and emotional states: Being in an ideal physical and emotional condition can boost self-efficacy. For example, having had a good night's sleep gives one confidence they can be on top of their game during the day. Having a hangover would cause one to feel much less confident in their capacity to perform to potential. Being able to imagine the ideal mind/body state for the task in question, however, will enhance the likelihood of the condition; if only due to the likelihood of behaving consistently accordingly.

All of the above would not only affect our belief in our abilities, but also in the amount of effort we might be willing to expend, and thereby affect the outcome, which can create a vicious circle. With mental imagery practice you enhance your capacity for improvement and success, leading to a cycle of confidence upon which you can build and build.

Summary

In this chapter I have provided an overview of several major positive psychology strategies highlighting how integral mental imagery is to gaining benefits. It is early days in compiling evidence for positive psychology interventions, but the data is promising. If you would like to maximise results of applying positive psychology strategies, then it makes sense to more consciously engage your imaginal processes to augment and consolidate any benefits. This will also increase your inner resources and reserves upon which your future is based — for how you think, feel and act — for being and doing better.

Chapter 3

The Science —
How Mental Imagery Works

Everything you can imagine is real. – Pablo Picasso

This chapter covers the scientific evidence for the efficacy of mental imagery in practice, providing an overview of:

- Indirect evidence based on what we know about the placebo effect and how biofeedback works

- Recent findings that the new neuroscience technology has produced

- How the field of quantum physics explains the power of mental imagery

- And finally, what is probably of greatest relevance to you is the proof how the mental imagery process is much more powerfully linked to our emotions than words and language, and therefore a far more effective tool for producing best results and change

Mental imagery advocates have long conjectured that the brain cannot tell the difference between what is real and what is imagined. We have relied mostly on theory and anecdotal evidence, with a smattering of applied research along the way. Unfortunately, it has been very difficult to test with standard imagery protocols, as firstly, imagery works best when tailored to the individual; and secondly, there is no way to objectively measure the actual quality and quantity of mental imagery. It would be fantastic if we could get inside your head and videotape your images, but this is not possible.

With the advent of new technology in the field of neuroscience, however, we now have direct and incontrovertible evidence for our claims. I will first cover the older and more indirect evidence based on behavioural medicine research about the placebo effect and biofeedback; to be followed by the more recent evidence based on neuroscience. The best evidence, however, will be based on your own experimentation with the practice — your own trials and observations.

Mental Imagery in Action

My own personal proof that I enjoy sharing is about how mental imagery got me to do something. Since the state of meditation provides fertile mental ground for the practice of mental imagery, I attempt to capitalise at the end of every meditation. On one particular occasion, I couldn't decide what to focus on, so I just picked an easy task, but one which I tend to have a deep resistance to. When I got up from my meditation, I found myself standing in front of the sink washing dishes as if in a trance. It wasn't long before my natural resistance kicked in, practically shouting: 'What are you doing here? And how did you get here?'

I didn't remember deciding to be there doing that! But was already halfway through, and so finished the job. It was only later that I remembered that I had deliberately primed myself by picturing the dishes done in my post-meditation mental imagery. While doing dishes is not a very challenging task, what is challenging is how much I normally hate the job, and put off until absolutely necessary (even though I have a dishwasher that I do not use). This is not atypical of the many behaviours most of us need to change in order to live healthier and more productive lives (not to mention happier). All too often the 'behaviour' is completely within our control and ability, but we resist for one reason or another. Despite being a great believer in the power of mental imagery, what was so profound to me is how the imagery practice overcame and overrode my strong resistance. If it can work in this case, it can work for anything!

Until the turn of the current century, we relied mostly on theory to explain how mental imagery works. Most notably, Psychoneuromuscular Theory had the greatest credibility. It refers to the fact that brain activity for mentally imagining an act, and actually performing the act are very similar. Many went so far as to suggest that the brain doesn't know the difference. We are now able to demonstrate this in the lab. Not only is the brain activity very similar, although far more pronounced when actually active, nerve firings are also in evidence in the muscle groups that would be involved in the activity. This is something that has long been well accepted and implemented in the sport and performance psychology domain.[31]

Indirect Evidence: Placebo Effect and Biofeedback

The findings from medical research on the placebo effect and biofeedback provide some of the most convincing evidence for the power of mental images. The key mechanism involved in the effects of placebos and biofeedback is via the images triggered, which in many cases the person is not even aware of!

Placebo effect

The placebo is a sugar pill with no medicinal value, except for the suggestion of the pill's function. For example, if I were to give you a pill and tell you that it was a pain reliever and you believed me (because I'm a trusted doctor or pharmacist) your pain would likely go away. This is called the *placebo effect*, which refers to healing brought about by belief in a treatment that actually has no medicinal value.

You've probably already experienced this effect yourself. How many of you have been sick or in pain when booking an appointment with your doctor, only to find your symptoms disappear en route? This is based merely on the suggestion that help is on the way, and your body responds accordingly. Almost any physiological or psychological condition responds to the placebo. Merely the suggestion that the medicine will work sets in motion the image of what the medicine is designed to do. The placebo can be so effective as to be dangerous in terms of the side effects and addiction potential.

The placebo effect is so powerful that all drugs must be tested in comparison to it. In most drug trials, the placebo effect accounts for up to 50% or more of the results. In fact, the more potent the drug is suggested to be, the more profound the results. In the case of analgesics (pain relievers) the placebo effect is stronger — the stronger the analgesic effect is believed to be, e.g. when comparing aspirin/ ibuprofen to morphine. Unfortunately, doctors are not permitted to actually prescribe placebos for several ethical and indemnity reasons. But that need not stop you from drawing on your inner chemist via mental imagery!

In his book *Spiritual Evolution*, George Vaillant likens the placebo effect to the sacrament at the end of church services. 'The placebo serves as the physician's communion wafer and sacramental wine', which is not unlike how the 'prescription at the end of a clinic visit seals the contract between two individuals who are committed by faith and love to hope for the patient's recovery.'[32]

Biofeedback

Biofeedback involves the process of amplifying the signals (feedback) of your body (bio) in a way that you can see and/or hear. Electrodes are placed at the regions of the body that you wish to control, e.g. heart rate monitors (EKG), muscle contraction monitors (EMG), brain wave monitors (EEG), etc. and hooked up to a machine that registers the activity and emits a tone or picture on a computer screen. You are then asked to change the tone or picture. It is now well documented that individuals can adjust their neurophysiology merely by use of the feedback. For example, people can raise or lower their blood pressure, increase or reduce their heart rate, and increase temperature in their hands (called hand-warming).

Interestingly, when early researchers Elmer and Alyce Green were experimenting with hand-warming they inadvertently discovered that migraine sufferers found relief. By increasing temperature in hands migraines tend to go away. This is due to the increased blood flow to the hands (and away from the head) that is generated by the heat imagery, which is what causes the relief. While the researchers provided suggestions of images to engage in to produce the desired hand-warming effect, it is ultimately up to each individual to use what works best for them. Some of the participants reported drawing upon images of hands near a fire or stove, or sunshine warming the hands. Others focused on hot colours infusing their hands (hues of red), or imagined heat waves radiating out of their hands. The biofeedback indicator lets them know whether they are on track or not.[33]

The biofeedback and placebo research provide two functions in relation to mental imagery. Firstly, imagery appears to be the main mechanism by which biofeedback and placebos work, and also provide the evidence for the physiological impact of the purely imaginary experience. What is most amazing is how quickly this mind–body process works. In the case of the placebo it can be almost instantaneous; and in biofeedback, within minutes.

Neuroscience

With the advent of new technology in recent years we are now able to document and prove what was previously only possible theoretically and indirectly. We can now measure and directly observe mental processes and corresponding changes in the brain. We used to say that the brain cannot tell the difference between what is real and what is imagined, but we couldn't prove it. Now we can.

Neuroplasticity

Neuroplasticity is the technical term for what is also referred to as *cortical re-mapping* (i.e. brain remapping — the capacity of your nervous system to develop new neuronal connections). It refers to the ability of the human brain to change as a result of your experience, including imaginal experience. Previously automatic patterns that are resistant to change can be switched off by creating newer and more adaptive patterns to override the old. This can only occur with mental practice that creates new neuronal pathways. Translated, this means you can rewrite your script. Whatever you can imagine can become your new more preferred repertoire to replace the old.

Mirror neurons and the power of observation

Mirror neurons are a small circuit of brain cells that explain the phenomenon of 'monkey see, monkey do'. They come in to play whenever we observe another, and can be indistinguishable from when we engage in the same behaviour ourselves. Our brain virtually *mirrors* what is being observed, and activates the same brain centres for actually performing the action observed.

The same parts of the brain light up when planning and controlling actual actions, as when simply imagining the same actions, albeit to a lesser extent. This overlap between what is imagined and what is actually performed increases with practice. It explains how observation of a performance directly improves one's own performance of the same action regardless of one's intentions while watching, e.g. a professional tennis match can enhance your own tennis skills regardless of whether this is your purpose for attending the match. This is further enhanced with deliberate mental practice of a performance, and is accentuated the more skilled you are in the act you observe. If you're already skilled you become more so. If unskilled, you will still improve, but to a lesser extent.

This explains an all-time peak performance of mine: how I was able to execute a spectacular winning shot behind my back in squash. This is something I normally would not have dreamt of attempting, let alone expect to be successful with. It occurred the day after watching several hours of high level exhibition tennis featuring Jimmy Connors and John McEnroe playing doubles with local pros, horsing around with plenty of trick shots on display.

This also explains how involved fans become in the exploits of their favourite athletes or teams. You would probably have also noticed the frequent scene of friends and families tossing the football around during half-time of a championship game with great skill. Which is why watching those more expert than ourselves before stepping onto the field ourselves is recommended and, conversely, why it is not recommended to watch others of lesser skill level just prior to stepping onto the field or stage.

It is also important for athletes who participate in sports where others preceding them are likely to falter before their turn to perform, e.g. falling on the ice in figure skating, to either not watch if possible, or quickly correct the negative images. This explains the Bradbury effect, which refers to the case of Aussie Stephen Bradbury, who was able to win the gold medal in a speed skating event at 2002 Winter Olympic Games. He was fully prepared mentally to not be affected by others falling in front of him, as this often causes a domino effect even without contact. His greater incentive for being prepared was because he also knew that his best chance of winning would only be if those ahead of him were to fall, and he to remain standing. And fall they did in the final — and Bradbury won by being the 'last man standing'.

Not only are our brains wired to simulate whatever we observe without conscious thought or intention, but also the motivations and emotions underpinning those actions. This explains how emotions can be contagious. For example, when you observe someone else smiling, your mirror neurons for smiling are also triggered, leading to the sensations that you would normally associate with the experience of smiling. You do not have to think about it to know the other person's intentions; you experience them directly and naturally.

Mirror neurons, therefore, explain the experience of empathy and sympathy. How it is that simply observing the emotions that another exhibits stirs similar feelings within us? It used to be believed that this was due to the logical thought processes for interpretation and prediction of other people's actions. It is now clear that what we come to instinctually understand about others arises not from the cumbersome process of thinking about it, but more reflexively with feelings via the mirror neuron process. This is why we cringe when someone else stubs their toe, and why our heart races in the dying moments of a close game, why we laugh or cry in the presence of another doing so, or how our heart breaks at witnessing another's sorrow. This also explains how we become devoted fans hooked on the adrenalin rush of watching our favourite team in battle. It's almost as if we're out there doing battle alongside them.

The mirror neuron process adds weight to the power of drawing upon role models, as discussed in *Chapter 5*, and how the power of imitation creates greater chances of replication for you.

This also raises the issue of what we witness in the media. The direct implications are that you become more of what you choose to watch, in the same way that 'you are what you eat'. Being wired to automatically internalise the movements and mental states of others suggests we ought to be more careful about what we watch. As leading expert on mirror neurons Lacoboni attests: 'Mirror neurons provide a plausible neurobiological mechanism that explains why being exposed to media violence leads to imitative violence'.[34]

This process can either work for you or against you. It is up to you to be more aware and choose more consciously. You do not have to be a passive participant, but can more consciously utilise this process to activate and/or deactivate accordingly.

We can exploit this natural process by creating new images for changes and improvements we desire in ourselves. By imagining a new way of being, we are activating our mirror neuron mechanism, which in turn becomes stored as a new memory, and becomes part of our repertoire. This is facilitated by watching someone else we admire, hence the power of role models.

If our brains are engaged as if executing a particular move then why don't we actually move? The most plausible explanation for why the brain mirrors the action without actually engaging in the action is that there has also evolved a mechanism for switching off the motor action, when the actually relevant sensory input would be missing. So the brain sticks with merely 'as if' while not actually doing.

Functional MRI studies

It is thanks to magnetic resonance imaging (MRI) technology that we can now definitively demonstrate what we've long claimed and believed: that our brain cannot tell the difference between what is real and what is imagined. So real that according to leading researchers 'imagining something can later be mistaken for having seen it'.[35]

You are probably familiar with MRI as a diagnostic device that yields far more valuable information to medical professionals than X-rays and other types of scans. The MRI translates magnetic fields and radio waves to produce high quality two- or three- dimensional images of brain structures (without injecting radioactive tracers as with PET). A functional MRI (fMRI) further enables the observation of changes in the brain, by measuring the quick, tiny metabolic changes that take place in an active part of brain.

Research comparing visual perception to visual imagery shows that both draw on similar neural regions of the brain.[36] Studies find that the brain regions used for imagining visual images are the same ones used in actually seeing them. The overlap is as high as 90% and most pronounced in the frontal and parietal regions of the brain (more so than in the occipital and temporal regions). The degree of overlap goes up with the level of skill and practice: the better your imagery skill, the less difference between the real and imagined. As with all skills, this can be enhanced with practice.

This indicates that the mental (aka cognitive) control processes function similarly in both perception and imagery. Whatever gets laid down as memory from an actual perceived experience is little different from what gets laid down in memory from an imagined experience. Both processes become our frame of reference, influencing the filter through which we perceive and therefore experience all future events. We can become more 'experienced' without actually having had the experience! We can, therefore, take greater creative control over our destiny by changing the memory bank upon which we filter and thereby influence our perceptions and reactions, i.e. we can shape our future experiences. The psychotherapeutic implications are that we can reverse the effects of traumatic memories, which is currently being applied to treat PTSD (called 'rescripting').

The fMRI research has involved mostly visual imagery and perception, but also to a more limited extent auditory, tactile, and even kinaesthetic — fine motor movements (e.g. finger tapping). There are obvious limitations to studying the brain during gross motor movement while contained within the fMRI contraption. There is extensive biofeedback evidence, however, of neurological firing in muscles being imagined moving, thus confirming a neuromuscular connection during imagery.

It is reasonable to surmise that given there is a proven overlap with visual imagery and perception, the same would likely occur with all senses, including what is best referred to as a visceral sense that is most aligned with emotions, thereby adding weight to the power of imagery for emotional regulation.

Transcranial magnetic stimulation

Transcranial magnetic stimulation (TMS), alternatively referred to as transcranial direct current stimulation (tDCS), is relatively new technology that is still in its infancy. It involves placing a coil over a location on the skull that is known to have a specific function in the cerebral cortex. An electrical signal is then passed through the coil that produces a magnetic pulse activating neurons to fire.[37] This results in slight muscle twitching when this electrical current is directed at parts of the brain in charge of fine movement control. When a person is engaged in mental imagery of the movement, the amount of TMS required to cause muscle twitching is reduced. 'The mental practice activates the appropriate brain area to a slight degree, which then requires less TMS to trigger the muscles'.[38]

Quantum Physics and Evolution of Consciousness

Mental imagery engages your power of intention that creates a real metaphysical change. According to quantum physics our evolution relies on raising our level of consciousness and thereby better access and utilisation of 'information' (i.e. the database of all that is, was, and potentially can be). Therefore consciousness = information. The more information we have access to, and are able to sort through and apply, the better for our evolution.

Applying quantum physics to the metaphysical

By actively engaging in creating your preferred reality via mental imagery, you create a new base of information from which to draw (remember: change of consciousness = information). The imagery provides more order to the less organised system of your mind and various agendas, and provides the opportunity for introducing greater clarity and coherence. This leads to greater awareness of your positive options as well as generation of possibilities leading to more conscious (positive) intention, which will affect the filter by which you take in new experiences. Your frame of reference changes.

The experience played out in mental imagery of preferred choice modifies future capacity for more adaptable perception of choices in behaviour/performance. This is not dissimilar to the neuroscience explanations earlier, but arrived at from another perspective that does not involve the brain as such.

Mental Imagery = Applied Quantum Physics

According to quantum physics, consciousness evolves by decreasing entropy (i.e. disorder and complexities, e.g. competing inner agendas), and increasing organisation and coherence of information (i.e. database). Mental imagery creates new 'data', or re-organises existing data in a new way that is more conducive to your wellbeing and aspirations. This then alters your frame of reference as you encounter new experiences, allowing you to exercise more free-will rather than reacting in habitual ways (or re-enacting) reflecting old maladaptive patterns of behaviour.

In summary: Mental imagery has the effect of changing the database of your reality and experiences, and thereby greater freedom to change and evolve.[39]

Mental Imagery and Emotions

Mental imagery has a far more powerful and deeper impact on affect (aka emotion) than verbal processes (e.g. self-talk, affirmations, etc.), which are more superficial[40].

A picture is worth a thousand words.

Interesting case in point is the now iconic 'I♥NY' promotion for New York City, which is far more evocative than the words (i.e. I Love NY).[41] The word 'love' alone is empty without an associated image.

Images have a more direct route to emotions, and are therefore a far more effective strategy to employ when attempting to trigger or change how you feel. This is due to the fact that there is a direct link in the brain from images to emotions that bypass the language centres of the brain.[42]

This is why I always emphasise to my clients that any self-talk strategy is limited to the extent they evoke an appropriate and effective image. Images serve as an emotional amplifier (positive and negative) for the verbal meaning and information upon which you would wish to draw from. Conversely, invoking verbal meaning will serve to diffuse emotions, thereby reducing negative impact of negative emotional reactions, e.g. by labelling an emotion or experience you enable your ability to detach from it, thereby gaining relief from the negative (also referred to as dissociation).

The reason for this is that language has appeared much later in our evolution, and is therefore not as well connected to our perception-reaction link essential to our survival, especially with respect to danger. This mechanism had basic evolutionary survival value that enabled us to quickly (automatically) generate the requisite neurobiological resources with which to act efficiently (fight or flight; aka stress) in reaction to fear/

danger. This is why so-called talk therapy is so limited in effectiveness if we are not able to tap into the deeper more emotional and visceral components of our minds. While this link between perception-imagery-emotions may seem inconvenient when attempting to access via language, it does nevertheless offer up a direct link to also (re)gain control over our emotions. So, as I like to say: Dive in to soar!

Theoretical Mechanisms for Mental Imagery – Emotions Link

There are three mechanisms to explain the process of mental imagery as follows:

Bio Informational Theory. Imagery signals go directly to emotional centres that bypass higher cortical regions such as language. As mentioned previously, this had basic evolutionary value with respect to fear and survival, which has now become a liability with respect to stress effects on our bodies and minds. This process is in evidence even when the threatening stimuli (triggers) are not even within range of conscious awareness or attention. It can be so automatic that conscious awareness is unnecessary for the survival mechanism to kick in (fight/flight). For example, you might find yourself slamming on the brakes while driving before realising why — that you were about to be side-swiped by an erratic driver. Thank goodness for that!

This works against us, however, when we overreact to whatever we perceive (consciously or unconsciously) is highly associated with an intense past experience, such as in the case of PTSD. You do not need to have experienced trauma for this mechanism to maladaptively operate in your life. Any painful experience will do.

Imagery-perception link. Given that imagery and perceptual processes overlap in the brain (see the fMRI section above), the brain signals the emotions similarly. Therefore imagery is a conduit to your emotions just as if really being perceived.

Imagery and autobiographical memory. Imagery draws on, and triggers links to, memory and relevant associations. The mechanisms for both remembering your past as well as imagining your future overlap. New images will draw upon your existing repertoire of autobiographical memory (as same processes are involved)[43]. Interestingly, people who report lower levels of detail when describing memories or images are also more likely to avoid emotional expression.[44] Conversely, imagery vividness (aka clarity) of memories as well as of the future is highly correlated with emotional intensity and expressiveness. This indicates the strong link between those with more active imaginations and emotionality.

The implications of the above section is that while self-talk techniques are brilliant at short-circuiting the downward spiralling effect of negative emotions that are typically fear-based (and therefore more intense thus requiring 3:1 positive emotions just to counterbalance, re. positivity ratio) — they are short-lived and stop short of being fully effective.

You might get temporary respite from the tyranny of what holds you back. You might find inspiration that motivates and energises you, but such inspiration and greater force of will eventually runs out. It is not sustainable and the subsequent inevitable setback (inevitable especially for challenging goals) will only lead to more frustration, disappointment and worse, despair, and giving up (and the downward spiral that we're so familiar with).

Simple exhortations such as variations of 'Yes you can!' and 'You can do it!' help to refocus attention away from 'No you can't' internal dialogue, but you need to fill in the blank that follows with more specifics and imagery for the 'can do …' element. And focus more on what is within control in the immediate future — the better to prevent any frustrated/disappointed descent again … while obviously keeping in mind the more distant aims — to keep it meaningful and purposeful. Mental imagery is the way!

Imagery Beyond Words: Putting Words in Their Place

In *A Final Word about Words*, Holmes and Mathews conclude that 'emotional effects of imagery are greater than those of alternative language-based representations, and under some conditions verbal processing may even cause deterioration of an existing emotional state.'[45] And: 'In summary, we propose that mental imagery acts as an "emotional amplifier" in both negative and positive emotional states and in many emotional disorders.'[46]

The implications, therefore, are that mental imagery is a useful tool for changing negative emotional patterns, and for enhancing change and fulfilling our potential!

Summary

Mental imagery has the effect of changing the database of your reality and experience, which has been borne out by evidence from medicine, neuroscience and quantum physics. Moreover, the research has proven how important it is to engage your mental imagery processes (versus verbal processes), for accessing and changing how you feel — for creating your best emotional state of mind — upon which so much of your wellbeing and success depends.

PART 2
Setting Goals and Practising Mental Imagery

Chapter 4

Charting Your Course — Setting Goals

Setting effective goals is a natural first step before practising mental imagery. This chapter will provide:

- Ways to avoid common goal setting pitfalls
- Guidelines for how best to implement goal setting ranging from dream goals to the nitty gritty of everyday pursuits
- The basics and essentials

Goals set the stage for what it is that you will imagine unfolding. The process of goal setting may seem quite simple and straightforward, but consistently doing so effectively is not. To get the most out of your mental imagery practice, therefore, you need to nail your goal setting practice to springboard your success.

You would probably never set out on a road trip to a new destination without a map. You might choose to go the scenic route or the fastest route, but you will likely have a well-charted course and set of directions. There will also usually be clear signposts along the way to inform you whether you're on track or not. When you veer off track, you will soon know it, and be able to find your way back with a good map. What about the journey of life? While there may be well-defined pathways to many life goals, they need to be personalised to you and your circumstances. In many cases, we're dealing with uncharted waters, so you might need to develop better navigational sense to read the signs to adjust your direction accordingly.

Many of you may now be relying on GPS technology for real road travel. Wouldn't it be wonderful if we could have a GPS set up for our best life? Developing your own inner navigational skills, however, is ultimately more empowering, than relying on external programming. In fact, you are already responding to a program that is not of your conscious making (based on your genetics and upbringing). Goal setting is about taking more deliberate and conscious control over your destiny, and mental imagery is what will give you a turbo boost.

What is your life course? Do you know where you're going, and how to get there? Without a well-charted course we are likely to end up easily side-tracked and even lost at times; or worse, as many do, end up going in circles. You are also more vulnerable to succumbing to someone else's plan and agenda when you do not have a well-established one for yourself.

If you would like to be more in control over your destiny, you need to have a well-developed set of goals and plans. Some goals come more readily than others and are well-established signposts for how we're doing (e.g. getting a degree or job, buying a car or house, winning a game, beating cancer, etc.). Many meaningful life goals, however, are not as concrete, and have no reliable and objective 'yardstick' for determining how we're doing, e.g. in social situations. At such times, we tend to veer into the neverland of social comparison that usually leads to greater anxiety rather than boosting confidence and wellbeing.

For long-term resilience and a sense of security and confidence that will enable you to enjoy more of life's challenges and opportunities, you need to better articulate the basis upon which you rate yourself, or the criteria on which you base your sense of self-worth, or of being good enough (including, but not limited to, being attractive enough). This is tough and few of us, when pressed, can define quite what these criteria are. Only that we don't meet them! Perfectionists are particularly vulnerable because their 'enough' is 'perfection', which does not exist![47]

Whether you're a perfectionist or not, the key to becoming free from incessant self-doubt, and the stress and quest for extrinsic reassurance that comes with it, is to define clear personal standards (criteria) that work for you. In doing this, ask yourself what your values are, or what's truly most important to you, as the two should align. Also define a basis upon which you'll know you are achieving your criteria, as otherwise life becomes a constant guessing (and worse, second-guessing) game. Nowhere is this more nebulous and insidious than in social situations.

Here's how you can apply developing your own compass in a social situation (in addition to focusing on what's good about you). Before you head out, establish your criteria for being and doing well, specific to the situation. What's your criteria for displaying your best features and attributes? For staying calm and focused? For exuding warmth and confidence? Then when you're in the situation, if you're going to make any comparison, you'll make it according to your own checklist, not to other people. You don't need to be the best in the room — just the best you. It is, after all, your best chance of being likeable, and all you have control over anyway.

This chapter describes how setting goals are linked to mental imagery. You will learn about the different types of goals you can set, and which types are most conducive to performing and doing well. While long-term goals may be obvious, it is necessary to break them down into more intermediate time frames and ranges to be more manageable and achievable.

The better you can get at applying goal setting effectively, the better your images will be. Keep in mind a couple of your most cherished goals as you read this chapter, and see how much more value you can add to them by following the suggestions. Consider both professional type goals as well as more personal goals.

Avoiding Goal Setting Pitfalls

More and more people are becoming disenchanted with the concept and practice of goal setting. This is often due to incomplete or flawed application of the process, and lack of following through. Nowhere is this more in evidence than in the tradition of New Year's resolutions, which highlights the issues.

There's good reason for putting off making resolutions until a major prompting occasion such as a brand new year. It's a time for us to look back as well as forward with greater hope and optimism hence the lasting tradition of New Year's resolutions (NYR), even though the resolutions themselves rarely last beyond the first week. It can feel great to declare our goals and aspirations buoyed by the moment and the crowd, but the enthusiasm quickly gives way to discouragement over time in facing our challenge on our own. We lose our resolve, and give up on evolving.

The major reason for this is that we tend to overshoot and under-commit to our goals. This is especially the case for goals related to changing or breaking bad habits that are characteristic of New Year's resolutions. As we all know, change of any kind is difficult. Old habits die hard, and the best predictor of future behaviour is past behaviour. Most New Year's resolutions are therefore destined to fail from the start. But your destiny need not be controlled by your history. You can seize control by harnessing the power of your imagination to increase your chances of successfully changing and evolving; or you can leave it all to chance.

The first step is committing to the change or goal.

> *Losers make promises they often break. Winners make commitments they always keep.* – **Dennis Waitley**

Promising, and even getting started, is the easy part (relatively speaking). The commitment to staying the course is not. If you fail to develop and commit to a plan for a challenging goal, then you are planning to fail. There are several other major pitfalls and antidotes to making and keeping NYRs.

NYR pitfalls and antidotes:

Minding the (goal setting) gap — most worthwhile goals are challenging, but goals too far out of reach highlight the gap between where you are now, and where you want to be. This can be too disheartening.

Antidote — set goals in steps and increments and celebrate the little successes along the way. Daily goals are most powerful, as they are all you have immediate control over, and you get a morale boost from achieving them. More importantly, foster the conditions (mentally, physically, socially) conducive to the process of achieving goals.

What you taketh away must be replaced — many NYRs involve giving something up, such as a bad lifestyle habit, e.g. smoking, sugar, alcohol, etc. Taking something away without replacing with a better alternative sets you up for failure. Focusing on what not to do inevitably conjures up more of the same rather than the reverse; not to mention creates a sense of deprivation.

Antidote — focus on what to do, and on positive alternatives that can serve a similar purpose in healthier and more self-nurturing way.

Changing for the wrong/external reasons — changing to please others or to meet another's expectations may provide some incentive, but is ultimately demotivating.

Antidote — pursue change for the right and internal reasons — establish and remind yourself of the benefits to your own wellbeing.

Relying on willpower — willpower may work temporarily, but inevitably runs out as we encounter the inevitable setbacks.

Antidote — develop and harness your personal strengths and resources (such as mental imagery discussed below), and create detailed plans (including and especially contingency plans) for sustainable gains and maintaining momentum. And/or recruit a goal buddy or coach!

Goal Setting Basics

Many of you have probably already heard about the SMART goal system, which is a handy acronym for remembering any goals you have in mind. The basics are below:

SMART goals

There are a few variations on the SMART goal theme, but below is what is most commonly espoused. Some people are now adding a couple more components to bring the acronym to SMARTER. See below.

Specific: The more specificity you can bring to your goal, the better and more clear your images can be. Vague goals yield vague results.

Measurable: How will you know that you've achieved your goal if you do not have any measures in mind.

Action-oriented: Having set a goal, you need to develop a plan of action in order to achieve your goal. Alternatively, the 'A' refers to being 'Accountable', which enhances commitment.

Realistic: Your goal needs to be within reasonable reach otherwise you are setting yourself up for perpetual frustration. Alternatively, the 'R' refers to 'Resonating', which creates more meaningfulness.

Time-bound: Setting deadlines prevents procrastination. An alternative to the 'T' is thrilling, which is energising, and would stem from heartfelt goals.

Energising/**E**ngaging: The goal ought to be engaging enough to sustain the energy required to stay the course. This is also associated with the concept of 'Flow' (covered in *Chapters 2* and *7*) that requires ample challenge as well as skill level to achieve.

Rewarding: Setting up a reward structure supports the endeavour for working towards a goal. The 'R' could also refer to setting a 'Range' of goals from minimum to maximum.

HARD goals[48]

A newer acronym to apply to goals has recently appeared on the scene, coined by Mark Murphy, who has raised the bar on the above by developing the HARD goals system, which includes incorporating mental imagery in the process (see 'A'), recommending that goals also need to be:

Heartfelt: Goals generated from the heart are more likely to generate the will and motivation to achieve them. The more emotionally invested you are in your goal, the more likely you are to take the steps necessary to achieve the goal.

Animated: Refers to picturing your goals, bringing them to life with mental imagery.

Required: The more urgency you can bring to your goal, the more energy you will also bring forth that creates greater likelihood of achievement.

Difficult: Challenging goals tend to be more engaging and meaningful, and therefore more motivating and satisfying when achieved.

Goal Setting Essentials

There is so much more to understanding goal setting than the basics described above. To garner the most from the process, you will also need to keep in mind the following recommendations.

Keeping goals positive: Do's versus Don'ts

What applies to all types of goals is to state them in positive terms. Do not set goals for what you *do not* want. Only set goals for what you *do* want. For example, if you set a goal to not fail at something you are actually setting the stage to fail, as that will be the mental image associated with such a goal. Our minds do not follow the directive of the word 'don't', but do follow the directives of the image generated. Therefore, set a goal for success, and the image to come up will be more positive. This can be trickier to accomplish with certain goals.

For example, if the goal is to not drop the ball while running down a field with a bunch of burly guys chasing you to tackle you, what image comes up? More likely than not, it's you coughing up the ball! If you had a goal to not bite your nails the related image to come up would be of you biting your nails. The ball example would be much easier to adjust. You would simply set a goal for holding on to the ball (maintaining good ball possession). The nail example requires a bit more creativity, e.g. setting a goal of long and healthy nails, and a positive alternative to biting your nails, such as using the impulse as a cue to taking a couple of deep breaths and stretching or shaking out your hands and loosening your jaw (as nail-biting can cause problems for the temporal-mandibular joint that then leads to headaches), to relieving any stress that might be the triggering impulse.

Dreaming to manifesting

There are several types of goals that can be set. There are *outcome* goals that relate to the desired end result of an endeavour. There are *performance* goals regarding what you need to accomplish to achieve the outcome you want. And then there are *process* goals, which relate more to your state of mind and body as you pursue your goals.

There are also dream goals, long-term goals, and intermediate goals. The most powerful, however, are daily goals, because they are what you have most control over — what you can accomplish today — and are therefore also most motivating, as they are more immediately within your grasp and therefore encouraging. Daily goals also provide the best information about whether you are on track or not.

Dream goals

> *Go confidently in the direction of your dreams! Live the life you've imagined. As you simplify your life, the laws of the universe will be simpler.* – Henry David Thoreau

Dream first, compromise later. Think about what might be possible if you were to completely stretch your limits, and if all the stars were aligned in your favour. As the famous Swedish sport psychologist Willi Railo suggests: 'Imagine the possibilities of unlimited possibilities.'

Highly successful individuals tend to shoot for the stars in any pursuit. Not everyone can reach the top, but it is very difficult to attain without having set your sights on it. You might never reach your dream goal, but you might reach one even better suited to you because of the fork in the road that pursuit of your dream led you to. We don't always know what is in our best interests, but if we don't set out on the journey, we may never find out what was ultimately possible and achievable.

Most people fear even daring to dream, but in denying the dream we also deny any chance of the goal coming to fruition. It might seem too daunting or too unrealistic, but it is the dream that sets in motion the efforts in the direction of realising the dream. It costs nothing to dream, and no one need know what you are dreaming of. Some of the most successful individuals, however, whether in business, sports or the arts, will often relate how they imagined living out their heart's desire many times before ever getting there.

Daring to follow one's dreams takes courage, but keep in mind that the root meaning of the word courage stems from 'cour', which means heart in French (from the Latin 'cor'). To have courage, therefore, means to have heart. This brings the prospect more within the realm of possibility, as the heart is a muscle that gets stronger the more we use it. I take great heart in the following quote attributed to the poet Goethe (who was, incidentally a great friend to Beethoven whose music inspires me more than any other).

*Until one is committed, there is hesitancy, the chance to draw back —
concerning all acts of initiative (and creation), there is one elementary truth
that ignorance of which kills countless ideas and splendid plans: that the
moment one definitely commits oneself, then Providence moves too. All sorts
of things occur to help one that would never otherwise have occurred. A whole
stream of events issues from the decision, raising in one's favor all manner
of unforeseen incidents and meetings and material assistance, which no man
could have dreamed would have come his way. Whatever you can do, or dream
you can do, begin it. Boldness has genius, power, and magic in it. Begin it now.*

Begin with setting what your all-time dream goal would be in your career. What is ultimately possible for you to achieve if you were fully committed and stretched your capacities to the max? Here is where role models can come in. Is there someone who has already achieved the top rung that you might reach for? What are they like? What does it seem to take to get there? What can you learn from this person to emulate on your journey? What additional qualities and attributes could you bring to the table? What will you need to further develop and master? Answers to these questions point to what you need to include in your mental imagery.

Then set an all-time career goal that you would be minimally satisfied with. It might not be the dream goal above, but one that you would be content with. You would then need to break down these goals into more palatable chunks, within appropriate time periods.

For example, you may need to reach a sales quota in your job. In fact, you may even get a bonus if you exceed that quota. That is a very clear and definable goal, and you will know if and when you achieve it. In the meantime, however, how will you know you are on track? And what can you put in place to keep you going? What do you need to do today in order to be on track towards your annual goal? Maybe it means making a certain number of cold calls? Maybe it means doing your paperwork, so that you are better organised for your next round? Maybe it means cultivating your business relationships? Maybe it means working better in your team? It might also mean looking after your health and family life better in order to maintain the strength and tenacity for the long haul.

The list is endless, but in every case likely requires being the right frame of mind to increase your capacity. Identifying the key determinants leading to your success profile layer by layer will give you focus and direction. This will also provide the source for images you can develop to foster your capacity to stay on track towards your goals.

Range of Goals

It is best to set short term as well as long-term goals, as well as a range of goals from minimum to maximum. What is the minimum you would be satisfied with, and also the maximum imaginable?

Long-term goals

Long-term goals refer to your ultimate destination in any endeavour. What is the end game for your particular pursuit? It is important to define in order to determine whether you are on track along the way. If you have a clear idea of where you are going, then you will quickly notice when getting side-tracked. If you are unclear, you may find you have veered so far off track as to give up on getting to where you wanted to go originally.

Staying on track can be as easy as staying in your lane on the highway once you know exactly where you are going. Veering aimlessly out of your lane can spell disaster.

Having set your long-term goals, you can then establish all the milestones en route. Breaking down the journey into intermediate goals increases capacity to manage the journey. More about this in the section on stepping stones following.

Outcome goals

Outcome goals are the kind of goals that are directly measurable. They are also referred to as end-result goals. Nowhere is this more obvious than in the world of sport, e.g. score, ranking, win/loss record; or war (in which case it can be life or death, as well as territory and resources). Examples in business are: hitting the sales target, negotiating the deal, creating a new product, and the financial bottom line. In health, it would mean full recovery from an illness or injury. In relationships, it could mean marrying the man or woman of your dreams and starting a family. Professionally, it could be as simple as getting a promotion, or a degree. In other areas, it is not always so obvious.

Clearly specified goals provide the focus required to pursue them, as well as benchmarks for feedback on how you're doing, i.e. to determine how on track you are.

Outcome goals are not necessarily within your control, however. In sports, for example, you cannot control the score as you cannot control your opponent. In business, you might have performed brilliantly in a proposal meeting, and still not win the prize account. This is why outcome goals are often not recommended, and performance and process goals are therefore more advisable. Nevertheless, outcome goals provide the ultimate standard by which you can measure your progress.

It can be challenging coming up with clear and measurable goals in relation to personal issues. For example, the perennial goal to be happier. How will you know? How do you rate something as subjective as that? Each one of you will need to develop your own internal barometer, your own scale. For example, how confident on a scale of 0–10 would you like to be when performing a certain surgical procedure for the first time solo? Your answer might be a '10' if open heart surgery. How will we know if your '10' is the same as my '10'? What would it look like? How would it feel? How could it be verified? Once you got started, your confidence would probably be evident, but by then it might be too late!

Performance goals

Unlike outcome goals, performance goals are directly within your control. You control each move you make, whereas you cannot control the actions of others who also impact on the end results. In sport, performance goals refer to execution of your various skills. In business, a performance goal could be making a certain number of viable contacts at a business conference. In health, a performance goal might mean adhering to a certain treatment or fitness regime. In relationships, a performance goal might involve paying more attention, expressions of kindness and appreciation. These are all within your direct control, and all may increase your chances of achieving your best outcome.

Process goals

Process goals relate to creating the optimal conditions mentally and physically, e.g. developing the mindset required in order to get the best or the most out of your mind and body, and to choose the actions that are in your best interests. For example, being relaxed, positive, clear, and focused may be conducive to bringing out your best performance. Being able to stay positive and focused only on the here and now is a skill that many aspire to. Many performers refer to the elusive ability to get out of their own way to shine.

Lifestyle goals might require an improved attitude towards the desired changes. Consider the example of including more fresh fruit and vegetables in your diet. For many, if they were put in front of you, you would eat them with zeal. But if you're like most people, you need to take more time to stop in at the shops more regularly. You then need to bring the produce home, clean and chop and then cook or prepare for consumption. If you find yourself getting irritable at getting to and fighting the crowds in the shops, this won't be conducive to reaching your goal. If you resist the chore of having to spend time and effort preparing your veggies, then that is not conducive to following through on your goal.

Creating and staying in the optimal mindset can be an important goal in order to ensure that you achieve your goals. If you can achieve the process goals of being patient and cheerful as you go about it, then you will more likely achieve the desired outcome. A classic example of this is to check in with your inner dialogue. Look out for the stressful self-talk that stems from the 'have to's', and 'should-ing all over yourself'? and 'must-erbation'. To take the edge off, try converting to: 'want to' or 'need to' … and better yet: 'get to'. Be more self-nurturing by preparing more nourishing options.

Exploring Attachment versus Detachment

It is important to have a goal to strive for, but if you become too attached to the meaning of that goal it is likely to elude you. This can be likened to the previous example of holding a bar of soap. If you hold on too tight, what happens? It slips from your hands. If you don't hold on enough? You drop it. Finding the right touch is essential so that you do not become overly anxious about the outcome, which will ultimately distract you from what it will take to make the little steps towards your goal. Be ready for the best, and prepared for the worst!

This is also related to the motto that appears before players step onto centre court at Wimbledon: *'If you can meet with triumph and disaster and treat those two imposters just the same …'*, which is an excerpt from the poem 'If' by Rudyard Kipling:

'If you can keep your head when all about you are losing theirs and blaming it on you; If you can trust yourself when all men doubt you, But make allowance for their doubting too; If you can wait and not be tired by waiting, Or, being lied about, don't deal in lies, Or, being hated, don't give way to hating, And yet don't look too good, nor talk too wise;

If you can dream — and not make dreams your master; If you can think — and not make thoughts your aim; If you can meet with triumph and disaster, And treat those two imposters just the same; If you can bear to hear the truth you've spoken, Twisted by knaves to make a trap for fools, Or watch the things you gave your life to broken, And stoop and build 'em up with wornout tools;

If you can make one heap of all your winnings, And risk it on one turn of pitch-and-toss, And lose, and start again at your beginnings, And never breath a word about your loss; If you can force your heart and nerve and sinew, To serve your turn long after they are gone, And so hold on when there is nothing in you, Except the Will which says to them: 'Hold on';

If you can talk with crowds and keep your virtue, Or walk with kings — nor lose the common touch; If neither foes nor loving friends can hurt you; If all men count with you, but none too much; If you can fill the unforgiving minute, With sixty seconds' worth of distance run — Yours is the Earth and everything that's in it, And — which is more — you'll be a Man, my son!

Can you picture it?

Any time you set a goal, follow it up with this question: Can I see it/ picture it? Can you imagine achieving it? And how it would feel? If you cannot, then there is a lot of work to be done, or you might need to reconsider your goals. If you can, this is a very good sign.

In every case, and for whatever type of goal, ensure you can imagine it with all or most of your relevant senses.

Stepping Stones

Once you know your ultimate destination, you can then set yourself more intermediate level goals, i.e. the steps you need to achieve along the way. For example, let's say you have a goal to save up for a down payment on house or an overseas holiday. The long-term goal is easy to set (though not necessarily to attain). You might decide that you would love to have saved the required amount within a specified period of time, but a longer time frame might be more realistic (and depending on any unexpected expenses along the way). You might also decide on a certain amount to have saved up, e.g. 30% for the down payment on a home, but would settle for a minimum 10% depending on the house and other circumstances (e.g. ability to pay the mortgage, interest rates, etc.).

You would then need to set a goal for how much to set aside each year, each month, each pay. This might mean there will be less for other discretionary items and luxuries that you have become accustomed to. Keeping your eye on the prize (the big picture) will help to motivate you to take all the little steps that will help you build your home or travel fund (little pictures along the way). These little steps can be represented in the accumulation of small savings by cutting back (e.g. on take-away meals and coffee) or being more frugal, which you can build on to secure the entire amount. You will likely find that these little steps will beget more little goals required to reach those steps; for example, goals to bring your own lunch to work from now on, go to the library instead of buying books, go for romantic walks in the park instead of lavish dinners in expensive restaurants. This process can be applied to most goals.

You might start off with a focus on one area, which eventually when broken down, brings to light many little pictures. You discover many little steps that might seem unrelated to the big picture goals, but upon which the big picture goal depends. Focusing on the big picture won't help you get there, but focusing on all the little pictures will, while also giving you a greater sense of control over the journey. Remembering why you are performing all the little pictures will help motivate you. Keep your eye on the prize as you go about taking one step at a time.

A journey of a thousand miles begins with a single step

Long-term goals can be awfully discouraging and frustrating when goals seem so far in the distance, even if you are truly on track to where you are keen to be. Setting intermediate goals brings them more within reach, and gives you a better idea of whether you are on track or not. You don't have to do it all today, but you can begin today.

Daily goals are the most powerful of all. The many steps and intermediate goals that lead to your ultimate goal or full potential can seem quite daunting. Breaking your goals down into more manageable bits can make it all seem much more feasible and worthwhile. This is probably because they are the only ones you have any control over in your immediate future. They are also motivational when achieved.

For example, if your doctor tells you that your cholesterol and blood pressure put you at high risk for heart attack, and that you must radically change your diet and exercise and drop 40 kilos — the enormity of the task before you can seem impossible. But once you break the goals down into smaller chunks that you can achieve on a daily basis, you can breathe easier as you begin to see the light. You will know that if you managed to walk for five minutes longer today than yesterday, you have achieved success and are on track.

If you managed to also choose a healthier snack than previously, again you have achieved success that you can build on. This helps to now be able to picture the possibility of what once seemed impossible. As suggested in previous chapters, if you also have good examples of others before you who have been successful, and model the lifestyle changes you need to make, this too will boost your confidence. Celebrating the little successes along the way is also uplifting (rather than dismissing them as we often do).

Yesterday is history; tomorrow is a mystery; today is a gift; that's why they call it the present.

We have no control over the past, and the future is full of uncertainty. What we do today determines our tomorrows. What are you pleased with having accomplished yesterday that improved your conditions today? Imagine your tomorrow and look back at today? What would you have been proud of that you achieved today?

Summary

Your journey is unique to you, and as such — it takes you into uncharted waters. Goal setting creates your personal roadmap to where you most want to go, and helps to keep you on track. With practice you will get better at breaking down the process and applying the strategies, which will then increase your chances of doing what you set out to do, and getting to where you want to go. Setting your goals naturally stimulates your mental imagery processes, which you can then build on as you embark on your adventures in life.

Chapter 5

Guidelines for Practising Mental Imagery

This chapter contains general guidelines for mental imagery practice. You will learn about:

- The what, who, where, when and why of mental imagery
- The importance of perception and what you focus on
- How to set the stage with a relaxation exercise
- Tips for what to incorporate into your mental imagery practice
- Drawing on role models
- How to overcome imagery challenges
- Caveats and warnings

Unlike the need for guidelines for most other skills and practices, such as embarking on a new fitness regime or learning a new computer program, mental imagery is not about getting started with the practice. The fact is that you are already using mental imagery whether you are consciously aware of it or not. You need to start getting the images to work better for you rather than against you. By being more consciously aware and in control of your images, you can create more of what is in your best interests in alignment with your goals and values.

Think of a goal that is important to you and try to bring up the image of you being successful with it right now. Keep this particular image in mind as you read on and apply the guidelines.

The chapter begins with a 'W5' of mental imagery (why, what, who, when, where) followed by how. I explain how a relaxed and focused mind is imperative to imagery effectiveness, and how music can help get you into the right mood. I then cover how to use all of your senses, and provide tips for ensuring you get the most out of your imagery practice.

W5 of Mental Imagery

The previous chapters have already covered a great deal about the 'why', which in essence is to simply accelerate your capacity to achieve goals and facilitate change that leads to better wellbeing and success.

What: Mental imagery skill

Mental imagery is a skill, and like all talents and skills, some people are better at it than others. But like all skills, everyone can get better at it. Children seem to be more receptive and adept at it than adults. They have an easier time suspending judgement and allowing their imaginations to run free. Imagery is standard child's play.[49]

Who: You

Every one of you carries a unique history of experiences from which to draw, and unique paths to follow. There is no one size fits all. What is best for you to imagine in order to achieve your goals is very individual in nature. The main thing to keep in mind is that your images contain the essential and evocative ingredients that will lead to achieving your goals. Like any talent or skill, however, some are better at it than others. It comes more naturally for some than others. But like any talent or skill, everyone can improve. Everyone can benefit from the process.

When: No time like the present

The great thing about mental imagery is that it is an inner mental resource that you can draw upon at any time. While regular practice will yield best results, both towards your goals as well as in developing your imagery skill, you don't necessarily need to spend a lot of time at it. What it does take, at a minimum, is to merely be conscious of what images are playing in your mind and directing them according to your best interests; simply practising *mindfulness* in your daily life and pursuits.

While imagery can be practised anytime and anywhere, you might need to experiment with it until you get the right timing down for any particular purpose or event. Because the practice of imagery requires effort and concentration, you might want to practise it at a time when you are fresh mentally, but not practice it too much before needing to perform the task. If you put in the practice time well before the event, there will be no need or temptation to *cram* right beforehand. And everyone knows that cramming does not yield the best results possible.

I am reminded of an example relayed to me by a sport psychologist working with a high level basketball team who practised too much imagery right before a game. While the intention was to improve performance, the opposite was the case as the players were mentally worn out by tip off.

Where: Wherever You Are

Mental imagery can be practised anywhere you are. Some conditions are more conducive to quality practice than others (not unlike with meditation practice), but once you get better skilled at it, you will be able to call up effective positive images anywhere.

Change your mind to change your life

Most people are too focused on improving their material wellbeing rather than their well-*being* and *doing* well. They have it backwards. It is by creating the right inner mental conditions that provide more fertile ground for taking the right actions that eventually lead to having the experiences that one desires, and getting the things that one wants. This is supported by the tenets of quantum physics, which claim that it is only by changing your *being* (i.e. your mindset) that you can change your experience.

Perception is Nine-tenths of Reality and What You Focus on Grows

I'm sure many of you have heard of these expressions and how they might apply. Have you ever wondered how it actually works beyond the popularly espoused Law of Attraction theory, which suggests that your outer experience mirrors your inner experience?

The education of attention would be an education par excellence. –William James

Imagery is a form of information processing that begins with what you focus your attention on in the present — on what you are perceiving and *choosing* to perceive — which will then become the memory that becomes the foundation of future experience/s and perception/s. What memory/information would you prefer to file away and act upon? Keeping in mind that it is previous (dominant) memories or perceptions that will be most available (based on the concept of the *availability heuristic* to you in the future.[50] This is especially important when it comes to making decisions and determining direction at the proverbial forks in the road of life. Remember that the best prediction of future behaviour is past behaviour (along with the associated psychological impressions). Therefore if you would prefer to make better choices and react differently in the future, you need to pay more attention to what you focus on in the present. Hence the *power of now*[51] and *mindfulness.*[52]

Your imaginal processes are at work whether you are consciously practising mental imagery or not. The process begins with what you focus on in the present moment, and this is what registers in your mind. These mental representations then get laid down in your memory banks along with the associated feelings. What you focus on now influences your experience of the now hence the nine-tenths reality proverb (perception is nine-tenths of reality).

Your future experiences depend on your take on present experiences (not to mention all those previous to now), so that in a future similar situation you will have the tendency to think, feel and behave consistently with this internal programming that was registered previously. So, what you focus on grows. Negative experiences and perspectives tend to dominate this scenario as our evolution depended on getting our attention for survival. We've come to the point in our evolution where this process is actually killing us now with the accumulation of the effects of stress on our systems; and we now rely on creating more positivity for our evolution.

Our brains have evolved to be extraordinarily adept at constantly monitoring our perceptions and assessing for danger. We unconsciously judge whether what we're experiencing is good or bad, safe or threatening, positive or negative, pleasant or painful, right or wrong. This is an automated function that has developed over thousands of years. Our survival has depended on it. The consequence of not heeding fear in our ancient past was death. This is why negative emotions like fear are experienced so much more intensely than positive emotions — the better to get our attention to act accordingly.

While this assisted our survival and evolution in the past, this stress process is now killing us; our evolution would now appear to depend on shifting the weight towards greater positivity. At this stage in our evolution, however, it appears that we need at least three positive experiences to counteract just one negative, which is why the positivity ratio is set at 3:1 as the tipping point for reaching equilibrium.[53]

The constant monitoring and judgment is largely an unconscious and automatic process that alerts us to action when necessary. It is the same process that kicks in during the fight or flight response that we talk about in relation to stress. In this day and age, however, we are increasingly likely to 'freeze' given that acting on the 'fight' or 'flight' impulse is no longer a viable or necessary option. This has dire consequences on our systems that are detrimental to optimal focus, health and performance.

The residual problem is that we engage in far too much judgment about factors that are completely irrelevant to our safety and wellbeing.

This is what I refer to as 'gratuitous judgment', although judgment can also be gratifying, in that it gives us a sense of control over that which we have little to none — other people, for example. We may not be able to change others to conform to our rules or agenda, but we can damn them all to hell, which seems to bring great satisfaction to some folks but ultimately perpetuates ill-being.

This is where the practice of mindfulness has enormous benefit — the number one foundation for which is the practice of non-judgment (see Kabat-Zinn's book *Full Catastrophe Living* as a leading resource on the topic).[54] Letting go of constant vigilance and judgment can free up valuable headspace to focus and engage in that which is truly relevant and brings greater wellbeing.

Having good judgment is also important for our wellbeing and success! But this is not facilitated by engaging in gratuitous judgments. It is fostered by cultivating the mental state of being that will enable our perceptual faculties to hone in on the more relevant, useful and positive elements of our experience (such as mindfulness practice and mental imagery).

Complaining is a case in point. There are times when it is productive — when it leads to desirable change and when preferred alternatives are articulated and actionable. Most of the complaining engaged in, however, is not productive, and more often than not is destructive and contagious. It can be a favourite, albeit toxic, pastime in unhappy workplaces and families. When you complain, you are focusing on your negative impressions and feelings. So that next time you encounter that same situation, those impressions and feelings come to the fore being more readily available, rather than a more positive alternatives. Hence perpetuating the negative that you've been complaining about (similar to the self-fulfilling prophecy mechanism covered in *Chapter 1*). By adjusting your focus in the present you have the opportunity to change your future experiences of the same.

If there is a behaviour or reaction you would prefer not to repeat, try the rewriting history exercise in *Chapter 8*. If there is a new behaviour you would like to repeat and become habit, you need to get better at catching yourself being good and doing well. Then take the opportunity to tune in and amplify the positive association — to strengthen your resolve for the next time, especially when there is pattern of competing bad habits. Taking up exercise is a typical case in point. Despite knowing it is good for us, exercise has negative and painful mental associations for many of us so we avoid it. We humans tend to be more motivated to avoid pain than to approach wellness.

Turning Negative into Positive

I live at the crest of a hill overlooking Avalon valley with glimpses of Pittwater beyond. It is a ten-minute walk down to the shore of Paradise Beach. Sound pretty good so far? It truly is fabulous! But it is uphill most of the way back! The steepest and longest hill is the final one that we must climb to get home, which most of us who live beyond it refer to as a 'killer hill'. As much as I enjoy getting down to the water's edge with my beloved chocolate Labrador, I will sometimes opt for going in the other direction rather than tackling that hill, short-changing both of us as we live on a cul-de-sac — a literal dead end.

The great thing about writing such a book is I notice more opportunities to practise what I teach. I've been noticing how much I engage in inner complaining as I climb that hill. It can be rather painful as my lungs, heart and muscles make themselves noticed. But as I inwardly complain it only seems to get more arduous. But! If I adjust my focus to reaching the top of the hill, using better technique and breathing that is more efficient, and I notice how good that feels and how proud and pleased I am with myself and my effort, then the experience actually becomes enjoyable, and I feel much better about myself.

Rather than focusing on how hard and painful it is, I focus on what will make the experience easier and better — more rewarding — and this then becomes my memory/image. Next time I contemplate which direction to take, the aversive memory/image will have faded and better ones replaced it. I will feel more keen and confident about climbing the hill, and now look forward to it! Not to mention the fact that the more often I do it, the easier it will get anyway.

In summary, what you focus on becomes perception and therefore your reality ⮕ gets filed away as memory ⮕ registers as an image/information ⮕ which forms the basis for future perceptions and experience.

Energy flows where attention goes. – Anonymous

By becoming more aware of your perceptions and what you are focusing on now, and adjusting accordingly, you are not only improving your present experience, but also more likely to create the basis of a better one in the future. As Rick Hanson, co-author of Buddha's Brain[55] puts it:

'Scientists believe the brain evolved a "negativity bias" that makes it like Velcro for negative experiences but Teflon for positive ones. This helped our ancestors survive, but it's bad for children (and parents) today — leading them to overreact, hold onto hurts and resentments, and have a harder time developing inner resources. Because neuroplasticity is heightened for what's in the field of focused awareness, attention is also like a vacuum cleaner, sucking its contents into the brain. Directing attention skilfully is therefore a fundamental way to shape the brain — and one's life over time.'

Harnessing the Power of a Relaxed Mind

Developing the ability for relaxed focus is important for developing your mental imagery skill. Relaxation clears the path for your imagination to roam free. You're far more able to sustain focus and generate positive images when you're relaxed than when you're stressed with lots on your mind. Plus, your mind is also far more receptive to suggestion when in more relaxed state.

Relaxation fosters an open mind that is better able to conceive and consider the possibilities versus limitations. Most of us are too quick to compromise on our heart's desire and end up short-changing our potential. Relaxing enables you to 'be in the moment', and helps to suspend your fears and worries, and negative thinking patterns so that you can envision more of what is possible. You can think of it as clearing the decks of your mind, thus creating the blank canvas on which you can project your best images.

Your mind is like a parachute — it works best when open!

Relaxation increases your openness to positive suggestions much like hypnosis does. When you're relaxed, the blood flow in your brain changes to reach creative centres of the brain, away from and quieting the more self-critical, negative and judgmental areas. Your brain then has increased access and ability to harness the power of your imagination.

Practising meditation and relaxation techniques on a regular basis will strengthen your mental capacity to relax and focus at will, raising your mental fitness, not unlike physical fitness training, and strengthening the wiring (synaptic connections) of your brain. And just as with physical fitness — use it or lose it! For an overview of relaxation and meditation techniques, see Relax to Max in *Appendix B*.

When you get good at relaxing and focusing, you'll only need to take a couple of deep breaths to bring yourself to a relaxed state of mind that readies you for imagery practice.

Mental imagery as self-hypnosis

You might be wondering what the difference is between hypnosis and mental imagery. The answer is that the processes are virtually the same. They both involve an induction phase; a relaxed and receptive state of mind followed by focused attention. The physiological systems all play out virtually the same as well — what happens to your brain and nervous system, cardiovascular system, immune system, for example. When you practise relaxation followed by mental imagery, you are virtually practising self-hypnosis, with similar benefits. The best part about it is that you are in the driver's seat. You are actively in control and self-reliant. Whereas when you are being hypnotised, you are being passive and reliant on another person being in charge.

We regularly slip in and out of a hypnotic state throughout the day. For example, whenever you catch yourself daydreaming you are probably in a bit of a trance. Instead of snapping out of it when you catch yourself daydreaming, I suggest that you go with the flow, and engage in a bit of mental imagery instead. Take advantage of this state of mind.

Facilitating new learning and change

Relaxation facilitates your ability to take in new information and store it for future use. You're able to absorb much more when the mind is still and quiet. Have you ever noticed that when you are stressed or in a hurry you have to read a paragraph over and over, and are still not able to absorb the content? Or that you check your watch several times in the space of a few minutes and still don't know what time it is?

When relaxed you'll find it much easier to focus your attention and to remember what is relevant and important. Being anxious disturbs your concentration.

Unlearning old habits

It can be far easier to learn new habits than to unlearn old ones. Oftentimes the goals you're trying to achieve through the practice of mental imagery are in direct opposition to old negative patterns and images hard-wired in your brain.

Relaxation allows you to quieten down the old wiring, so the new wiring has a chance to take hold. You can liken it to a well-worn path. Water flows more readily in the direction of the grooves. We all have a tendency to gravitate automatically to the familiar routes, even if the destination is not our preferred one. Laying down the groundwork and creating a new path can be challenging.

Have a clear image of the new destination you want to reach so you can stick to the correct pathway and better realise when you have veered off track. A relaxed state of mind is more conducive to the discernment required when faced with resisting our old programming and running with the new.

An Autobiography in Five Chapters

Mental imagery can help you chart a new course for your life, and can be especially useful for breaking bad habits and patterns, and creating new directions. You can break the vicious cycle of repeating mistakes and painful experiences (revolving) and establish a more positive way of life (evolving). The steps it often takes to find new direction are illustrated in the following poem. The original author is unknown, but the poem can now be found in various sources and is used in many positive thinking programs.

1) I walk down the street.
   There is a deep hole in the sidewalk.
   I fall in. I am lost...I am hopeless.
   It isn't my fault.
   It takes forever to find a way out.

2) I walk down the same street.
   There is a deep hole in the sidewalk.
   I pretend I don't see it. I fall in again.
   I can't believe I'm in the same place. But it isn't my fault.
   It still takes a long time to get out.

3) I walk down the same street.
   There is a deep hole in the sidewalk.
   I see it is there. I still fall in...It's a habit
   My eyes are open; I know where I am; it is my fault.
   I get out immediately.

4) I walk down the same street.
   There is a deep hole in the sidewalk
   I walk around it.

5) I walk down another street.

— Anonymous

Mental imagery gives you the opportunity to practise that for which life has yet to provide. To first take the path in your best interests, plus feel you have the capacity to do so, may not be easy. If your images are clear, however, you are a step closer to achieving your new direction/s and goals.

Soundtrack of your life

Filmmakers have long understood the power of soundtracks to set the scene and create the mood that keeps you engrossed. Take the music away and the plot can seem far less intense or gripping. You probably already have a list of tunes that bring back cherished or perhaps bittersweet memories. You can take this a step further by creating the playlist or soundtrack for your life. But first, consider being choosier about what music you are exposed to and listen to. If you're to take a more active, creative hold of your life, you need to be more aware of what you're allowing into your consciousness.

The effects of music on our mood, health, wellbeing and performance are well documented. Athletes often use music to get them into the right frame of mind and energy level for their event. Theme music for special events such as the Olympics is designed to be inspirational and lift your spirits. But what works for each person is unique to them. You might be surprised by what some famous athletes choose to listen to before a big competition. For example, a champion boxer likes to listen to classical music before a bout, a famous golfer chooses that old crooner Frank Sinatra's *My Way*, and a shooter goes with Whitney Houston's rendition of *One Moment in Time*.[56]

You can use music to enhance the power of your mental imagery practice in several ways:

- **Open up your creative mind.** Listening to music can open up the channels to your creative mind. By pairing up your imagery with well-chosen music you can enhance the power of your images. Songs with lyrics that match your desired result can be especially beneficial.

- **Help set the right mood.** Playing a song that makes you feel the way you want to feel makes it easier to generate the kind of images you desire. Music is one of the most powerful mood boosters — find the music that resonates with you — songs to energise, inspire, uplift, soothe and relax you.

- **Keep you focused.** With practice, you develop a strong association between the music and your imagery. Eventually, all you need to do is listen to the music, and the images will appear naturally with minimal effort.

- **Set the pace.** Find a special song that sets the correct rhythm for your training or performance. Athletes often have a song or songs that keep them training at the optimal pace.

Engaging All Your Senses: Once More With Feeling!

Even though mental imagery is often referred to as visualisation, this draws upon only one of your senses, albeit a dominant one. We live in a highly visual world that constantly bombards our visual sense. We often compensate by adding auditory stimuli — look around and see all those people with wires coming out of their ears on public transport! So much so that we've become detached from our other senses. Becoming more aware of all your senses enables you to more readily imagine and create sensory experiences that are more effective and intense — more real. Interestingly, the sense that is our most potent link to memories and emotions is our sense of smell — the one we tend to be the least consciously aware of.

To achieve best results with your mental imagery practice, you need to use all of your senses to keep it real: seeing, hearing, smelling, tasting and touching, as well as feeling your body in motion if applicable, which is called the *kinaesthetic* sense. Some senses may be more relevant than others — depending on what you are attempting to achieve with your imagery. For example, when I was preparing for my first scuba dive as a novice out on the Australian Coral Sea, what I found most helpful was to mentally imagine being comfortable breathing solely through my mouthpiece (as nose would be blocked by the mask). To 'hear' the rhythm of my breathing (which is pretty much all you hear below the surface) — slowly and deeply — to ensure I got maximum usage of oxygen from the tank. I mentally imagined remaining calm while trying to remember all the essentials of safe diving (because you cannot talk and ask questions under water!). This worked very well for me, despite diving being more about the visual extravaganza.

You may find that certain senses are more effective than others for you. For relaxation, your sense of hearing (e.g. the sound of a babbling brook, ocean waves and/or in combination with relaxing music), or smell (e.g. lavender aromatherapy) might be the most effective for producing how you want to feel. In the sport of golf, for example, you might begin with hearing the crack of the club hitting the ball just right, plus the visual image of the ball arcing in flight, before focusing on the kinaesthetic feel, and/or having the right grip on the club.

You need to imbue your imagery with the appropriate intensity of feeling to strengthen its meaning to you. While emotion is not technically one of the senses, how you are feeling can be the most critical element to your imagery to get the best results. Imagine you're watching a scene in a film — it's not just the execution of the words and movements that create the scene — the depth of emotion you feel when watching is what leaves the most lasting impression. The more intense and visceral, the more real and effective. As the saying goes in showbiz: Once more with feeling!

Below are examples that illustrate how to use all your senses when practising imagery.

Using all your senses to relax

When practising imagery to improve your ability to relax by imagining being at the seashore for example, you need to include the view of the water and/or the surf (the colours, waves, light reflection); hear the rhythm of the surf, see and hear the birds, feel the wind and hear children giggling; smell and taste of the salt air; feel the sea breeze caressing your skin and blowing your hair; feel the ground or beach beneath you, including the sand between your toes, or the water lapping at your feet. All the while feeling peaceful and content, and that all is well in your world. This comes more readily if you've actually experienced such sensations before that might then be filed away as a peak experience memory (see *Chapter 7* for guided peak experience recall imagery).

Using all your senses for sport imagery

When practising imagery to improve your golf swing, for example, you need to picture the arc and direction of the ball in motion, after first seeing the ball being struck; hear the crack of the ball being hit, as well as other sounds associated with the swing; smell the turf; feel the entire swing from the backward swing to contact with the ball and follow through, and the rhythm and twist of the swing; and feeling powerful and self-assured.

Beginning With What You're Good At

The best way to start mental imagery practice is by using what you're already good at and what you most enjoy before attempting more challenging images. Beginning with your strengths and favourite aspects of your performance or goal activity also sets the standard for your imagery skill. You will probably be much better at imagining what you most enjoy.

For example, you might feel really competent at speaking to a group of your peers or colleagues at a social function, but then get nervous when asked to speak more formally at a business meeting or presentation, even if the subject matter is the same. Imagining the first scene — being comfortable and at ease — and then gradually picturing feeling the same way in the second scene, will enhance your imagery, and make it more likely to actually happen. If you tried this in reverse, you might have difficulty getting the imagery going without the associated nervousness. You would then be practising being nervous!

Once you have a good feel for clear and vivid imagery of what you are already good at, be sure to continue on with the other more challenging aspects of what you're trying to achieve — to cover all your bases. All too often, people will run the images that come easily and neglect the ones that do not. Even champions are guilty of this. They sometimes only imagine their favourite and best moves or abilities and what they're already good at, and neglect that on which their performance really depends — putting it all together in one seamless performance.

The chain is only as strong as the weakest link.

You don't need to dwell on your weakest links, but you do need to strengthen them to reach your full potential. Seeing yourself perform what you're already good at is useful to give you the confidence to also generate the picture of what you are working on improving as well.

Inside out: Internal versus external perspectives

It is generally considered best to engage in imagery of yourself from the inside out. That is from a first person point of view, just as how things would be experienced in reality. First person images also evoke a stronger emotional response, and is therefore better for generating, regulating and changing your emotions. Imagining yourself from a third person perspective, as if a video view, detaches you from what the experience is really like.[57] Interestingly, a common concern among performers who are beginners at the practice of mental imagery, is that they cannot see themselves. I reassure them that this is just fine, as when you are going about your business, you do not usually see yourself either, nor do you usually need to.

You are aware of yourself, but you are not actually watching yourself. There are occasions when it is necessary to have a good idea of how you appear to others, and so it might be good to incorporate that view, but it is ultimately best to keep it as real as possible, and therefore maintaining an internal versus external perspective. This has been borne out by the neuroscience as well, demonstrating that first person images produce far more pronounced results in the brain than third person images.

Keeping it real

You may think I'm stating the obvious here, but your mental images need to be accurate for best results. You don't want to be practising something incorrectly — even if only imaginary! If, for example, you are using imagery to enhance healing a broken bone, it won't help to imagine a cracked bone, which will only perpetuate the image of injury. What you want to see is the bone mending   getting smoother and stronger, and handling all the weight you put on it. If you are using imagery to improve your technique, and it's incorrect, then you've only made things worse, and are potentially risking injury. This is why it is important to not rely solely on your imagery practice, but to regularly test yourself in real situations.

Imagery ought to be carried out at the correct pace as well — in real time at the correct pace. If your images are in slow motion, you might find it hard to keep up with the pace of the real event. Same goes if your images go too fast — you might find yourself rushing which hinders performance. Getting in touch with the correct rhythm is helpful to keep things as close to 'real life' as possible. Successful athletes have a very well-developed sense of inner timing because, in most cases, their performance is time dependent.

I remember witnessing a remarkable incident as a graduate student at University of Ottawa with Terry Orlick. He had a world champion kayak pair time their imagery of their 500 and 1000 metre races as they each held a stopwatch timing themselves. They both crossed the finish line in their best time, within one-hundredth of a second of each other.

Accuracy trumps speed though. You might, therefore, need to begin your imagery in slow motion to get it right first, before then gradually speeding it up to real time pace.

On the other hand, speed may not be important for what you are hoping to achieve, but taking your time might be. When people are under pressure or feeling nervous, their minds tend to race as well as their speech. Mentally imagining yourself breathing and taking your time will prepare you to flow more naturally in your delivery, and allow others to better take in your message in the case of presentations.

Playing out your imagery in a natural sequence — just as it might actually unfold in real life — is recommended for best results. This helps you stay in the flow in real life. For example, if you're preparing for an important meeting or interview, imagine what it will be like beforehand as you enter the scene. Imagine a smooth transition from being called in to the first question, so that it won't be such a shock once the meeting or interview begins. And then imagine the different combinations of questions and answers — flowing easily from one to the next.

You might also find it useful to imagine how you want to be and feel after an event. What do you want to have accomplished? How do you want to be feeling? I also recommend that if you were to imagine only one aspect of an event, just imagine the aftermath. How do you want to be and feel immediately afterwards? Your mind will fill in the blanks to be consistent with that image. This is called 'end result imagery'.

Remember, you tend to behave and feel according to your self-image. If you can maintain a strong image of how you want to be and feel walking away from an episode that means a lot to you, you are more likely to feel and behave as you'd hoped **during** the episode. It is also sometimes easier to play out the imagery in reverse, as imagining yourself having emerged successful, can foster the confidence to face the challenges that may be involved.

Finishing with a flourish

Be careful not to lose focus towards the end of your practice. Too often, people stop just short of the finish in imagery practice, perhaps feeling they've done enough. See your imagery through to the conclusion of your event or experience.

The finish can be the most important to practise because this is the time when you're most likely to get distracted and take your eye off the ball so-to-speak, and be affected by fatigue, mentally, emotionally and physically. You need to stay sharp, focused and feeling great right through to beyond the finish, to give yourself your best shot. This will also prevent you potentially getting blind-sided if you drop your guard on the playing field, or missing an essential point in a board meeting, interview or the like.

Accentuating the positive: Do's and don'ts

Be careful to ensure that your imagery is focused on good execution and not on avoiding mistakes. Try not to engage in negative self-instruction that begins with 'Don't…', such as 'Don't be nervous', or 'Don't stumble' (I'm imagining a model on a runway or diva teetering on stillettos on stage), or 'don't drop the ball'. What you actually end up doing is strengthening the very thing you are trying to prevent! Your imaginal mind won't understand the 'do not' part, and will only conjure up the image of what you want to stop. When you catch yourself with such do nots admonishments, cue to taking a deep breath and refocusing on what best to do and how to be, with positive self-instructions and images.

For example, if you're trying to stop biting your nails and you keep berating yourself to 'Stop biting your nails! Stop biting your nails! Stop biting your nails! …' you'll only bring up the image of biting your nails. Coaching yourself to imagine long, healthy, beautifully manicured nails is far more effective. You could also imagine yourself engaging in a more beneficial substitute for the nervous habit of biting your nails, such as taking a few deep breaths to relax (and you'll likely find your urge to bite will have dissipated).

Or say you keep telling yourself: 'Don't drop the ball!', or 'Don't double-fault!' You'll just keep bringing up the image of dropping the ball or hitting into the net or out of bounds. If you do end up dropping the ball or double faulting then you've actually executed perfectly! You've performed the move just as you had imagined! Your body will have followed the directives of your imaginal mind.

The game of golf is designed to mess with your mind in just this way. The golf course is a deliberately created obstacle course with hazards built in all over the place, e.g. ponds, bunkers, trees, etc. It is abundantly clear what a golfer does not want to do. There is no need to be reminded. Nevertheless, the course hazards are a constant distraction if you let them be. I remember a golfer client playing for a major championship telling me of a particular hole with three bunkers in view en route to the pin. It got from bad to worse, when the last thought on his mind before the first shot was to not hit the ball in the bunker.

Well, this player is particularly skilled at hitting out of bunkers, however, his next thought was to miss the next bunker … and then the next … so the shots went: bunker, bunker, bunker … The poor player was humiliated by being such a 'bad player', which of course only serves to make it more difficult to refocus on to the positive. My take on it, however, was that it played out perfectly! He had the bunker on his mind, and so in the bunker went the shots. Plain and simple. Players of such high skill just need to ensure that the last image before taking a shot is where they want the ball to go.

Another golfer I have worked with used to be distracted by the fear of hitting into the trees en route to the hole in what is called a dog-leg set-up (when you cannot see the pin around the corner). Even though there is plenty of room between the trees for the ball to travel, he kept worrying about hitting into the trees that were between him and the pin. It got to the point where he began to view the trees as his enemy. He reframed this issue to focus on the trees as his friends guiding the ball down the middle of the fairway (rather than sucking the ball into their evil lair). This enabled him to hold the image of the ball going where he most wanted it to go.

Personally, I have a bad habit of interrupting people when I think I know where they're going with what they're saying (or because I get impatient when I notice they are simply being repetitive or providing more information than I need or want at that moment — even in my practice with clients!). If I were to keep admonishing myself: 'Don't interrupt!' or 'Stop interrupting!' the image that comes to mind is of me interrupting! I therefore focus on taking a breath … paying attention and listening intently with good eye contact.

It also helps to understand that my bad habit of interrupting only interferes with good outcomes, and often only serves to prolong the process of arriving at best outcomes. Interestingly, I hate being interrupted myself, which also motivates me to get better. I am happy to report that I've gotten much better, i.e. more patient and attentive; and when I'm not, I am quick to catch myself and apologise.

If you're working on stopping a certain behaviour, therefore, you need to focus on a positive image of what you're trying to achieve, and not what you're trying to stop. Watch out for those negative instructions, take a deep breath, and refocus to more positive images. Refocus from a 'don't …', to a 'do …'

You Get What You Focus On

Here's another story from my days studying for my Master's degree in sport psychology. A bunch of us grad students were invited for lunch up at our professor's cabin on Meech Lake, Quebec (just outside Ottawa). After lunch activity options included kayaking on the lake across from the cabin, or hiking in the woods behind the cabin. A couple of us opted for the hike, while the others joked about tipping over in the kayaks all the way down to the lake. I warned them not to joke about it, but to focus on paddling and staying afloat instead. They admonished me for being too serious.

Sure enough, upon return from our hike, we noticed a wet trail of footprints leading from the lake to the cabin and lots of wet clothes hanging over the porch railing. When we got into the cabin and found our wet and bedraggled colleagues, we had to laugh when we learned that they hadn't been in their kayaks more than a minute before they tipped over into the water. I told you so! Moral of the story — if you focus on what can go wrong (even in jest) you are imagining what can go wrong, which tends to lead to you behaving consistently with the image. Focus on the positive!

Role Models

Whenever I am working with a client going for a challenging goal, I always ask whether they have any role models to draw from. Without a role model, it can be extraordinarily difficulty to conjure up an appropriate image. Having a role model can foster belief in ourselves and in what can be achieved, i.e. 'if they can do it, than so can we'!

Leading mental imagery researchers Kosslyn and Moulton have remarked that: 'Imitation is in fact an amazing, almost miraculous, feat: Visual input (watching someone else) somehow gets converted to a "program" in the observer's brain, which then allows that person to make the same movements. How can observing someone else perform an act that allows you, with your different body and different point of view, to do the same?'[58] The answer lies in the power of mirror neurons discussed in *Chapter 2*.

We cannot learn hope without experience and without models.
We must see seeds grow before we can believe in sowing.

– George Vaillant.[59]

Faking it till you make it

Having a role model to emulate can be helpful when the image of your best self seems to elude you. Think of someone who demonstrates the qualities you wish to achieve in yourself. It could be someone you know personally, or know of, or even a fictional character. Carefully observe them, and then see if you can embody those key characteristics. Make them your own, and according to your personal style.

Fake it 'til you make it.

This is why mental imagery can be such a powerful technique for self-development and transformation, providing the opportunity to practise being the way you wish to become.

Interestingly, those we admire the most often embody the qualities we most seek to develop in ourselves. Same goes for those who annoy us the most — often they possess the qualities in ourselves we most dislike. Role models therefore can be useful for your self-growth and to improve your image of yourself.

Strike a Pose

Faking it 'til you make it is related to the evidence from body language research that indicates we can reverse engineer how we feel by engaging in a pose or posture associated with how we'd prefer to feel. For example, when we are feeling happy we tend to smile. The act of smiling is associated with feelings of cheerfulness. But if you were to reverse this process with faking a smile, the associated feelings are likely to be triggered. This also works by simply holding a pen in your teeth which triggers the smiling muscles, and which then generates positive feelings. It can actually be difficult to arouse negative feelings when holding such a pose.

If you would like to feel more buoyant and confident then simply striking a pose and walking with bounce in your step not only gives you the appearance of being confident and in good form, but can also make you feel more confident and good within yourself. It is hard to exude and feel confidence when slumped and head down. But if you stand tall with head held high it is near impossible to feel down.

Accepting before expecting

A word of warning about attempting to live up to role models — we might hold unrealistic expectations of ourselves, which begets or uncovers an underlying lack of self-acceptance (and worse, self-loathing). Lack of self-acceptance will blind you so you can't see what you need to see. This limits your possibilities of moving forward. It also suggests that you might have too much riding on the success of your goal, which will actually impede you.

If you skirt over essential details from the start, then you would be opting for remaining unaware and therefore stuck, rather than growing and evolving. In fact, you would be deluding yourself and avoiding what is actually in your best interests to address, before rising above it. You cannot change what you are not aware of; and furthermore, you cannot change what you do not accept. In short, it takes accepting how you are now, before *expecting* improvements. Otherwise, you will be constantly undermining yourself.

Another thing to watch out for is to make sure the image is your own and not somebody else's dream. Be careful of looking up too much to your role models and putting them on a pedestal as they will invariably topple. And don't look down on them when they do (remember: that which you react to in others, you create in yourself). As Jesse Jackson says: 'You should never look down on another, unless it is to help them up.'

Simulation and Rehearsal

Just like actors, you can benefit from rehearsing how you want to feel and be, as well as perform at an upcoming event. In some professions, this is called *simulation*. For example, in the airline industry, simulators enable pilots to test out their skills for various emergency and contingency situations in a real cockpit, without leaving the ground. The more real the simulation the better. Accidents have dramatically reduced since the use of simulator training. Simulation is also used a lot in sports. At practice a coach might put two minutes left on the clock with the score tied, and get the team to practise a particular play (or series of plays) under pressure.

Businesses will now even employ actors to provide such practice opportunity for their management staff — to improve how they manage difficult employees or customers.

I often role play with my clients during consultation sessions, so that they can prepare and practise responding more effectively to challenging situations, and to prevent reverting to negative reactions and patterns of behaviour.

Quality versus quantity

What is most important when you practise mental imagery is that your imagery is vivid and clear, within your capacity to perform, and with no competing or interfering images.

An episode of imagery practice should last as long as the actual event you are preparing to experience or perform. For longer events, you can break down your imagery into key sections of the event. You can practise the entire episode at least once a week, and concentrate on different parts or certain skills throughout the week — much like training for a sport.

If you only feel like doing a short imagery practice then it is recommended that you just focus on the end result; picture the outcome that you desire, and how you want to feel at that point. Your brain unconsciously works out the rest.

Try to do your mental imagery practice during the same timeframe that the event will actually occur. If you have an important event (e.g. meeting or presentation) that takes place at 10 am, do your practice at that time if you can. So that when that time rolls around on the big day your execution will unfold more naturally. Our bodies maintain an internal clock; for example, when you wake up just minutes before the alarm goes off.

Some people like to practise imagery for five to ten minutes every morning to set the tone for the day, or practise performance imagery before training or a competition. Practising before going to sleep increases the likelihood of you dreaming about it, which will deepen the images within your unconscious mind. The more you practise the better you get at it. Remember: use it or lose it!

Preparing for the worst

Things rarely go exactly as we would wish or even plan. Even the best laid plans fail to unfold exactly as we'd envisioned. What if something or someone distracts or upsets you? You need to have a plan and image in place to quickly refocus and get back on track; back to your best mindset for what it is that you want to achieve.

If you prepare for all the things that could go wrong, then you will more likely remain unfazed by them, or failing that, to recover quickly. Practice makes perfect in this area. Life doesn't always afford us the opportunity to practise coping with all the various possible obstacles. But you can mentally rehearse dealing with them in your imagery. This will increase your confidence going into any situation, and you'll feel well prepared and ready for anything.

The ability to bounce back is what people say made Tiger Woods such a great competitor when at his peak. He doesn't just have great golf skills, he has developed the ability to recover quickly from bad shots or other distractions and get back on track immediately. He got so good at it, and so far surpassed his fellow competitors that they would report playing for second place (rather than winning). His mastery seemed to have reached such a point that he needed to create a larger challenge/obstacle beyond the sport — to overcome and master on his life course. There is every chance that he will successfully apply his mental skills to regain top form on the golf tour once again.

Recovering or maintaining your focus and confidence can be especially important when you're faced with a major incident when minutes or even seconds count. Preparing for all that could go wrong is empowering, and will help you get back on the path to success again — quickly. Many professionals in high risk jobs (airline pilots, surgeons, astronauts and police officers) train to be prepared for crisis situations; situations where getting it right quickly can mean the difference between life and death. The rest of us can benefit from 'preparing for the worst case scenario' and work towards minimising regret and remorse, and creating more satisfaction in our lives.

Troubleshooting Imagery Challenges

Sometimes, no matter how much you try, you may still have difficulty controlling your imagery, or even imagining what you are seeking to practise. This can be due to a number of factors, such as having competing inner agendas, underlying resistance, fears, intrusive negative images or memories, investing too much emotionally in the outcome, and other blocks.

Competing inner agendas

It can be challenging to create new more desirable images when an old outmoded one is still in play. It might simply take more practice to lay down the new path to overcome the more familiar one. Ensuring you are in a relaxed state is also helpful. If you continue to have difficulties, then it could be that there are unresolved feelings that might need to be addressed before proceeding. This can be a good thing! By engaging in your mental imagery, you may have uncovered an issue that requires further attention, which had likely been sabotaging you previously. Now that you are aware, you can do something constructive about it, rather than denying or avoiding it.

You may have perfectly clear and vivid images running in your mind for a certain goal, but that might not be enough if you have strong underlying competing images. For example, you might have great images of being slimmer and fitter, but also of indulging in your favourite high caloric meals and deserts or comfort eating. In which case, you would need to add more to your positive repertoire, such as making better food choices, finding alternate sources of comfort and pleasure, etc.

Or, you may have all the best intentions of remaining calm and positive when faced with criticism, but when you feel the feedback is unfair or unjust, your inner warrior may be stronger. In this case, you might need to include more elements to your positive images as well as step up your imagery practice. It also helps to break down your goals into smaller and more manageable steps. You might also need to consider consulting a professional to sort out and unravel any underlying issues that might be holding you back.

A classic competing agenda most of us contend with is on the one hand being keen to pursue and fulfil our potential, and on the other hand being keen to stay safe and avoid failure and humiliation. More about this in *Chapter 8* on rewriting history and creating change.

Worrying or planning?

Remember, what you see is what you get (WYSIWYG). So, beware of negativity, as negative images can beget negative effects. Ensure positivity and accuracy. While the risk of things going awry may have dire consequences, worrying about things that are out of your control is futile, and will distract you from your best focus that would increase likelihood of success and prevent such worrisome distractions.

When you catch yourself being negative, try to refocus back on the positive and what is within control. Worrying is a form of mental imagery — programming that which you most want to avoid! So, ask yourself: Am I worrying or am I planning? And go with planning. If you have well-developed plans for all contingencies, and have rehearsed them mentally, this tends to quell the worries. You are free to then go forward with greater confidence knowing that you are well prepared; and to focus on the positives and what is within your control.

If you fail to plan, then you are planning to fail.

Resistance

Resistance is similar to competing agendas. If, for some reason, you find yourself resisting imagining your best self, or acting in your best interests, there may be a competing interest. While this interest may be well intentioned and ostensibly on your side, it may prevent you from going down your best path. Sometimes the source of the resistance has had many pay-offs in the past, such as protecting you from disappointment. Once you can address those pay-offs, you may be freer to pursue your desired images and goals.

Again, the beauty of practising imagery is that it may unearth underlying issues that were below your conscious awareness (and that may have been seemingly sabotaging your efforts). Once such issues emerge on the surface, you are a step closer to overcoming their power over you, and in a position to choose your path with better intentions.

Fear

Fear can be a great motivator as well as a great deterrent. Some fears are real and legitimate and serve as fair warnings. Most fears, however, are merely figments of our imagination that serve no useful purpose. As Mark Twain has famously said: 'I've seen a great many catastrophes in my life, but few of them ever happened.'

Many of you are probably well acquainted with fear of failure, which is often more to do with the fear of the (imagined?) consequences of failure that hold you back. Keep this old saying in mind: most regrets are based on failing to try, and not on trying and failing. Some of the most painful regrets have more to do with missed opportunities; and some of our best opportunities for success arise from lessons learned from our missteps.

Some of you might also experience fear of success and all that might entail. You may fear heightened expectations and pressure, or you might fear what others will think and if they think your success may have been deserved or not. Or you may fear becoming a target. I suggest that a worse fear would be letting such fears prevent you from fulfilling your true potential.

The only thing we have to fear is fear itself. – Franklin D. Roosevelt

Most fears stem from a sense of there being too much at stake, which can lead to desperation. As previously discussed, this then interferes with your imagery effectiveness, as it naturally brings up the counter images that you intensely wish to avoid. Consider giving yourself more permission to flourish and embrace your potential, rather than languishing and resisting it by playing it safe. Keep this quote in mind from spiritual advisor Marianne William: 'Our worst fear is not that we are inadequate, our deepest fear is that we are powerful beyond measure.'

Life begins at the edge of your comfort zone. – Dean Donald Wash

Shaking off negative images

It is often difficult to imagine changes to what is familiar and habitual, or to imagine accomplishing something that you fear. For example, let's say you have a habit of being shy in large groups, which results in you not contributing or fully participating, whether at an office meeting or at a social event. Shaking off the image of becoming embarrassed might interfere with feeling and being comfortable sharing your opinion about something that is being discussed. This is especially the case if you've had bad experiences in your past, such as being teased, bullied or ignored. You avoid the uncomfortable feelings if you remain quiet, but in the process you have deprived yourself of being fully authentic and happy, not to mention giving others a chance to get to know you and potentially like and love you.

When struggling with such issues, it can sometimes be helpful to run your imagery in reverse. Begin by picturing what it would be like *after* you have accomplished your goal. For example, a figure skater I worked with was tackling a difficult jump, and had fallen many times in the past. It was therefore difficult to shake off the painful image of falling in the lead-up to the jump. So, rather than replaying the painful image, I suggested she break up the entire sequence into sections, and then practise them in reverse order. To begin with, we got her to imagine just landing strong. She was able to do this if not preceded by the lead-up to the jump and spin. Once she was confident with the landing image, we gradually introduced each previous element of the jump, e.g. coming out of each spin within the jump, until she was able to imagine the entirety from the take-off. This helped in two ways: first by creating more positive images, and secondly by short-circuiting the negative image that coincided with the approach to the jump. Once the image was strong it extinguished the fear.

The above can apply to any situation. Play the scene in reverse. For example, walking out of a difficult meeting feeling well satisfied with how you conducted yourself under pressure, and gradually including more and more until you can picture it from the start. Sometimes playing a scenario from the start triggers the very automatic reactions that we're trying to eliminate, and there is no point in practising them! Playing out the scene in reverse can enhance better execution mentally and thereby increases our chances of execution in reality.

Conversely, another strategy is to wind back the image to well before the negative fear usually kicks in, and insert a pre-emptive positive suggestion. For example, a point guard in basketball feared turning over the ball when he set up a particular play. We backed up to the point well before he was in position to pass the ball (upon taking possession of the ball), and planted a positive suggestion/image of a clean pass while dribbling down the court. This worked well by interrupting the previous pattern. It might take a bit of experimentation before you can get to the point of finally shaking off the negative and embracing the new and improved version.

Wide Right

Wide Right refers to the now legendary college football story of the legacy of a missed field goal, which perpetuated season after season for the Florida State University Seminole football team in the early 90's. The team had consistently been ranked number 1 at the start of the season, but struggled to maintain that position by season end. The legacy began with a potentially game winning field goal attempt from 34 yards that went wide right in the dying seconds of pivotal game between the Florida State Seminoles and rival team University of Miami Hurricanes in 1991. *Wide Right* dominated the subsequent headlines in Florida newspapers. The failed field goal was played over and over on TV and in everyone's minds, such that it became a dominant image and topic of conversation campus- and city- and state-wide. When FSU was again in the position to take the lead in the dying seconds of the game the following year against Miami, guess what happened? *Wide Right* was so deeply imprinted on the consciousness of everyone — even though a different kicker this time — that it was almost inevitable that the ball would go wide right again: *Wide Right II*. And so ensued the legacy year after year.

Investing emotionally in outcomes

Be careful of being overly attached to the outcome you desire. Being too anxious and desperate for a particular result interferes with your capacity to produce your best when you need it most. For example, in sports — if you're thinking of the score while in the middle of a play you will lose your best focus. In business, if you're thinking of what it will mean to your career and finances if you close a deal, you will lack the focus of attention during a negotiation upon which your success would hinge.

While the outcome may be very important to you, with major consequences either way, it is not helpful to dwell on that while in the process of pursuing that outcome. Marianne Williamson tells a funny story about a woman being too keen to attract a man she was interested in. What woke her up was the image of the guy telling his mates about meeting a 'fabulously desperate woman'.[60] Desperation is not attractive, and will do the opposite and push the goal away from you.

The best way to create your best future is to look after your present opportunities. If you're too focused on the future you might miss opportunities that are right before your eyes. There are times to keep your eyes on the prize, and to strive; and there are times to let go and focus on the present. Finding the right balanced approach is the key to success.

Think of your goals as you might a bar of soap. When you hold on too tightly, what happens? You drop it. If you don't hold on tight enough, then what? It slips from your hands. You need to find the right touch to hold on without squeezing the life out of it.

This is akin to the concept of trying too hard to make something happen which ends up eluding you. And so you try even harder with worse results. The trick is to catch yourself, and *try* softer instead, especially when things are not within your control, adopting a spirit of allowing rather than forcing.

> *By letting it go it all gets done. The world is won by those who let it go. But when you try and try, the world is beyond the winning.* – Lao Tzu

If you're finding it too difficult to let go of focusing on results, then you might need to revisit your motivation. It could be that there's too much riding on the outcome that might be better attended and addressed otherwise. You might be in it for the wrong reasons. And/ or to compensate for a sense of lack or neglect elsewhere in your life. If so, it might be worth consulting a professional to help you better resolve such issues.

As mentioned above, the advantage of mental imagery is that it can bring such underlying issues up to the surface, which ultimately creates a better opportunity for facing and resolving the problem, than otherwise if remained below the surface (and continuing to wreak havoc).

Removing blocks

Other contributing blocks to your imagery could simply arise from what you are trying to imagine being too far off course from what is genuinely meant for you to achieve? Or too far off track to what is in your best interests? This could signify a cue to steer in another more appropriate direction, just as you might when things aren't working for you in your real life. As one of the most famous authors on creative visualisation Shakti Gawain suggests: When the images go against your true inner nature or destiny, engaging in the imagery will serve to accelerate the goal eluding you.[61]

Imagery Tips and Tools

Generating the best images to match your dreams and goals is a skill. And like all worthwhile skills, it can be challenging to develop. It helps to have well-developed cues available to jump-start your images. Here are a few tips and tools.

Tailoring to individuals

What works for one person may not work for another. Imagery is a very individual and personal matter. What is evocative and effective for me, may not be for you. For example, one person might find water images soothing and refreshing, while another might find it distressing if they have a fear of water and drowning. Another example might be imagining that you are in a field of wildflowers. Such an image might be uplifting for some but conjure up an allergic reaction in others.

A person battling cancer might find the image of white cells being sharks gobbling up the cancer cells powerful, whereas another will imagine snow washing away the cancer cells. What works for one will not work for another. However, we need to be careful that the images accurately reflect the desired result. For example, is the 'snow' merely covering up and hiding the cancer? Or is it dissolving the cancer? In this case, the patient was adamant that it was the latter and is now cancer free.

In another case, a patient envisioned a vine growing up his spine; he rationalised that this was supportive and comforting, whereas I found such an image disturbing. I attempted to persuade him to consider alternatives, but he too was adamant, and died soon after as his spine was riddled with cancer (just as he had imagined). What this latter case reflects is that the patient was 'reading' his body rather than healing.

A cautionary note — we need to emphasise and accept that there are limits to what imagery can accomplish. Who knows where the line between what is realistic and what is not *lies*? But there is plenty of evidence that suggests that we are vastly underutilising the power of our mental imagery. The application of mental imagery to health and healing is also covered in *Chapter 9*.

Vision boards

Vision boards involve creating a collage that represents your goals. The first step is to accumulate pictures from magazines and other sources that best reflect what you aim to achieve. If you have any artistic flair, you might also draw pictures of your own. Once you have completed your collection, you then arrange your cuttings in a visual array that displays all that you hope for and dream of. You might like to mount your collage on a poster board and hang on your wall, or include in a journal or scrapbook. It can be as big or as small as you like. You can create one big board that includes all of your more valued and cherished goals; or create several smaller ones that represent different goals, and then post them where you will notice them to trigger inner images of becoming one with the pictures, and making them real.

This is why it is also inspiring to display any of your previous accolades and mementos. They remind you of where you've been, of what you are capable of accomplishing, and what you can continue to draw upon going forward.

Audio and video recordings

There are many generic recordings available in the market, including those associated with this book (see *Recordings* at the end of the Appendices and visit www.bigskypublishing.com.au for more information); however, personalised versions are naturally the most powerful. You might wish to adapt one of the scripts available in this book to your specific goals, and then have it recorded to enable you to relax and just listen and imagine.

If you have access to any video recordings of yourself in action these too can be very effective in generating the images. Nothing beats actual evidence — seeing yourself performing and being at your very best — to boost your confidence. Many professional teams and sports hire producers to compile peak performance videos for this purpose. They review game film or other video coverage, and compile, edit and set the video to theme music to create the desired result. Any performer who has access to video recordings of themselves can put together a compilation of their best moves too. Nothing beats real evidence! This would also be effective for tuning in to your role models if you have a good recording of them in action.

Rating your imagery skill

How is your imagery? Now that you have reached the end of chapter, take a moment to revisit the original image that you started with, and apply the guidelines to improve your imagery skill. How did you go? How well were you able to control your imagery? How vivid was your imagery?

An exercise to assess your visual imagery skill is to study an object in your surroundings, and then close your eyes and try to recall every detail. What colours and features can you recall? And then open your eyes and see how well you did, and find out what you may have missed. What you were trying to recreate in your imagery may not be critical to achieving your goals, but it does provide an idea of your visual imagery skill.

Another exercise you can try is to time a person entering and walking across a room (if inside), or across a road or garden (if outside), and then replay the movements in your mental imagery as you time yourself. How well do the times match up? You can also try this with images on television. Time a particular sequence of movements, and then time yourself as you replay in your mental imagery. How well paced were you? This reflects your kinaesthetic imagery skill. Most beginners would either replay in slow motion or too quickly. Tuning into your inner sense will strengthen your imagery skill. Champion athletes are able to imagine their event to within one-hundredth of a second. This is especially impressive when you consider that teammates in such events such as pairs in kayaking are able to stay in sync with each other throughout the entire event as it is playing out in their mental imagery.

When practising your imagery practice for the first time, try it on something simple and of minimal consequence at first, to keep the pressure at a minimum. For example, playing fetch with a pet dog. He or she is already happy to be playing so you're already in a win-win situation. You might try imagining your toss before you throw the ball, and see how well you reach your target. Watch for what comes up when you engage in this practice. How many principles were you able to employ from this chapter? If you caught yourself being negative or having difficulties bringing up the image, how well were you able to stop, relax and correct your imagery before trying to throw to your target again? Remember, mental imagery is a skill, and takes practice to master just as with any other skill. Take your time and be patient, and with diligent practice you will reap your just rewards.

Testing, testing, testing

Mental imagery is a powerful tool for accelerating your progress and development, but nothing replaces actual practice. It is important to test yourself in real situations, which may yield important information that you can then build on and utilise in your imagery.

Warning Caveat

Beware of the possibility that imagery will work too well for you! This warning is two-fold, and could perhaps be viewed as two sides of the same coin. On the one hand you might achieve your goals far sooner than anticipated, which challenges your underlying beliefs about yourself. Too good to be true? This could lead to creating a setback. This is why it is important to include feeling ready and prepared for the consequences of your success (e.g. getting a job opportunity before you're ready to leave your current location). On the other hand, imagery of success can seem so real and feel so good that you might trick yourself into believing it is already accomplished and behind you, and therefore get too complacent and not put in the requisite effort. The former could lead to self-sabotage, and the latter could lead to inaction.

Summary

Let's finish where we started — thinking of the goal you had in mind at the start of the chapter. How did you go applying the imagery guidelines? Keep the guidelines in mind as we move on to the next few chapters with more specific applications for imagery practice. Perhaps consider the following checklist as you go:

Mental Imagery Checklist

• Were you fully relaxed before starting your imagery practice?
• Did you have clear goals in mind?
• Were you able to control your images? Keep them positive?
• Did you engage all of your senses? Especially feeling?

- Was your imagery in first person vs third person?
- Did you cover all your bases? i.e. imagined all aspects necessary for achieving best results?
- Was your imagery paced well — in real time?
- Was your imagery accurate? Natural and realistic?
- Did you imagine a strong finish or outcome?
- Were you able to draw upon any role models?
- Did you become aware of any competing images or worries?
- Did you include practice for all contingencies?
- Were you able to maintain the right touch?
- Did you conclude with imagining successfully executing your very next step today?

Chapter 6

Imagery Loves Company — Vision Buddies and Groups

This chapter is about sharing the benefits of mental imagery, by enlisting others to join you in the process. You will:

- Gain an understanding of mental imagery practice as a form of secular prayer
- Make the connection between faith and mental imagery
- Learn how to best practice imagery with partners and groups
- Understand how imagery is a vehicle for practice of compassion

Imagery as Secular Prayer

The vision buddy practice is akin to the known power of prayer and prayer partners.[62] It offers a secular version of the practice for those outside of religious circles and institutions. One does not need to believe in a God or practice a particular faith in order to benefit from the known benefits for the power of prayer (e.g. see Larry Dossey's review of research on prayer).[63] In this case, the process incorporates the communal aspect akin to the fellowship that is found in religious gatherings, such as church services and at temples. Consider this oft repeated phrase (from Matthew 3:20 of the King James version of the Bible): 'For where two or three are gathered together in my name, there am I in the midst of them.'

The 'I' is variously interpreted to be referring to Jesus and/or God. Given that the primary message of Jesus was love and compassion for one's fellow man, it would therefore follow that whenever we gather with good will for one another (with loving kindness), we are embodying the spirit of the meaning of Jesus/God within. And as such are in a greater position for generating positive actions and potentially creating so-called miracles.

Neuroscience is now in a position to prove the above effect — of the synergistic effect of like-minded individuals gathering for a common devotional cause, whether that be in meditation, communion, choir, sports, etc. In fact, it takes less than a few minutes for our bodies to synchronise in many measurable ways neurophysiologically (e.g. biofeedback measures). This works in both directions — positive and negative; for good or for bad/evil. The effects hinge on the intent.

Very little compares to organised religion for communal uplifting of one's spirits. Where do secular types go to experience such opportunities? There is obviously a dark side to religion that is beyond the scope of this book (and has been well explored by other authors, e.g. Christopher Hitchens,[64] and Richard Dawkins),[65] but why should non-believers be deprived of the same benefits? While the spiritual component may not be the primary motivation (e.g. many derive similar benefits through allegiance to a sports team, charitable organisation, or political party), why not put out an explicit call to gather and join in positive images, not unlike the call to prayer?

Isn't the concept of a God, Higher Power, the Divine, Allah, Buddha, etc., just an image of the *best friend* one could possibly have? Christopher Hitchens was fond of referring to a believer's concept of God as merely an *imaginary friend*. Well, who among us wouldn't love to have just such an imaginary friend upon whom we can call at any time for encouragement and support? And miracles? And to answer our prayers? I propose that no one is better than your own best future self as a suitable substitute upon whom you can confidently rely.

The good news for secular types, whether atheist or agnostic, is that you all have access to the same process that believers do, which does not require faith in a god (suspension of belief), but faith in the process ... in fostering the transcendent power of mental imagery.

Prayer among the religious is based on belief in a higher power beyond oneself. It is common religious practice to also gather in prayer circles for the benefit of others. Knowing that someone is praying for you seems to foster hope and belief more readily than attempting to pray/imagine for oneself. The advantage of faith in a higher power (aka God and angels) is that it fosters belief in the process that might be missing in the non-believers. Nevertheless, it is still a powerful process regardless of the source of one's belief, whether the power resides in a 'higher power' or in the power of mental imagery that science is now bearing out.

Generating new images from within is naturally more challenging to our beliefs than in the case of imaginary sources from without. The placebo is a case in point (see *Chapter 2*) — the effects can occur in an instant due to the ready belief in the process, i.e. in the power of medicine (i.e. in pharmaceuticals). This facilitates imagining the desired result with greater ease, which sets in motion the cascade of chemical changes from within.

Belief in a higher (god-like) power facilitates the ease with which we are able to embrace and run with an image generated by prayer. It is far more challenging to believe in our own power to create a desired result, even though this is precisely the process underway with the placebo and prayer effects.

Teaming up with others as vision buddies can also be viewed as a substitute or secular form for the benefits accrued through the combination of fellowship and prayer that goes on in churches and the like. We know that those of faith (regardless of religious affiliation) tend to be happier and healthier. This can be attributed to many factors included in religious practice that others miss out on; as well as missing out on the known benefits of faith per se, e.g. the power of fellowship, rituals, sense of connection, etc.

The vision buddy exercise provides an alternative for secular types to benefit from the same process without needing to be part of a religious movement. Interestingly, there is a parallel movement afoot for doing just this, e.g. Alain de Botton[66], who calls for providing reverential venues for secular people to gather in contemplation. I would suggest adding reflection and projection such as occurs with mental imagery to the menu, as well as a venue/forum for the imagery buddy groups.

Faith and Imagery

What is faith after all but a belief one imagines to be true? That one takes comfort in; that instils confidence? (According to the *Macquarie Dictionary:* confidence or trust in a person or thing …)

We can foster our belief by buddying up with others to assist in each other's process. This is, after all, how it is done at Lourdes, the legendary centre for miracles — where the pilgrims pray for each other and not for themselves, which inspires greater hope and therefore positive images. It seems we are far more receptive to the image depicted in prayer on this basis. Likewise, having a vision buddy also fosters the sense of support in our goals which frees us to focus on the positive more than if on our own. Research has also shown that the social support factor is among the most powerful in creating and sustaining changes in behaviour. Being supported increases our sense of enthusiasm and confidence towards our own goals. Coincidently, the word 'enthusiasm' derives from the Greek meaning to be filled with God.

We all like to be inspired, but inspiration is often short-lived once the source of the inspiration fades — unless we continue to stoke the fire, and invoke the key principles and attitudes from which it originated. The word 'inspire' incorporates the concept of 'in spirit' — to infuse one with enthusiasm essentially. But, as is inevitable with high aspirations whether in work, love, or play, there are challenges and setbacks to contend with — the point at which many become disheartened and give up, or revert to old maladaptive patterns of behaviour. Only the most confident and optimistic maintain the requisite tenacity and persistence to keep going, to regroup, to stay the course and/or embrace the changes necessary.

Having and being able to hold the clear image and the pathway forward, plus having the wherewithal, is the definition of hope; consistent with the process of mental imagery.[67]

Vision Buddy Guidelines

This exercise is based on imagining goals being achieved. It is, therefore, recommended that you keep the goal setting guidelines in mind as you embark on your vision buddy practice. As with goals, daily practice will yield best results. This is gratifying in so many ways, as the simple practice generates an array of positive emotions conducive to wellbeing, health and performance in general.

The exercise can be conducted in pairs or groups. You get the benefit of increasing synergy with increasing numbers, but only up to a point — probably five people at a maximum (beyond five may get tedious as each person must wait their turn). The advantage of groups is that greater numbers takes the pressure off individuals to come up with what is called for.

Vision buddy steps

Remember to keep in mind the guidelines for practising mental imagery that begins with relaxation and clearing our minds.

Step 1: Choose a vision buddy or group carefully from among people or community you know you can trust. While your closest friends or relatives might seem a best choice, it is sometimes more beneficial to practise with someone who is not so close, yet of like-minded values and commitment to the process. Groups may form around the practice, while not necessarily maintaining personal relationships outside the group.

Step 2: Each individual takes a turn at stating their goals that they would like support for. Generally, and especially after dream and long-term goals are established, it is best to focus on what is within immediate control; and immediately achievable by next meeting of the pair or group. It would be appropriate to ask questions to gain greater clarity and specificity to enable the buddy's conceptualisation of the goal. But do resist the temptation to offer advice.

Step 3: Once the goal information has been articulated and received by everyone, each vision buddy will wait for a positive image to emerge in their mind relevant to the goal in question. It is important that you do not force this image to appear, but to engage in the spirit of allowing an image to form naturally.

If you draw a blank (or recognise mental interference), then it is best to pass, and not offer up what might be an inappropriate and useless image. While this might seem a bit disconcerting, it is the respectful thing to do. This requires an element of trust that while your best intentions may well be in play, the images are not. The focus is on quality and not quantity. Having said this, this is less likely to be an issue among the more skilled and practised among you. But the only way to get better is to keep trying even if you still get it wrong. There is no failure; only feedback.

Step 4: Each vision buddy expresses and the image that came to mind of the goal being achieved. A suggested sentence stem would be: 'I hold the image of you ...' fill in the blank with specific images regarding goal success and how it would feel. The intention by the word 'hold' is that you will not only share the image, but also commit to holding that image for an agreed period of time. The idea is to not only express the image directly to your partner when gathered together, but to also take time throughout the near future to hold the image (to imagine for another — just as you might pray for another) until you next meet up again. The prescribed or agreed amount of time depends on what suits your partnership or group. This could be once/day or more over a period of a week or longer. Obviously this requires a strong level of commitment and trust. The synergist impact well fuels the effort though.

Step 5: Seek feedback for how well the image shared by your partner/s resonated. And return the favour, until everyone's goal has been attended to.

The emphasis is on *allowing* an impression to take shape as this engages your more intuitive mind, and you will therefore be likely to come up with more appropriate image that will resonate with your partner. Sometimes these images will make no sense to you, but it is not up to you to decide, only to express. The image or information you provide may be more on target than you realise, and you may be pleasantly surprised! This is where the process can seem quite magical. (See the Vision Buddy Guidelines provided in *Appendix D*).

A great example of this was when I tried this activity out with a group of students for their first time. One of the students (A) was despondent over a new flatmate who was imposed on her by the owner of the house she lived in. This turned out to be a most fortuitous circumstance, as it pushed her to seek and find far more suitable accommodation; something that she had put off pursuing until this issue was brought to a head (crisitunity?).[68] Her goal was to be happy and content in her domain — whether at the same place or in a new abode in a neighbourhood she had been contemplating but procrastinating about. When we went around the circle sharing images that came to mind relevant to each other's goals, the student (B) sitting next to A shared that when she attempted to tune in to A and her goal, only a song came to mind (audio image), but no visual image.

Now, this student was not at all musical, and this particular song didn't have any particular meaning for her, but came through loud and clear. She didn't question it, and so she shared it: 'Sitting by the dock of the bay'. Little did she realise that this song was a favourite of A's and most meaningful as the place where she dreamed of living was on a lake. As you can imagine, the impact of this revelation was amazing for both A and for B.

This experience spurred A on to set in motion her search while keeping the song in her head. B and others in the group also reported keeping the song in mind as well for A to find what she sought. A subsequently found the perfect place for her budget in the space of just one half hour (by advertising her wish on an online site, which was quickly responded to by a property owner whose tenant had just vacated). The song kept A calm, positive and focused while she embarked on her search and efforts.

This image was highly effective and allowed A to maintain her own image which, without the vision buddy exercise … well, who knows?

During this same vision buddy exercise, a number of deeply moving and resonate images were shared, but a few students also came up blank. This was well accepted and appreciated, and allowed the best to flow, such that everyone was well pleased and cherished the experience. If any of them had not passed on certain individuals, it would likely have marred the experience. Best to keep it pure and genuine. It is not a competition. Maintain a spirit of openness and wonder, and you'll be amazed at what transpires. Trust the process, and it will work for you! I have run the vision buddy exercise many times now with many different groups — and the experiences have been simply astounding, attesting to the benefits of imagery in company.

On a personal note, when I attempted the exercise with a group of workshop participants, I was pleasantly surprised to be on the receiving end of a powerful image — not only because I was not anticipating being included in the process, but also for the image that came up. One of the participants expressed seeing a flash of me signing her copy of this book! I cannot tell you how powerfully evocative such an image was for me. I would never have thought of it myself, and yet it so inspired me — catapulting my belief in the project to another level. I have been holding that image ever since, and it made me more determined to make it happen and share the real event with her. When it came from another who believed in me it was far more potent than anything I could have possibly conjured up for myself, and believe me, I imagined plenty! This is my hope for all of you.

Practical and Positive Spirituality

George Vaillant sums it up in *Spiritual Evolution*: It matters not how one arrives at a positive spiritual experience (e.g. meditating on an eagle feather or praying over a rosary). What is important is that it brings comfort and generates positive emotions for the healing benefits to occur. He describes at length how the success of AA and the 12-Step Program fits the bill. He notes how AA is now embraced across the world, e.g. in Hindu India, Buddhist Japan, and atheistic Russia. This is testament to what he considers genuine spiritual value in action. His litmus test, in a nutshell, for a good theology or spiritual practice is if it leads to *practical compassion.*[69]

Engaging in the vision buddy activity can demonstrate practical compassion and positive spirituality, invoking the best within us to create the best experiences among us.

Summary

This chapter featured the benefits of practising mental imagery with partners and groups, and getting to experience the power of secular prayer. This can enhance your imagery experiences, not only due to the synergistic effects but as it also extends to the beneficial reassurance generated by supportive others.

I am now holding the image of you, dear reader with this book in your hands … considering who you might first recruit to join you as a vision buddy … imagining how playful and meaningful the practice can be … telling others about it … and committing to the adventure of being vision buddies! I am further imagining that you will share your wonderful stories online (e.g. find the facebook page via www.bigskypublishing.com.au). It is my hope and dream that vision buddy groups will spring up everywhere to the benefit of everyone involved. Remember: *imagery loves company!*

PART 3

Drawing from the Well of Your Best Past and Future Self

Chapter 7

Back to the Future — From Looking Back to Moving Forward

The best place to start in your mental imagery practice is to draw out the best from your past in order to project to a better future; as well as how to be your own best friend. In this chapter, you will:

- Learn more about being in the flow and how to get there and stay there
- Be guided to recalling previous peak experiences and projecting to the future
- Learn how to be a better friend to yourself
- Be guided to connect and relate better with your future best self

As I continually remind my clients, you are your own best teacher. The best way to start when creating change and reaching for your potential is by understanding, accepting and appreciating where you are at now, and how you got here. This means reflecting back on previous patterns (best and worst), pulling out the lessons, and then projecting to future scenarios of how you would prefer to think, feel and act — to the best future self you can be.

It is also a lot easier to generate positive images by drawing on past positive experiences already stored in your memory bank. This requires less imagination, and is good for establishing as a reference point or benchmark if you will. You can then build from there — ever extending and expanding as you grow and evolve.

Looking Back: Recalling Peak Experiences and Performances

Drawing from your existing memory bank by reviewing previous peak experiences or performances is one of the best ways to develop your mental imagery skills. Recreating an image from your past is much easier than creating a new one from scratch.

Once you can reconstruct a previous optimal experience and reconnect with the associated peak state of mind, you can then project that image onto future events and draw upon this repertoire in your day-to-day life. Being able to relive a previous experience where you felt or performed at your best is a great way to generate feelings of confidence in the face of uncertainty, challenge and pressure. By reviewing such positive experiences, you strengthen and reinforce self-belief in your capacity, and minimise any room for the self-doubt and anxiety that is counter-productive to bringing out the best in you. You've done it before so you can do it again!

In this section, I cover peak experiences and performances and the state of mind that usually accompanies them. I then look at how to recall and re-create a feeling and experience to enhance your present wellbeing and prepare for upcoming challenges such as a big presentation at work, musical performance, sporting match, or to simply feel relaxed and confident in an interpersonal encounter, such as a first date or job interview.

Being in the flow[70]

Peak experiences and performances share much in common, but are also distinct processes. Peak performances are often the result of achieving what we refer to as the state of being *in the flow*. 'Flow' is a term coined by renowned Hungarian psychologist Mihaly Csikszentmihalyi to describe a serene state of body and mind that is achieved when fully focused and engaged in a challenging activity that matches your level of and ability — you need to be involved in something that is not too difficult and not too easy, yet challenging enough to require your full attention.

A *peak experience,* on the other hand, is often also referred to as an optimal experience, and is usually associated more with participation in a more passive pursuit that brings spontaneous pleasure and joy; more of a sensory experience. You could just be taking in a beautiful scene or environment, receiving a spa treatment or listening to music. It can also be related to a moment of awe or inspiration. Such rapturous and enchanted experiences can often take on a mystical quality, to which only spiritual terms seem to apply, classified as a sacred or holy moment, and being connected with the divine or one's God if religiously inclined.

A *peak performance* is something that is more actively pursued. You are actually engaging in a meaningful and challenging activity that leads to a transcendent moment, such as executing a difficult dance routine for the first time, composing a musical piece, playing sport, and even in conversations. This can be extended to performance in the board room or brilliant negotiations when you feel completely on top of your game, bobbing and weaving effortlessly — hitting the proverbial sweet spots.

Being in the flow means being totally immersed in the task at hand to the exclusion of everything else, without a worry or care about the result or consequences. You lose yourself in the moment, and time seems to stand still. Your mind and body are as one, working in concert, which produces an experience of pure joy and fulfilment. Fears and concerns seem to fall by the wayside, and hope and optimism reign supreme. Such peak or flow experiences can also involve feeling at one with the universe, such as the awe-inspiring experience of watching a beautiful sun rise over the ocean. Such transcendent experiences create a natural high because of real and positive changes to your brain chemistry and brain waves.

In addition to the characteristics already given, people who have been in the flow in a variety of domains — on the playing field, in the classroom, on stage, or in the garden — have reported the following common features of their experience:

- **Merging of action and awareness:** People in the flow report feeling as one with the action. For example, a pianist reports: 'The music just seemed to flow out of my fingertips'; a hockey player recalls: 'I felt as if my hockey stick was an extension of myself …'.

- **Holding clear goals:** Knowing exactly what it is you wish to achieve and how it facilitates being in the flow — keeping your eye on the prize. If the direction isn't clear, then the focus of attention is fuzzy too.

- **Receiving unambiguous feedback:** Similar to holding clear goals, is being aware of how you're doing when in the flow. You need ample information to let you know that you're on track to achieve your goal. This can be obvious in sports, but not as much in other endeavours. But you may still have a good sense that all is going well. For example, 'I could sense the audience was with me', or 'The emerging painting seemed to speak to me'.

- **Experiencing a sense of control:** When in the flow, there is a feeling of mastery and invincibility. You feel like nothing can stop you, and you can handle anything thrown your way. For example, 'I was able to anticipate my opponent's every move'.

- **Being joyful:** Autotelic experience refers to the pure joy of the experience for the experience's sake; being fully immersed in the process without concern about consequences. While paradoxical, the best results eventuate when you let go of any concern about the results.

Beware of the difference between going with the flow and being in the flow. Remember even dead fish go with the flow! Be clear about your direction before following the process. Don't take your hands off the wheel! Or your eyes off the prize. As the famous quote from one of the all-time great Formula 1 drivers Ayrton Senna advises, 'The car follows the eyes'.

Troubleshooting Roadblocks to Flow

Becoming aware of yourself or others while you're pursuing an activity is the worst foe of flow. If you have a nagging fear of how you might appear to others and what others might think of you, you won't achieve flow. Being self-conscious triggers your inner critic — we all have one — which tends to stop us from reaching our full potential. Peak experiences and flow transcend such constraints, which frees you to experience more of the extraordinary.

Another obstacle to achieving flow is becoming aware of being the flow. If your focus shifts to what can be accomplished with it, you are back in the realm of the ordinary. You can get 'psyched out' when someone notices that you're performing at the top of your game, and they stop you to ask how you're doing it, or what you've changed in your technique. This makes you focus on mechanics and results and tears you away from the state of consciousness of flow.

If you're out on the golf course, for example, and your golf buddy notices that your swing has vastly improved, she might exclaim: 'What a great shot! How did you do that?' or 'You're swinging so much better! Are you taking lessons? What are you doing differently?' You start thinking more about what you're doing rather than how you're being, which is sure to mess up your golf swing.

The best way to react to someone who is — intentionally or not — pulling you out of peak performance is to first recognise the diversion, avoid being analytical, take a breath to keep you in the present moment and refocus on your rhythm and positive image. If necessary, you can simply tell your playing partner that you'd prefer to talk about it later, after you've finished playing.

Reliving highlights from the past

Remember the last time you looked at some of your favourite photos or recordings of family celebrations or holidays, or of a sporting or other performance-related event? Remember how it felt to view them? Perhaps you were sharing the images with others who may have been at the same events or places? What did it feel like to review the experiences? To recall the warm and glowing feelings associated with reliving such events?

Once you can vividly recall a previous highlight, peak experience or performance, you can then easily project it to the future. In other words: review in order to preview. Think about some of the most memorable times of your life. Can you remember how they felt? And how you now may enjoy reminiscing with those you have shared the experience with? Some of our best times with others are spent reminiscing, and waxing nostalgic. We can extend this same process to not only review such events, but to proactively draw from them to apply those same feelings to an upcoming event — to preview and create how we want to feel and be (rather than merely react).

Boosting self-confidence

The best source of confidence (also known as *self-efficacy*) is prior experience of success. Positive images of ourselves in the past provide a ready place to go mentally — to remind us of what is right with us, and what we are capable of (instead of what is wrong and worrisome). Your self-confidence increases as you choose to replace negative memories and feelings with positive ones.

Don't be awed — be grateful!

Too often people are awed by a peak experience or performance, suggesting that it might be too incredible (in other words, not credible), or not worthy of you. Such a feeling suggests you were not in control of the event; that it somehow occurred by chance. And if it occurred by chance you had nothing to do with it, right? On the other hand, the attitude of gratitude is entirely within your control — while acknowledging and savouring the exceptional nature of the experience, you also bring it back into the realm of what is possible — what is within your capacity and control to experience and perform again.

Reflected Best Self Exercise™ being employed in the workplace by the Center for Positive Organizational Scholarship is a variation on the same theme, which begins with expressing peak performance observations of fellow employees/colleagues; and projecting future positive images.[71] Such practice in the workplace, as you might imagine, certainly boosts morale of not only the individuals in question, but also improves the collegiality due to the sharing of good will.

Peak experience/performance recall imagery guides

This section covers how to practise recalling peak experiences and performances. First, take a moment to carefully consider what experiences you want to recall. You might wish to choose parts of different experiences and performances, or stick to one at a time.

The first step to practising mental imagery is to get into a relaxed or hypnotic state. Research has shown that the mind is more open and receptive when in this state. Positive suggestions and imagery are more likely to take hold.

I've used generic instructions here that you can adapt to your own imagery. See the *Peak experience and peak performance recall sample scripts* in the *Appendix* for more on how to create this detail. The more you can personalise the guides, the better your images will be. Take a moment to reflect on your own personal experiences, and how they might compare or differ. Remember, your experiences are the ones that counts.

Ellipses ('…') have been inserted to indicate when to pause — to allow the image to take shape before moving on to the next step.

Peak experience recall imagery guide

Once you've relaxed (see the section on relaxing your mind and body in *Chapter 5*), follow these steps to practise a peak experience recall.

1. **Imagine that you have arrived at a door or gateway to the time and place where you experienced your all-time peak experience.**

   A place where you felt at your very best … most serene … most happy … most joy … most blessed … could be what some consider a 'holy moment' … take in the sights and sounds of this time and place … what do you notice? What do you see? What do you hear? What do you feel? What do you taste? What other sensations are you aware of? Totally immerse yourself back into this wonderful experience of your life … savour and immerse yourself … feeling great appreciation and gratitude as you do so … savouring this peak experience of your life … there is great power in recalling all of the details and sensations of this wonderful moment in time … when time seems to stand still …

and all is well in your inner world … Continue to savour and enjoy recalling this experience … remembering your breathing as you do so … slowly and deeply … exhaling fully and steadily … as you continue to immerse yourself more deeply and intensely into the experience … What are you feeling? What are you thinking? Is anyone joining in with you? What are they doing or saying? As you continue to focus on this image … try to gradually strengthen and intensify it … strengthening and intensifying.

2. **When you feel you have fully re-created the experience, give it a name.**

   Think of this as a kind of file name … to file away in your mind to be recalled at any time you wish to feel this way again. Repeat your file name to yourself as you continue to engage in your imagery.

3. **Picture feeling this way in an upcoming situation, challenge or event where you would like to feel this way again.**

   Once you have practised a strong image of this experience, you will be able to merely repeat the file name to generate this wonderful feeling of wellbeing again — on cue. Promise yourself that you will revisit this experience often.

4. **When you are ready to close the file on this image, and to return back to the here and now begin your ascent back up from one to ten.**

   Count back up the steps the way you came … taking your time back up to full consciousness … remembering your breathing … as you count back up from one to ten … Open your eyes gently before refocusing on the here and now.

Peak performance recall imagery guide

Once you've relaxed (see the section on relaxing your mind and body in *Chapter 5*), follow these steps to practise a peak performance recall.

1. **Imagine that you have arrived at a door or gateway to the time and place where you experienced your all-time peak performance.**

   The time where you performed at your very best … a time when you felt optimally ready and prepared … feeling confident and self-assured … relishing the challenge before you … Take in all the sights and sounds as you (try to) recall all the thoughts and feelings as you approached the event of this great performance … what were you thinking? … What were you feeling? wWhat do you notice? What do you see? What do you hear? What do you feel? What do you taste? What other sensations are you aware of? Who, if anyone, are you aware of?

2. **Now take yourself back to a peak moment of this event.**

   Choose one that epitomises the experience for you … bring up all the feelings and sensations ….Totally immerse yourself back into this great performance of your life … where is your attention focused? … What are you doing? What sights and sounds are you aware of? Who else is in the picture (if anyone)? What are they doing and saying? … Fully immerse yourself back in the key moments of this all-time great performance … when you were in the flow … feeling strong and flexible … totally engaged in what you are doing and performing at your very best …

3. **Now recall what it was like afterwards.**

   How did it feel? Imagine any applause or congratulations … imagine the celebrations … What are you thinking and saying to yourself? What are others saying and doing? Savour this peak performance of your life … there is great power in recalling all of the details and sensations of this excellent moment in time … this great memory … recalling all of your strengths and capacities … your skill and talent… Continue to savour and enjoy recalling this experience … remembering your breathing as you do so … slowly and deeply … exhaling fully and steadily … as you continue to immerse yourself more deeply and intensely into the experience … what are you feeling? What are you thinking? Is anyone joining in with you? What are they doing or saying? As you continue to focus on this image … try to gradually strengthen and intensify it … strengthening and intensifying … and when you feel you have fully re-created the experience, give it a name … a file name so-to-speak … to file away in your mind to be recalled at any time you wish to feel this way again. Repeat your file name to yourself as you continue to engage in your imagery.

4. **Once you can fully re-experience this peak performance in your mind — you can project it to a future event where you would like to feel and perform the same way again.**

   Bring up the scene of an upcoming event ... and picture yourself feeling and performing at your very best again ... Imagine approaching the event the same way ... performing the same way ... and finishing strong and with a flourish at the upcoming event. Continue the image with what you expect and hope to occur after the event. Clearly imagine the aftermath with the applause and congratulations ... And congratulate yourself on creating yet another experience and performance ... of fulfilling your potential.

5. **When you are ready to close the file on this image, and to return back to the here and now begin your ascent back up from one to ten.**

   Count back up the way you came ... taking your time back up to full consciousness ... remembering your breathing ... One ... Two ... Three ... Four ... Five ... Rising back up to the here and now ... Six ... Seven ... Eight ... Nine ... Ten — back to the here and now. Open your eyes gently before refocusing on the here and now.

To recall and relive a peak performance, you need to imagine the aftermath as well. Recall what happened after the result, the congratulations and any applause. Remembering the praise and celebration supports your self-image as being successful and worthy of such attention and recognition. If you're not comfortable and prepared for the accolades, you might shy away from success, which could prevent your goal from becoming a reality.

Defining Luck: Preparation Meets Opportunity

If you're able to draw on past powerful images of yourself where you are strong and confident, you can then more quickly grasp opportunities as they arise. Being mentally prepared and having a positive image of yourself being successful makes it easier for you to first recognise opportunities, and then secondly to actually seize them. Too often we become aware of missed opportunities too late!

For example, say you're at an event and the CEO of a company you want to work for happens to be there too, or you're at a party and you notice the man/woman of your dreams, but get too nervous and tongue-tied to go up and introduce yourself, let alone offer your card (or phone number). Missed opportunity!

Not seizing opportunities happens to athletes all the time. Just when a dreamed-for moment arrives — such as beating someone for the first time in a match — they get distracted by the novelty of being in this position. There's something wrong with the picture. It doesn't fit their image of themselves. The distraction causes them to let up or slow down, if only for an imperceptible amount. This may be just enough to be passed or beaten on the next move. Ah, now that's better — the experience now matches the inner pictures of their mind! Of course, they kick themselves afterwards at the missed opportunity! Practising mental imagery helps foster the readiness to recognise and seize the moment.

Moving Forward: Best Future Self

Drawing from your inner database is the best way to create your best future self. You may not know it or believe yet, but you already contain all within you to take your next best step and build towards a flourishing future. Back to the future!

It's about just taking one step at a time, one foot in front of the other.

A journey of a thousand miles begins with a single step.

You don't have to do it all today, just begin today. All this requires is the simple decision to move forward … to embracing your potential with greater optimism. This also entails engaging in activities that can boost your skills and knowledge and thereby the confidence to go in the right direction.

As discussed in the first section of this chapter, you already own one of the best sources of confidence, which is your memory of prior successes of meeting and overcoming a challenge — no matter how large or small. I know you have tasted success in your past just because you've picked up this book; and you have an appetite for more. By drawing upon the best within you from looking back, you prepare yourself for more of the same going forward.

To begin with, what do you think a younger version of yourself would think of you now? Keep in mind what you are most proud of to date. Don't you wish you could have the wisdom of your present self to encourage and support you back then? If you knew then what you know now, what would be different? Would you have made different choices? Taken more chances? Or taken better chances? What was the basis upon which you made your best choices and your worst choices? Might you have been less worried and more relaxed and optimistic? What do you want to keep going forward?

Imagine if you had the benefit of hindsight about your current life — right now.

Your best shot in the present is to act in a way that is consistent with the image of your best future self (BFS). As the acronym suggests, your best future (BF) self is your own best friend. Who better to count on? Imagine an older and wiser version of yourself; one who is more accomplished, with their fondest hopes and dreams fulfilled. Wouldn't you love to have a conversation with him or her? On the other hand, you are probably more acutely aware of being your own worst enemy. Isn't it time to turn the tide? And allow for a more positive influence?

Remember though, it is not about being the best, but being your best. Just being and doing better is enough to know that you are on track. Rushing it will only lead to unpleasant set-backs. On the other hand, holding back will only keep you stuck and frustrated. Finding the right pace is important but this may not be within your control. Certainty is certainly not within your control. So, allowing for a bit of mystery makes for a greater sense of adventure. Think about it. If you knew the ending to a mystery film or novel, or to a sporting match, would you still watch? And remain as engrossed?

It is also not about becoming someone you are not. It's not about living up to someone else's standards or programming, but about following your true calling. It's not about a fantasy self, or even an idealised self, but about your best possible self. It's your true self living up to your potential, and allowing your own aspirations to unfold naturally and efficiently. This is something most of us fall well short of. Your best shot at getting on track and staying on track is to be true to yourself, and creating the best supportive conditions possible and removing hindrances — internally and externally.[72]

The following quote from Michelangelo about his genius sculpting is an apt illustration of the above point: 'I saw the angel in the marble and carved until I set him free.'

Rodin when asked how he is able to create such an amazing likeness of someone (let us say you in this case), would reply that he simply carves away what is not you. The point I'm bringing home is that it is not about becoming what you are not, but about allowing the inner light in you to shine forth.

If you bring forth what is inside of you, what you bring forth will save you. If you do not bring forth what is inside of you, what you do not bring forth will destroy you. – Jesus

I believe this applies equally to what is good and bad within us. Quite simply, if you are not true to yourself, you will suffer — whether this is merely not expressing your true nature, communicating your real feelings, or developing your talent. As Tony Bennett likes to say: 'To not cultivate one's talent is to sin against one's talent.'

And the day came when the risk to remain tight in a bud was more painful than the risk it took to blossom. – Anais Nin

Some people might say that this process also taps into your intuition or inner wisdom, or even to premonitions and clairvoyance. Going to a psychic has become quite a popular activity these days. Fess up: How many of you have sought out psychic counsel? I would hazard a guestimate of at least half of you. And how much of what most resonates in those sessions is simply reinforcing what you already 'knew'? Truthfully, isn't the main purpose of your visit to get reassurance? To enhance your confidence in what lies ahead for you? What is their source of information? They are relying on tapping into you! Even if they report that it's your guardian angels, master guides and family members who have passed away, you are nevertheless the conduit. And if this is correct, then why not access this information yourself?

There is now a strong body of evidence demonstrating that we have an in-built and largely unconscious system in place for premonitions. While this faculty may have developed and evolved to predict and prevent the bad, i.e. impending dire circumstances and events that is necessary for our survival, we can also draw upon this ability for predicting the good. Such pre-cognitions seem to register in the body well before the mind, and are more pronounced for danger versus the more benevolent. Studies at Stanford and Princeton Universities have shown that our bodies give off signals well before conscious awareness is possible. Too often, however, we are switched off to the signals becoming conscious, unless intense enough in the case of danger; or unless we actively and consciously cultivate this capacity.

Premonitions might seem quite extraordinary, but they are actually extremely common. Many of you, I'm sure, have had the experience of someone coming to mind just before they ring you. And how often have you rung someone out of the blue, to hear them tell you they were just that moment thinking of you? Despite how natural this process may be, it is not one that can be forced and controlled. We can only invite it and allow it. Trying to force it seems to prevent it. In most cases, premonitions come unbidden, but that is not to say that we cannot open up the channels for them to come more readily.

Many premonitions occur while we are asleep and dreaming (including some of the best scientific discoveries), so keeping a dream journal can facilitate better access to this capacity. Try recording your dreams as soon as possible upon awakening. It helps to first lie still and allow the impressions to re-form in your mind. If you move too abruptly, the conscious access seems to dissipate quickly. It is suggested that premonitions will become more frequent with this practice.[73]

Learning to still and quiet your mind will also foster the conditions for accessing your unconscious and hence intuitive faculties. Meditation and relaxation techniques are the simplest way to develop this skill. Furthermore, focus on breathing that is central to all meditation and relaxation techniques is also considered the portal to our unconscious minds — the bridge between the conscious and unconscious, given the inextricable link that our respiration has with our emotional centres.

Language resides in a completely separate part of the brain, which is why thinking too much interferes with intuitive processes. Beware, however, that the mind can play tricks on you, and what you perceive as premonition, may not be true at all. This is similar to the fact that we can also have false memories of the past as well as false impressions of the future. Also, things can change. The information that exists at one point in time can be different at another. So, it is more a matter of probabilities.

Guidelines for best future self

Imagine yourself as your best self possible at some point in the future, after all has gone as well as you'd hoped. You are living your dream life, having accomplished your dream goals. You have fully capitalised on your talents, skills and knowledge ... fulfilled your potential ... living your life as you ideally imagined it ... It is probably best to write it out first — to generate the picture as fully as possible. Then spend time imagining yourself as this person.

What is it like? What do you notice? How does it feel? And probably most importantly, what did it take to get here? By practising this image you will more likely act in accordance with it — in alignment with the values and aspirations it represents. This will facilitate overriding negative images that prevent you from taking your best courses of action and achieving your best life. It might also, bring to light what is interfering — the better for you to attend to and resolve.

Conversations with your best future self

Imagine this older and wiser version of yourself; one who is more accomplished, with fondest hopes and dreams fulfilled. Wouldn't you love to have a conversation with him or her? Who better to support you and to count on than your inner best future self? While external supports are always wonderful to have, nothing builds confidence and security like being able to rely on your own internal resources.

Making a direct connection with your BFS can short circuit any inner saboteur that may reside within. It can also fast track making the choices that are more closely aligned with your BFS.

A variation on the above theme is to write a letter from the BFS. Try to focus on receiving the message without thinking too much about it. Just write what first comes to mind, remembering that intuitive impressions often don't come in words, but in more sensory impressions. Allow them to speak to you ...

Best future self imagery guide

1. Get yourself into a comfortable position ready to relax and tune in to the inner calm within yourself ...

2. Now take yourself to a certain point in your future. This could be one year, five years, to the end of your years in this lifetime ... Decide this before you settle in to your imagery.

3. Imagine yourself at this future date, being and having accomplished all that you'd dreamed possible ... having accomplished your best at whatever endeavours you've dreamed possible ... feeling and being as you would wish to become by this stage of your life.

4. Imagine having overcome all obstacles in your path with great aplomb ...

5. Imagine the kind of attention you are now receiving from others ... in your professional life ... and personal life ... who are you biggest supporters? ... who is closest to you? ... imagine what it feels like to be surrounded by such support and love ... who believed in you most ... and likely new players in your life as well (and while you might not be able to imagine them specifically,

you can imagine what it feels like to have them in your life).

6. Imagine having fully capitalised on your potential to this point ... and maybe even discovering new talents and endeavours to apply them to ... how your achievements have opened up new doors to great new opportunities and adventures ...

7. You are living your life as you ideally imagined ... and with ideal companions along the way ...

8. Spend time fully imagining yourself as this person ... how it feels ... emotionally ... energetically ... what you see ... and hear ... and any other sensations ...

9. What is it like being here? And probably more importantly, What did it take to get here? Fully explore looking back at how you got here ... the paths you took ... the choices you made ... the strengths and talents you developed and built upon ... the new skills and abilities you developed ... the changes you made ...

10. Once you've made a good connection with your BFS (your best future self and your new best friend), you might like to ask a few questions so you can benefit from her wisdom. What are her impressions looking back at you now? What is she proud of? Grateful for? Sympathetic about? Does she have any advice for you? Any guidance for how to overcome any perceived challenges? Any words of encouragement? Words of wisdom? What do you need to let go of? And what do you need to build on? What are the small steps that you can enact today towards reaching this brilliant future self? Ask her to show you the best way forward ...

11. Ask your BFS to stay accessible always ... to nudge you when you need nudging ... to draw courage and strength when you need it ... to direct you to soothing and comfort and when you need it ... and to take time for self-care and rest when you need it ... promise to heed her guidance and advice ... and to rest easy in the knowledge that her newfound and well earned wisdom and confidence is yours for the asking ... be receptive to it, and willing and committed to move towards it and all that entails ... to move towards greater good fortune ... and flourishing wellbeing ...

12. Take a few deep breaths, and with every out breath/exhale, release whatever no longer serves you towards this path to your best future self ... and with the next few in breaths embrace this new and better you with every inhale ... and conclude with thanking your BFS. Then move on with your day enacting whatever next steps are on the course of your best future self.

After completing this exercise, be on the lookout for any impressions that come to mind connected to your BFS ... they may arise as memories, but of the future (and not from the past). When you bid such information you are on the verge of tapping into your more intuitive self, your clairvoyant self ... you are drawing upon the reservoir of (potential) information that is yet to be fully explained though confirmed by science, and considered another dimension that is information. By bringing more conscious awareness to this process, and actively engaging with it, you can take better advantage of the opportunity to create a better future for yourself.

Summary

As you now realise, you are your own best resource. You contain, and have access to, a rich reservoir of information that can facilitate your mental imagery and reaching your goals. Practising recalling your previous best experiences will enhance your chances of creating better experiences in the future. By (quantum) leaping ahead to your best future self you also get to become a better friend to yourself in the present, supporting your efforts on your journey ahead, and moving forward successfully.

Chapter 8

Rewriting History — Creating and Sustaining Change

Mental imagery is increasingly being recognised as a powerful tool for reprogramming your brain — essentially rewriting the impact of your history. In this chapter, you will:

- Become more aware of how history dictates your future
- Understand why negative emotions have such a strong grip on us
- Learn how to recalibrate emotional reactivity
- Be guided to create positive changes that rewire your brain

We are all a product of our history. The influence of the conditions in which we were born and raised tends to follow us long into adulthood — creating hard-wired patterns of reactions influencing the choices we make. Some of these patterns may serve us well, and some not so well. The worst part about it is that much is below our conscious awareness, and therefore harder to control and to change. While on the surface you may be consciously making a decision and plan for change, you may also be stymied by an unconscious resistance to such change, which we've come to know as the *inner saboteur*.

This is what I refer to as the effects of having competing agendas within that we need to get on the same side. Or at least get them in sync with your best interests and to recognise that we're all on the same side. Now, we might have come to hate and despise our inner saboteur, but it is not going to go away quietly unless it gets due recognition and reassurance. This entity might also come across as our *inner critic,* who is generally not out to hurt us so much as to protect us from danger (e.g. from the pain of humiliation and disappointment).

So, instead of hating, it is more conducive to welcome it to the table, thanking it for looking out for you, and then reassuring it of how you can more safely navigate the way ahead with your plans. This alter ego needs to realise that its way only leads to more languishing, and that it is time to relinquish its grip to explore a new way that leads to flourishing. While you may be getting protected from the pain of failure and defeat, short-changing your potential is also painful.

Most of us do not regret trying and failing
nearly as much as we regret failing to try.

Bruce Lipton puts it this way in his book *Biology of Belief:* that a cell cannot both protect itself and grow.[74] We need to make a choice, and if we are to grow and evolve, then we cannot do so within the confines of our safe cocoon. We need to stretch beyond our comfort zone if we're going to really flourish.

Life begins at the edge of our comfort zone. – Dean Donald Walsh

History isn't Destiny

As much as many of us would like to, we cannot literally rewrite our own history. We can learn and grow from it, however, and endeavour not to repeat the same mistakes, but to draw the lessons from them. Most of our greatest strengths have emerged as a result of our adaptation to painful and frightful experiences. You've probably all heard the famous Nietzsche quote: 'What does not kill me makes me stronger'. Many of those strengths, however, become our weaknesses in adulthood, when we over-rely on them to compensate for any sense of lack within (e.g. insecurity and self-doubt) or attack from without (hyper-sensitivity to threats of harm by others).

If our only tool is a hammer,
then we tend to treat everything like a nail.

This often plays out as a pattern of overreacting beyond what a situation warrants, e.g. going on the attack with abusive anger (i.e. 'fight' component of the 'fight or flight or freeze' reactivity) when someone hurts your feelings (best defence being offence). When this occurs, any legitimate complaint of yours gets lost in the mix, with you having to apologise, and your point of view overlooked (again).

Connecting the Dots from Your Past: Trace, Face, Erase, Embrace

Emotional reactions of disproportionate severity such as abusive anger and bullying can be a sign of unresolved pain from your past that has either been suppressed or repressed, and needs to be addressed. Otherwise it will find a way to surface, often at a most inconvenient time, which you'll find hard to control. Essentially there will be an automatic, hard-wired reaction facilitated by your brain firing off signals, urging buried pain to come to the party out of fear it may never see such an opening again. We're not just reacting to a present perceived slight/threat, but all the related unresolved issues from the past — we've got recovering to do! So if you can't tame the beast by keeping it bottled up, how do you break the cycle of over-sensitivity?

The answer lies in confronting what has been buried, rather than being dismissive, which can be false economy, as avoiding the issue only lets the pressure build ready for an even greater eruption.

That which you avoid controls you,
and that which you resist persists.

To overcome this you need to ensure you don't get distracted by another's criticisms, or allow yourself to be seduced by a debate about right and wrong, which may serve as a welcome diversion but is ultimately futile in moving on. Instead, recognise that anger is a surface safe emotion that covers up vulnerability and frustration, and commit to identifying and attending to the old unmet needs, hurts and fears. When you tend to the underlying needs better, you'll notice that your reactions become more 'reasonable'. You will respond more effectively (rather than react).

You will also become better at expressing your views and feelings, to being better heard and understood. This will free you to more optimally navigate any new issues you come across, rather than creating a new pile of unresolved pain. If your issues seem too overwhelming or entangled to sort alone, it may help to unload with a qualified psychologist or other professional to help trace back to the source, face and resolve the issues, and then erase the hold your past may have on you; so that you can then more fully embrace your whole self and potential.

Tending to the Inner Child Within

Much of who we are is a result of conditions and experiences from our past — both nature and nurture (upbringing and genetics). Much of this will have become hard-wired by the time we become adults — both for our strengths and our weaknesses. Many of our strengths and resilience may have developed by adapting to difficult circumstances, which then become our weakness when we over-rely and over-use them at the expense of developing a more well-rounded repertoire. Most of our weaknesses, therefore, are a result of our strengths out of control. We tend to go with them when facing life challenges. This becomes a habitual and automatic mode of being and reacting, which can shortchange reaching our full potential and wellbeing. It often manifests in attempts to (over) compensate for a perception of lack that may have served its purpose when it originated, but outlives its usefulness later in life.

We don't, however, want to throw out the baby with the bath water so-to-speak. When we recognise that a weakness is merely an expression of our strength out of control, we can learn to accept and appreciate the value of the strength and simply develop an ability to bring it down a notch, while also exploring balancing out our repertoire. Changing such a habit takes a good deal of conscious awareness and effort — to catch the moment — to turn off automatic and reflexive reactions and allow a more balanced one to take effect.

The same goes for when we find ourselves overreacting to circumstances. This can be especially apparent with angry reactions that are out of proportion to the transgression. While a certain level of anger and frustration may have been well justified, the overreaction often denies you the opportunity and satisfaction of being heard, and the legitimate complaint goes unaddressed. And worse and perverse, you end up having to apologise for being transgressed! When such reactions can be connected to their origins you can then address, heal and forgive, which allows you to move on. By tracing back to when this pattern began, and facing up to the issues, you get to erase the damaging effects and move on with developing a more effective responding capacity.

While the imagery exercises suggested in this book are helpful in this process, it is no replacement for professionally facilitated psychological support for exploring and resolving deeper issues. Inner Child work in particular can be highly beneficial in this respect.

It is important to distinguish who we have become, based on our essential goodness and deservedness (or lack of) and the conditions we grew up in that have shaped us. We cannot control the conditions of our past, but we can control the conditions we permit ourselves in the present and the future. In the case of this book, we can create better mental images from which to base our experiences and pursue our goals.

If it was easy to let go the impact of past wounds and conditioning, we'd all be doing it. It isn't, and we aren't. There's a good reason why negative emotions have such a grip on us. Our wiring is designed to pay attention to any negativity or threats to our wellbeing, as a cue for action upon which our very survival and evolution depended. What got us this far, however, isn't what is going to take us to a better place going forward. To paraphrase Einstein: The same mindset that

IMAGINE

contributed to the problem is not what is going to solve it. While some negative reactivity is appropriate and inevitable to real circumstances that require us to take remedial action, dwelling or overreacting causes us more harm.

In practice, however, the negativity grip remains strong. Researchers suggest that it takes at least three positive experiences to counteract a single negative — to bring us to neutral, or to what is referred to as the *positivity tipping point*. To deal with gratuitous negativity (the kind that serves no real adaptive purpose, other than the gratification derived from commiserating), try this mental strategy:

1. Recognise that someone else's behaviour is not within your control, but that you can determine the lesson you draw from the experience.

2. Focus on what you would have preferred. For example, you cannot control the fact that someone (appeared to) ignore you at a function, but you can control your response. You can take a deep breath to recover your equanimity, and be grateful that you value and demonstrate politeness and friendliness.

3. Refocus your attention on how you prefer people behave. Recall images of when you have experienced this, and resolve to be more aware and grateful in the future. By doing this, you will change a (potentially) negative experience into a positive one. Doing this changes your memory and frame of reference, upon which all your future experiences will be based (and likely draw more of the positivity to you in the process). Focusing back on what is within your control is a much more practical and positive way. This is how 'what you focus on grows' works.

4. Replay your preferred scenario in your mental imagery.

When we use and misuse our strengths to cover up and hide our vulnerabilities and insecurities we are invested in trapping ourselves which limits our potential. We can only be as truly strong as when allowing and tending to our vulnerabilities. The real strength comes in the willingness to face the dark. You can think of it like switching on a light, which flushes out whatever is lurking in the corners. From here there is greater possibility of putting any issues into perspective. Research has shown that those with the highest self-esteem embrace their own vulnerability, while others engage in numbing behaviours (i.e. 'flight', e.g. drinking, spending, eating, etc.).[75] You can run but you cannot hide!

Old Habits Die Hard: Recalibrating Emotional Reactivity

The reason old habits die hard is because they've become hard-wired in our brains — to the point of automaticity — making it hard to catch and control or change. This is a good thing for habits we want to keep and not have to concentrate too much on, which frees up head-space. It's not so convenient when the habit is bad for us. Neuroscientists estimate that we only have one-eighth of a second to catch the moment for reflexive reactivity. Most unwanted (over)reactions suggest unresolved issues worth exploring (as above). Something to explore rather than ignore!

The brain maintains such reactions even if unwanted and unwarranted because of whatever initial programming occurred that engaged fear and anxiety; the trigger that 'hijacked the amygdala'.[76] There's good evolutionary value for this process, just as for negative emotions in general — not listening to them in our ancient past had dire life and death consequences.

While such processes (i.e. fight/flight/freeze) still have merit in this day and age, more often than not they merely interfere with being more adaptive and productive, not to mention happy and content. Such automaticity as well as intensity makes it doubly challenging to change, but imagine the satisfaction of a breakthrough! In fact, your best shot at making a successful break from the hold of the past is to practise imagining it as you would prefer (as outlined above). This is when mental imagery can be most useful — it gives you the opportunity to practise catching the moment, which strengthens our capacity to respond better upon any eventual trigger.

Despite lots of practice, chances are you'll still miss the actual instant of opportunity to implement a change in response to a trigger. This is normal and natural considering how hard-wired your brain has become. Consider yourself lucky as your survival depended on this brain feature historically/evolutionarily speaking. What it generally takes to get better at this is catching the moment as soon as you can afterwards — perhaps minutes, hours, or even days later — and winding back the clock and reviewing, but this time noting the opportunity, slowing down the replay, and getting it right imaginally. The more you can do this, and the sooner — the better you'll be at catching the moment IN the moment! Research has found that 'rescripting' after an event within a half-hour is effective in reversing actual perceptions and memory of the event — in effect rewiring your brain!

Therefore even when we miss the moment (opportunity to (re)act differently), if we catch it relatively soon afterwards we can still adjust and self-correct. We can file away the experience as a memory according to the preferred scenario, thus creating new repertoire/database. We have recalibrated our emotional reactivity to a more optimal range.

As I tell my clients, if you recognise the opportunity later (no matter how much later) then you're already on track for change. The goal is to recognise sooner and sooner, until you are fully aware in the instant, and make the shift ... and then relish your success!

This takes conscious intention and awareness plus imaginal practice until it becomes a new pattern or habit.[77] Ultimately, this saves lots of valuable time and energy in the long run, as we no longer need to feel frustrated and/or remorseful.

Family interactions are best examples of hot button issues, and also the most challenging to shift as they involve our oldest relationships from a very young and more vulnerable age. Some people attempt to escape the family dynamics by distancing themselves, only to find the same scenarios playing out in their lives personally and professionally. The workplace tends to reflect families in many respects, not least of which because we spend so much more time with our work mates and/or clients than family?

People tend to play out their family of origin roles in the workplace. If you were the mediator in your family, then you will find yourself attracted to, as well as playing a mediating role in the workplace. If you were bullied in your family, then you will more likely attract and/ or tolerate bullying behaviour from others at work. If you tended to be the centre of attention in your family then you will tend to seek attention and centre stage at work and in social groups. If you would like to change such patterns, then mental imagery offers you the best shot at making this happen. Imagine yourself as you'd prefer to become in such scenarios.

Rewriting History Imagery Guide

Below is an imagery guide for rewriting history which is designed to help you transcend old (bad) habits and enact better ways of being and behaving (i.e. doing). It is best to try this out with minor issues and work your way up to the more hard core. This involves gradually building up your skill at either resisting an urge (e.g. to withdraw/ flee or attack/fight), or to build up the courage to assert yourself better; and to generally make better choices under pressure, and feel better accordingly.

The first step to applying the rewriting history script is to identify your triggers, in order to better catch the moment. This process might begin by first monitoring and journaling your experiences to get a better handle on the array of scenarios to then incorporate into your mental imagery practice (see *Appendix C* for the Stressor/Blissor Monitoring Sheet). You can then practise rewriting history accordingly.

1. Get yourself into a comfortable position ready to relax and tune in to the inner calm within yourself ...

2. Focus your attention on your breathing ... taking in slow deep abdominal breaths, and exhaling fully and steadily ... fully expelling all the used oxygen in your lungs ... releasing and letting go with every out breath ... releasing and letting go of all cares and concerns with every out breath ... detoxing with every out breath ...

3. And once you have cleared and refreshed your lungs ... focus on breathing in purifying energy with every in breath ... oxygenating your body and mind ... washing away any residual tension in your body and mind ... clearing space for your mental imagery ...

4. You might like to go to that special place from the peak experience recall imagery — where you feel at your very best — most at peace, alive, confident, loving and beloved ... most calm and focused ... with each breath bring yourself to this deep well of strength within yourself ... breathing slowly and deeply ... and exhaling fully and steadily ...

5. And when you are ready, take yourself back to the time and place where you experienced your most recent challenge ... when you might not have reacted as you'd wish ... the one that you'd like to do over ... take this opportunity to recreate the images of that time and place ... entering it with a state of calm and positive focus ... reconnect with the moment just prior to the event ... remembering your breathing as you do so ... and then picture it unfolding better this time ... imagine yourself responding better ... with greater equanimity and positive focus ... expressing yourself as you'd prefer ... acting and responding as you'd prefer ... making better choices ... Run through your preferred scenario and your more positive response ... taking your time as you do so ... you might need to slow it down, or press 'PAUSE', to feel more in control ... take a few breaths and try again ... and once you've become comfortable with your better response ... imagine it again in real time ... Replay the scene in real time — unfolding as you would prefer ... imagine the satisfaction of meeting the challenge well and the flow-on benefits ... and how good that feels? You might want to even congratulate yourself? Or imagine someone congratulating you?

6. When you have completed replaying this scene ... think of an upcoming situation where you might likely encounter such an opportunity again ... Flash forward to such a scenario, and practice responding well again ... making good choices ... allowing your best self to shine .... Imagine how good it feels

knowing you can meet this challenge well ... and to greater benefit for all concerned ... and allow yourself an inner smile as you connect to your best self in action.

7. When you have completed running these images through your mind thank yourself for engaging in such positive programming ... and then take your time coming back to the here and now. With every breath commit yourself to maintain this connection with your best self ... to feel and do better ... as you bring yourself back to the here and now.

8. Breathing slowly and deeply — bring yourself back to the here and now, and open your eyes and reflect on this experience.

The imagery guide above is a standard one you may follow, but if you encounter difficulty in controlling your images, then there are a few tips to try out as covered in *Chapter 5* on imagery guidelines. For example, because we're dealing with overriding some of your most hard-wired programming, it might work better to do the imagery in reverse. Not from start to finish, but from finish back to the start. This is to avoid the automatic reaction to the trigger even in your imagery (remember, the brain cannot tell the difference between what is real or imagined, see *Chapter 2*), by starting at the end after the initial trigger has passed, thus bypassing the trigger.

Try imagining how you would prefer to feel upon conclusion of the scenario ... walking away having made a better choice ... or having responded as you'd prefer ... better than ever before, and having been well received as well. Having said that, you cannot control the reception to the change in you, so best to also be prepared for the worst, and being fine with that. Hope for the best, and be prepared for the worst in the other — by being your best and not responsible for the worst in another. Remember, it is best to focus on what is in your direct control, and let go of what is not. You cannot control another's reaction, and oftentimes, they do not welcome the change in you as it might require a change or adjustment in them! Keep in mind what is yours and what is theirs. Own your own thoughts, feelings and actions, i.e. responsibilities, but do not take on another's.

If you find you didn't pull it off as well as you'd hoped or even imagined you can always apologise and explain your intention, and then try again. Sometimes, the pendulum swings too far in the opposite direction when we try to implement change and recalibrate, before we establish a more optimal range of emotional reactivity that works for us. This is especially the case when we have no good role models to guide us. Praise yourself for at least taking steps in the right direction!

Summary

This chapter has outlined how to reprogram your brain in a positive direction to override and transcend negative impacts from your past. With your mental imagery practice you are recalibrating your brain to becoming more adept at responding to triggers in a more optimal emotional range so that you can be in your best form/self more often.

Chapter 9

Embracing Your Potential — Achieving Personal Best

Mental imagery can enhance personal effectiveness in a broad range of domains and facilitate achievement of challenging goals, whether related to health and lifestyle, relationships, performance and general wellbeing. As has been discussed in previous chapters, there is little in life in which your mental images are not implicated.

This chapter provides a sampling of how you can take greater charge over your images to create better experiences in your work, life and play — towards achieving your personal best. We begin with a general overview of the array of applications followed by more specific suggestions for applying mental imagery for:

- Enhancing success achieving personal goals
- Programming business and professional success
- Motivating effort (because of the above)
- Getting in the mood — managing energy and emotions
- Learning and perfecting skills

- Enhancing focus and concentration
- Coping with pressure and evaluation (i.e. overcoming stage fright)
- Drawing on role models
- Projecting forward from present optimal experiences
- Flashing back to draw from a repertoire of past success
- Dealing with performance reviews and feedback
- Mental rehearsal
- Practising contingencies
- Coping with and adjusting to change
- Making decisions and developing intuition
- Jogging your memory — storing and retrieving information
- Breaking bad habits and changing behaviour
- Health and healing
- Improving communication and relationships

Mental imagery is applicable to any and every facet of your life. There is virtually no goal or endeavour to which mental imagery cannot be applied. You can think of it as being a more actively conscious scriptwriter for your life. There are limits to what can be accomplished with mental imagery however. As I keep reminding you throughout this book, it is best to stick to what is realistically attainable and within your direct control and potential.

Nevertheless, few of us spend nearly as much time contemplating and imagining all that can go right in our lives, compared to the amount of time and energy spent worrying and catastrophising about things that could go wrong. Mental imagery practice provides the opportunity to redress this imbalance. Not only that, you can also use mental imagery to prepare for how you can best respond to life's challenges when things do go wrong, rather than compounding the difficulty with negative images from the past and overreactivity as covered in the previous chapter.

I tend to draw a lot from sports as illustrative examples that can be readily understood. The beauty of sport is that the objectives are clear and apparent to all, as is the immediate feedback on whether you are on track or not. But applying mental imagery to our everyday lives can sometimes be a bit more challenging as the criteria are unique to you and your situation, the time frames are often longer, and many more factors come into play.

In addition, it is also more helpful to think of yourself as person in training as you embrace pursuit of your potential, rather than thinking of yourself as someone with problems to overcome.

It would be useful to first read the chapter in its entirety to get the scope of applications, and then return to those areas that are most relevant to you, and consider how they might play out for you.

Remember to keep in mind the goal setting and imagery guidelines outlined in previous chapters as you read on.

Unleashing Your Inner Performer

Mental imagery is a performance enhancement tool that you can use to release the best within you. By strengthening your images, you clear the path towards more efficiently reaching your goals. Whether you perform on the stage, playing field, kitchen, classroom or boardroom, each and every day presents an opportunity for building and improving your repertoire. The practice of mental imagery is applicable to your everyday performance on the stage of your life as you know it — to being and doing better.

Take a moment to stop and consider what it is you wish to achieve today — personally or professionally — and imagine all unfolding as you would most prefer; interacting and executing tasks as well as can be; and having the flexibility to adjust according to any emerging circumstances. How'd you go?

Programming Body and Mind

Mental imagery can be applied to developing a stronger mind/body connection for getting the most out of your body. This is important when facing health challenges, as well as for any physical activity for which a lot is on the line.

For sporting goals, a stronger mind/body connection enhances the ability to execute moves automatically (without thinking too much which hinders performance). It reduces the amount of interference that naturally occurs in the face of distractions and pressures, and paves the way to a more smooth and fluid performance.

For health goals, a stronger mind/body connection enhances your ability to have a more conscious impact on your healing. Your body is a complex system that is constantly striving for homeostasis and survival that does not require conscious thought. By consciously engaging your mind in the process you can enhance the system's effectiveness, as well as override any negative influences that arise from the stress of worrying about what is wrong with you.

Maximising Your Healing Potential

While your body is always naturally striving for recovery and homeostasis when faced with health challenges, engaging in mental imagery strengthens the mind/body connection with which to more actively work with your body to heal and mend itself. Those who do engage in mental imagery find that their healing potential is accelerated compared to those who do not, or worse, those who replay their injury or complain and focus on what is wrong with them.

By directing the mind and body for greater health, you mobilise the body's natural healing processes to the fullest. This has been shown effective in a number of ways, e.g. by improving blood flow conducive to healing, boosting the immune system, improving cardiovascular function, encouraging behaviour that is consistent with treatment and best outcomes, and much more.

Optimising Your Wellbeing Quotient

By focusing more on what is right with you than wrong will boost your sense of wellbeing. When you focus on your limitations, you tend to reinforce them with the flow-on effect of depressed mood. When you focus on possibilities, then they too become reinforced, elevating mood, confidence and wellbeing. You can use mental imagery to more fully utilise and capitalise on your strengths and develop new mental and emotional habits to enhance your happiness quotient.

Deepening Your Inner and Outer Connections

Have you ever had a gut instinct about something that you ignored much to your regret? Your intuitive faculties are closely linked to the images of your mind. It is how intuition gets your attention. Too often we will dismiss such images when they do not make immediate sense to our more logical mind. The more you pay attention to such intuitive flashes, the stronger and more reliable they will become.

The better your inner connection with your true self, the better your radar will also be for connecting with others. Optimally relating to others, however, sometimes requires the presence of mind to switch off overreactivity, to respond more effectively. This can play out in any number of ways, e.g. moving from being passive to more assertive; and the reverse, dialling down aggressive tendencies to communicating in a way that is better received. This takes mindfulness and lots of practice when attempting to change old habits resulting from automatic and sub-conscious reflexes developed in our childhood. Practising desired changes in your mental imagery will strengthen your capacity to catch the moment and respond more as you would prefer. See the section on rewriting history in *Chapter 8* for more about how to loosen the grip the past has on us.

From the Playing Field to the Boardroom and Beyond

Mental imagery is probably best known for applications on the playing field, but there are many more of you whose job takes place off the field. Your performance at your workplace can also benefit from the practice of mental imagery.

There is no doubt that mental images can exert a powerful influence on physical performance, a notion supported by a substantial body of anecdotal and empirical evidence[78]. Imagery is used for a variety of purposes in the world of sport, including the acquisition and performance of skills, to change emotional responses and cognitions, and the regulation of anxiety. Logically, all of these applications are equally relevant in the world of business.[79]

The beauty of sport as mentioned previously is that the criteria is clear and unambiguous, and immediately evident (to ourselves and anyone else who is watching) whether we're meeting them or not. It is, therefore, much easier to measure success, including success of practising mental imagery. Nevertheless, the same principles apply, and to a much wider range of endeavour and performance — to bringing out the best in us.

Insights from the Zone of Excellence[80]

Here are excerpts from the work of Terry Orlick a world renowned sport and performance psychology consultant and researcher.

Positive imagery is useful for guiding your belief, focus, and performance, and for creating good feelings about yourself and your capacity. Through positive imagery you can pre-experience and re-experience feelings, sensations, skills or actions that are important for the successful execution of your task. High quality images of high quality performances allow you to experience yourself following desired courses of action and help you to feel ready to perform to your highest potential. These multi-sensory images take you where you want to go and often where you have not yet been.

The specific nature of your pursuit and your personal history will dictate the content of your imagery and the extent to which you draw upon different senses. However, those who attain the highest levels of excellence experience clear, positive, process-oriented performance images as real 'feelings' in their mind/body.

The world's best performers (e.g., athletes, surgeons, astronauts, and classical musicians) have highly developed imagery skills that they use daily. They draw upon these skills to: prepare themselves for high quality performances, recall and refine technical skills, make corrections, relax, experience themselves as successful and in control, regain control when struggling, set a positive frame of mind and create a high quality focus.

Imagery for excellence is holistic in nature, allowing you to pre-experience and re-experience quality performances and desired outcomes with all your senses. This imagery serves to guide your actions, reactions, and experiences. It nurtures feelings of control and an integrated high quality mind-body connection. It sets the stage and focus for high quality performance.

In an elite fighter pilot competition one of the tasks was minimum time to intercept. You're simulating that you are sitting runway alert and you're scrambled to go intercept some sort of incoming threat. You jump in your jet and you launch minimum time and you're trying to intercept this person as far away as possible before they release whatever they're going to release. The purpose was minimum time to intercept and identify what they were. And so we set down on paper and figured out the most efficient and fastest way to do these things... We got maps of where this actual competition was taking place, mapped out all the possible routes, what the best way to get out there would be... We tried all different types of waiting patterns, you go into waiting until you can turn your nose and come in on someone... we practised identification on a bunch of airplane types so we would learn the best way to roll in and come up and be able to identify what it is we're looking at.. We just went over those, over and over and over, until the whole thing became very familiar so that the first time we ever did it in competition, it was, we'd been there before. (Elite Fighter Pilot)

When you are parachuting, you have an emergency procedure to go through... depending on what kind of failure you have with your parachute. You've only got a few seconds to go through that matrix... I spent a great deal of time visualising the scenarios and it happened to me. And it's incredible because you've got that matrix down flat, you just go through it. And by four hundred feet I had the problem solved and I didn't die. And so you get down on the ground and you go — I won. You touched death and you won. (Astronaut)

Towards the end of my emergency medicine program I was using more imagery to help me survive... Emergency medicine is a very unstructured environment... you can never predict what's going to happen to you... To minimize my stress... I imagine the department falling apart and being able to handle the problems when they arise... Imagine yourself with six problems on the go and dealing with it calmly and in an efficient manner. When I did that I would go in and work my shift and it would be great. It's the same patients, same volume, same problems and yet it would work out really well. (Emergency Surgeon)

Programming Goals

The most basic application for mental imagery is to imagine your goals being achieved. In fact, the mere process of setting a goal will involve some form of imagery. The best question you can ask yourself upon setting a goal is whether you can picture or imagine it? If you cannot, then there's lots of work to be done. Either that or the goal may not be appropriate or achievable for you.

Remember that we tend to behave consistently with whatever image is dominant at the time. Same goes for goals. With a strong and clear image of a goal being achieved, you will tend to act in ways that are consistent with achieving that goal. This is a form of programming you to act in ways consistent with achieving the goal, and override any images to the contrary. Otherwise, if your positive images are not strong enough, any competing negative images that are driven by fears, anxieties and self-doubt will tend to sabotage you. An added beneficial feature of engaging in the positive images is that the process may bring to light the negative images that you may not have been fully aware of. This then enables you to address any underlying issues that you may not have dealt with otherwise, in order to loosen their grip.

Sometimes this plays out as simply as being distracted by our negativity when presented with a positive opportunity that we miss the boat. For example, being at a networking function where a key person you greatly admire and are keen to meet is in attendance (or whose attention to a cherished project you wish to gain). While this may present a brilliant opportunity, if you are not ready for it, you might miss it if overtaken by competing images represented by fear and anxiety. If you are not mentally prepared to capitalise on such an opportunity, then you are likely to miss out. Rehearsing the scenario in your mind will lift your confidence, and reduce anxiety, which will enable you to flow with the opportunity more naturally. This is how 'luck', as defined by 'preparation meeting opportunity', plays out.

When we're unaccustomed to being in such a position we are less likely to act upon it. We are less likely to first recognise the opportunity, let alone have the wherewithal to seize the opportunity. Mental imagery will make such occasions feel more familiar and natural, thereby increasing your capacity to act accordingly.

Remember the classic sport example of beating someone for the first time. Upon this new event registering in the brain, the question arises: what's wrong with this picture? Such a thought can distract an athlete just long enough for the other competitors to catch up. There, that's better (i.e. conforms to the mental picture more readily available). They then kick themselves afterwards at the missed opportunity! As previously mentioned, we tend to behave consistently with our images. Naturally, if you have never beaten a certain competitor before, you would have no familiarity with the experience, and this may allow doubts and hesitation to creep in. But if you have a strong image of belonging out front, then you are more likely to maintain such a position, assuming that you have the requisite fitness and skills to remain out front (whether a race, match, game, etc.).

Even after achieving a breakthrough, winning can be too confronting and disconcerting, and many athletes will revert back to their previous image, and/or eventually drop out of their sport.

If you want to be ready to be your best then you need to practise being at your best in your mental imagery to ensure that you are not distracted by the novelty of the event, and to maintain the focus necessary to follow through on your intentions. There is always lots of time to digest and/or celebrate afterwards!

> *It's not so much that champions are special people,*
> *but that they do special things to prepare.*

One of my favourite examples to illustrate the importance of preparation is of an Olympic Gold medallist, who every day for six months prior to the Olympics would stand on a makeshift podium while his sister would hang a gold medal around his neck, and then play their national anthem. This guy came out of nowhere to win at the relatively young age of 19 (most peak in late twenties and early thirties in this particular sport). This story was told to me by one of his competitors who became a friend, and with whom I worked 10 years later.

Remember that while it is important to have clear long-term dream goals clearly in mind, bringing your goals and images closer to within reach in the present is most powerful — as it's all you have immediate and direct control over. It is also more immediately rewarding to see yourself being that step closer.

For example, a common goal for many is to become slimmer and fitter. If you have a strong and clear image of this (e.g. my goal of fitting into a size smaller jeans than when I began this book), then this image will guide your everyday choices and behaviours that will lead to you reaching your goal. This might mean making healthier food and drink choices, and becoming more active.

Another common goal example is to save more money. If you have a strong and clear image of this (it helps if you have a specific item you are saving for, e.g. in my case a trip to Tuscany to visit a dear relative who owns a fabulous villa there), then this will tend to guide your choices that will lead to achieving this goal. It might mean giving up on some unnecessary luxuries as you keep your eye on your prize. It makes the everyday steps necessary more meaningful, more imaginable, and therefore more likely.

Programming Professional and Business Success

Success in sport is easy to define, e.g. win-loss record. In the average workplace, however, success is not so easily defined. The beauty of sport is that you can always tell when you are on track to your goals or not, and is plain to see for all concerned. In some jobs, you could go on for months without realising how far you are slipping or achieving, and even longer before others realise. Having well defined goals in your profession will set the stage for keeping track of your progress.

For some of you, success may be based your annual performance review, and/or key performance indicators (KPIs). For others, it is based on how much money you make. What you might find most rewarding and meaningful also varies greatly, even for those of you in the same job! For example, a janitor may enjoy providing a clean and tidy environment for hospital patients, even rotating greeting cards to cheer up the patients, and drawing great satisfaction from a job well done; whereas an administrator of that same hospital may find their job boring and unfulfilling. Those who can find meaning and purpose in whatever they do are bound to be happier in their job, as well as good at it. It's the difference between approaching your job as a calling or merely a pay cheque.

Take a moment to reflect on what makes you happy in your job, and what is considered successful in your profession. Just as in sport, keeping your eye on the prize (so to speak) keeps the meaning and purpose of work in mind. Imagining your dreams and goals coming to fruition will inspire you to put in the work required to achieve them. If you aren't able to picture them, then why would you bother? On the other hand, if your sole motivation is the destination but the journey is dreary, then you'll need to find a way to perceive the process in a better light, or consider a change in direction.

When setting your professional goals, remember to ensure you follow the goal setting guidelines in *Chapter 4*.

Motivating effort

Being able to imagine your goals being achieved will fuel the motivation to begin taking action on the steps towards reaching your goal. When you can picture success, when it feels real, it will inspire more effort and perseverance towards making it happen. It is when we doubt our capacity to reach a goal that we tend to lose confidence, get discouraged and drop the proverbial ball. If your belief is strong as reflected in being able to see yourself being successful, then the effort involved becomes less daunting and more achievable.

Having a clear image of your destination and how to get there is motivating. It gives you a sense of control and reminds you that your effort is worthwhile. Drilling down layer by layer might also highlight the little things that you can do to build confidence which is energising. This may then provide the impetus to seek extra training, information or advice that may more effectively enable you to reach your goals sooner.

Not only is it helpful for you to picture success, it can also be helpful to remind yourself of what your rivals and competitors are doing in their preparation. Or, alternatively, how your role model/s prepared for their big challenges and successes. When tempted to slack off or give up, you might ask yourself what your role model would do. Having a mental picture of what it took for others to reach their goals and achieve their highest heights will foster belief in yourself doing the same.

What motivates you to get out of bed to get ready for work? It is sometimes not easy to feel excited to go sit in an office after a long commute in heavy traffic. Reminding yourself of your goals (as well as the meaning and purpose of your job), however, might give you a boost to energise you towards achieving your goals. So that instead of thinking: 'I *have to* go to work', you might think instead: 'I *get to* go to work.'

The Myth of Pep Talks

Ironically, many people outside the sport and performance psychology profession assume that much of what we do is about motivating clients. Nothing could be further from the truth. In fact, motivation is too often the problem — being too motivated that is, and trying too hard. Having said that, many people will feel more motivated after a consultation, not because we engaged in any motivational strategies per se, but because when you develop more of the tools (such as mental imagery) — hope and confidence are boosted, which is motivating and uplifting. You can see your goals becoming more within reach and within your capacity to achieve, which is energising. Whereas, when they seem too far out of reach or not within capacity it can be demotivating.

Fatique makes cowards of us all. – William Shakespeare.

Getting in the Mood: Managing Energy and Emotions

With an abundance of positive energy, everything seems possible. Challenges are more easily met and decisions more clear. With lagging energy, however, even the simplest of tasks can seem daunting. Looking after your energy requirements may need to be your number 1 goal, as all other goals depend on the requisite energy being available.

This means not only being up for major tasks, but also providing for major recovery time. Just like an athlete's performance depends on the optimal balance of quantity and quality training, as well as that of their Rest and Relaxation.

Do you have a clear image of how you feel and act when in top form? Do you know how to get yourself there? Do you also have a sense of how to pace yourself? How good are you at taking regular time-outs? Do you make the best choices for your health and wellbeing? I like to use the traffic light analogy of heeding the amber warning signal before getting caught running the red; and maintaining better flow in the green zone. Having strong images of these things and keeping them front and centre as you go about your business is important for achieving your full potential. You might not necessarily need to take extra time, but simply be more mindful/conscious.

Do you realise that you can choose how you feel? If not you? Than who? Or does what side of the bed you got up on dictate your entire day?

This process begins with catching yourself feeling good as a future reference point, and also identifying and replaying scenes from your past. Remember that you are your own best teacher. When you become more aware of what naturally lifts your spirits you can then draw upon these sources on cue. Building your repertoire of positive images and memories are helpful to elicit the level of positive energy and emotion you desire, and that is most conducive to what you seek to achieve.

It can also be helpful to identify what tends to throw you off your best mindset or mood, and practise maintaining your top form in the face of such challenges, and/or getting back on track quickly. This relates to the upcoming section about coping and refocusing. Just as in sport, in 'real life' there are critical phases of an event, e.g. in the workplace there can be critical moments during the day when you need to be on top of your game.

Here are some examples:
- Being cheerful and pleasant making a cold call
- Being relaxed and composed walking into a meeting with intimidating or difficult clients or colleagues

- Feeling confident during a presentation
- Communicating bad news clearly and with compassion, etc.

Most successful athletes know exactly how they want to feel on the day, and how to get there. They don't simply hope for the best, but actively create the mental and physical conditions most likely to give rise to their best mindset. They do not leave to chance what can be developed and conditioned with mental training.

One of the top mental coaches of golf, Bob Rotella, has famously claimed that being successful in golf depends on being able to get into an exceptionally good mood and then stay there. Sounds simple, but in practice it's exceptionally challenging to sustain over the duration of each five-hour round, over seven days. In fact, it extends well beyond to 24/7, when you consider the importance of diet, fitness, and sleep, not to mention social influences.

While it is important to imagine and prepare yourself for being in your best mood for the job at hand, it is also prudent to also be ready for the inevitable butterflies that come with the territory. It is unrealistic to expect yourself to not feel the occasion if the occasion means a lot to you, and/or there is a lot riding on the outcome of how well you manage and acquit yourself. As the old saying goes — butterflies need not be a problem as long as they're flying in formation. It is therefore wise to also anticipate some nerves (or a lot), and imagine feeling them, but not being affected by them — maintaining your focus and equanimity. This is a mark of a true champion, whether this has to do with becoming a champion, or to champion your own goals and dreams.

Too often people will notice their nerves and allow this to undermine their confidence. Being nervous need not be a bad sign. Plenty of champions have reported plenty of symptoms, such as vomiting and diarrhoea prior to important competitions. Such reactions are so common that they practically become routine; sometimes so much so that they become concerned if they do not throw up before a big game! Getting comfortable with such emotions and physical reactions are crucial to overcoming them. This needs to be kept in balance with imagining coping and performing well.

All You Need is Love

One of the quickest and most reliable ways to generate positivity is to think of someone or something you love — which is why it can be so painful to let go of a loved one when it's time to move on. What does it feel like to be filled with love? To give and receive love — on any level — whether it be romantic love, filial love, love of music or nature, animals, pets, certain experiences, etc, makes us feel good. The feelings generated from imagining a loved one is why family photos on one's desk are well placed. When your eyes fall upon such a photo, take a moment to feel the love it represents, to get the positivity hit (aka micro-moment of love).[81]

The same goes for beautiful scenes of nature that will trigger alpha brain waves. As you well know by now, simply imagining such scenes is enough to set in motion the effects on your brain of actually being there. And once the brain changes, everything else changes. All systems benefit: your immune system, cardiovascular system; not to mention how you feel, think, and behave.

Loving Kindness Meditation

A standard practice in Buddhism is to meditate on compassion and loving kindness, which is a virtual mental imagery exercise designed to connect with the love within yourself and extend beyond the self. Research has demonstrated major health and wellbeing benefits. There are many variations on the loving kindness theme, which begin with a focus on your breath and heart centre followed by imagining someone for whom you feel warmth and tenderness, love and compassion. This could be someone you are close to or a beloved pet (nothing beats unconditional puppy love!).

Savour and hold the feelings before then allowing yourself to direct the loving feeling inward toward you yourself — feeling the tenderness as deeply as you might holding yourself as a newborn baby. The next step is to extend this loving feeling outward to those in your inner circle … to your family and friends … allowing the warmth and tenderness to then radiate out to an ever widening circle of connections … and ultimately extending your feelings of loving kindness to your entire community, region, country, the universe. See *Appendix A* for two common variations.[82]

Learning and Perfecting Skills

Being and becoming successful typically requires ongoing accumulation of knowledge, development of new skills, and experience. This is especially the case with the fast pace of technological advancements. Each new lesson can pose a challenge to your self-image and perceived capacity (aka confidence) to rise to each occasion. Using mental imagery allows you more practice time (than might normally be afforded you) to accelerate the learning process.

Mental imagery provides a vehicle to consolidate any skills you have developed in real training or practice, without the wear and tear on your body in the case of sports. Mental imagery has the advantage of allowing you the extra practice opportunity for things that you may not have had enough experience, opportunity or access. This can give you an edge that you might not have had otherwise.

It also affords you the opportunity to practise executing that for which you may have little opportunity to practise, but upon which your best performance may depend. For example, in triathlon, you might need to practise a smooth transition in between swimming and cycling, or fixing a flat tire. In music, you might need to practise having lost your place or forgotten the lyrics and quickly finding your way back or ad libbing (as many famous singers have reported doing without the audience noticing). Can you imagine being up on stage with a full house before you, and forgetting the words to a song that you wrote and have probably sung a thousand times before?

In many other domains and endeavours, the opportunities for practising and developing skills that may be an essential aspect of your role may also be relatively rare, such as managing a crisis. This also involves high pressure situations (or as a friend of mine puts it — high wire act – such as speaking to the board, negotiating a contract, or other unpleasant and dreadful interactions such as managing a difficult employee or customer, firing an employee, etc).

While you may very well have a clear image of what to do, you may be missing practising where best to focus your attention, and how to feel and be in order to pull it off effectively. This is why even when those who do get to spend a lot of time in training and practice, as athletes do, they often do not perform to capacity unless and until they have accumulated enough experience to become more accustomed to being able to focus and refocus under pressure. Mental imagery affords you more such experience thereby accelerating your experience factor.

Any time you are taking in new information, try to picture how you will put this information into action. The more you can imagine applying new skills and knowledge, the more quickly you will be able to assimilate it into your repertoire. When in an educational or job training setting, listening to a lecture or presentation on a topic of interest or importance, try to imagine applying the information to your life and/or work. This applies to reading instructional material. If you can imagine implementing the instructions, you will more readily be able to when called upon. You've probably had the experience during an exam when answering a question that you know you studied, and you can even remember the position on the page (e.g. bottom right). When you concentrate on that image the information seems to come back to you, unless you are pressing and trying too hard.

This practice can also apply to remembering great ideas that come to you — seemingly out of the blue. Have you ever noticed that your best ideas seem to come unbidden? And when you're somewhere without access to pen and paper to write them down! Inspiration often strikes without notice and when our minds are on something else (especially when our minds are on something else!) You can file away that great idea by giving it a name and/or rehearsing a few key words combined with a colour, and then imagine them the next time you sit down to your desk — the images reappear. This programs your mind to revisit those ideas upon sitting down at your desk as you imagined.

Enhancing Focus and Concentration

Just as performers schedule dress rehearsals, mental rehearsals are easily applicable to any endeavour. Generating the imagery actually takes more concentration because it requires conjuring up more details that are more readily available during a real rehearsal. This then enhances the capacity to concentrate while on stage and under pressure.

Coping with Pressure and Evaluation

Unlike sport, the criteria for evaluating artistic performances are not nearly as clear, and often quite subjective. A performer may be technically correct but still lose their audience. Meanwhile, many performers also report how they might have their greatest audience connection/response despite feeling off technically. They suggest that the audience may pick up on the struggle, and thereby relate more readily to the emotional component of performance. Perhaps the performer is showing more of themselves and their humanity.

Wondering about whether you are measuring up to ambiguous criteria can be very distracting and hinder performance and flow. Picturing yourself being comfortable on the stage and connecting well with your audience enhances the flow. Ultimately, it comes down to an ability to focus only on the here and now, and what is within your control. You cannot control what just happened or what is about to happen. You can only control your very next move. Learning how to relax goes a long way towards being more fully present and focused in the moment and letting go of the rest. Imagine staying calm and composed.

It helps to catch yourself when things are going well to project to a future pressure situation and imagine being and doing the same then and there as well. Bring to mind all of the conditions in concert with your present wellbeing, and the two will become linked — so that once you enter those conditions the associations will more likely pop up and play out accordingly. This can work in reverse: under the pressure conditions, conjuring up the image of when executing your functions well in the recent past will enhance your capacity to engage in the present accordingly.

Flash Forward and Flashback

Whenever you catch yourself going well, take a moment to flash forward to an upcoming event or challenge — being and doing well again. Incorporate the details of the upcoming opportunity to enhance the image and thereby readiness to replay upon the occasion. For example, a golfer who is hitting really well in practice can flash forward to an upcoming competition (e.g. US Open) imagining hitting well there and then.

In the next scenario you can reverse this process by flashing back to the previous time you went well and integrate it into your current circumstances. Using the golf example again: on finding himself at the US Open (or the like), the golfer would then recall hitting well and recreate those shots in his mind to fit the current game.

Drawing on Role Models

More and more businesses are setting up employees with a mentor. This can be very helpful for fostering the image of what you need to become successful in your profession. If you do not have a mentor, or your mentor is not a good match for you, consider who you might look up to in your field. Who embodies the characteristics that you would like to develop in yourself? Take time to learn and observe more about this person or persons, and picture yourself emulating the key attributes that you admire.

We're not talking about copying or pretending, but drawing on a role model to help you lift your game. It is hard to create characteristics within yourself without a good role model from which to learn.

You might also like to keep in mind what kind of role model you would like to be and become. Think about what kind of image you would like to portray to others, and play this out in your mental imagery. The more you can make it real in your mental imagery, the more likely it will begin to show in reality.

Dealing with Performance Reviews and Feedback

Too often feedback and performance reviews focus on the negatives rather than positives. This is characteristic of game film reviews in sport settings. The key is to at least replay the correction. Coaches would do well to also point out where players performed well. In fact, some professional sports teams now produce peak performance videos for their players. Nothing beats watching the real thing for boosting confidence and generating best images!

The more specific information you can obtain in such reviews and feedback the better for utilisation in your imagery for the future (so that you learn from errors rather than repeat them). If receiving negative feedback, ensure you get more instructive/constructive information so that your lasting image will be more about the remedial choices before you, rather than avoiding mistakes (which we know only begets a negative image).

Even receiving positive feedback may be too vague to be useful for connecting with a clear and vivid image that you can then draw upon for future reference. If so, then it is appropriate to request more information. For example, sometimes I've been told a presentation of mine was 'inspiring', which is gratifying to hear but tells me nothing I can learn from. So I always ask what specifically they found inspiring, e.g. was it what or how I delivered my message? I can then file this away to be repeated next time. I try to do the same when I deliver praise to others. I have also found clients will tend to skirt over reports of good news and progress, which I like to catch them out on. I ask them to drill down to capturing the essence of what got them there, in order to better consolidate and ensure more of the same in future. Catch yourself being good!

Mental Rehearsal

Just as the term mental rehearsal suggests, mental imagery can provide valuable rehearsal benefits.

Routines, strategy, protocols

The most successful performers are known to have well-developed game plans and routines. Most are clear on what to do, but less often regarding their best focus. They know exactly what they need to do and when according to all that may be thrown their way; but maximising chances for execution relies also on well-developed plans for where their attention needs to be focused. This is the most crucial component of such game plans and is referred to as 'focus plans' — a step too often skipped over — in sports and especially beyond sports.

Such plans include having a well thought out strategy for all critical moments of a game, or for the particular style or strengths of opponent. In other domains this involves being ready for all potential plot twists and turns, which enhances anticipation and more effective execution of best intentions for optimising outcomes. For example, when enduring a long meeting with much at stake, and you know that you tend to get annoyed when certain people talk too much and repeat themselves, you might decide that the best policy is to sit tight and not interrupt. But where might your best focus be? On how much you dislike them? On wishing they would shut up? Or better: on maintaining your equanimity and patience? On attending to what they are saying in case you miss valuable information or insight?

I further emphasise imagining finishing with a flourish. This is important to remember, as this is too often the most neglected component of rehearsing a plan — even with champions. The proverbial finish line becomes a major distraction that can undermine best focus — especially in the dying moments of one's event when most fatigued physically, emotionally and mentally. This is when you really need to practice maintaining best focus, so you do not let yourself down in the end, and allow all your hard work and preparation go out the window.

Familiarising with venues and conditions

Many sports have venues that are reasonably standard and require minimal adjustment. Significant variations do exist, e.g. basketball courts on rubber or hard wood flooring; pools with different depths and gutters; real or artificial turf, spectator bleachers/stands near or far, etc. Other sports have many variations that are purposely designed to require adjustments, but maintain certain key standards, e.g. golf courses, race courses, etc. The more familiar you can be with a venue, the less distracting any variation may be for you. Especially in the case of the latter when limited access is permitted, mentally rehearsing your sport within the specific environment will enhance your familiarity so you can concentrate on the task at hand, rather than be distracted.

Much has been learned from how the Soviets prepared their athletes back in the early days of sport psychology last century. For example, in preparation for the Montreal Olympics, photographers were sent to all the venues to take photos, which they blew up and placed around the training venues in their home country so that the athletes would be accustomed to the Olympic environment. Soviet hockey players also trained to loud noise and boos as this is what they learned to expect when they competed in North America.

The idea is to find out as much as you can well in advance. This could include the route to your event; time of day; the layout of the room or venue; where you will be; where others will be seated or situated; in as much detail as possible, so that you can be comfortable and ready for anything and everything, and be at your best.

Executing tasks well on time

Time management has very little to do with time, and more to do with enjoying the time we spend. If you find yourself struggling to fit in a task or activity because you are running out of time, this is likely illusory. It is more likely that you really were not that keen in the first place? If you find yourself procrastinating this is another clue to factors that need attention. We all tend to avoid those tasks that we find too difficult, boring or painful. We put them off until another time will offer temporary relief, which actually increases the pain factor. If we wait until we feel more up to the task we may be waiting forever. It is not realistic to wait until the perfect time, or until we feel perfectly able as that time will never come.

Sometimes the tasks are actually something that would bring the opposite of pain and boredom; they could actually lift us out of a bad situation, or better — could help us achieve a major goal. Getting help to process the mental obstacles can help overcome the issues, but sometime this only leads to paralysis by analysis. Here is where imagery can help override the negative influences (whether in your head or not).

Next time you face a task that you might be dreading, such as making a cold call, asking a favour, calling the bank for a loan repayment extension, facing an ex, breaking up (no wonder more and more are resorting to the cowardly text message), try imagining yourself executing the task well. Remember to not just focus on the doing, but on your being — feeling calm, composed, confident, etc. — and then the relief and satisfaction upon conclusion of the task. And then the self-praise for finally getting something done that is good for you (rather than avoiding which is ultimately bad for you).

It does help to change the associated inner dialogue that goes with the dread, to more positively encouraging language. For example, changing the standard 'should', 'have to', 'must' to 'need to' 'want to' or even better 'get to' … imagining the benefits of executing the task. Imagine the satisfaction of finally getting done what has stood in your way.

Practising contingencies

You may spend a great proportion of time imagining (worrying about) all that might go wrong. But how much of that practice involves responding well versus catastrophising? While the purpose of positive mental imagery is to focus on all that can go right; being prepared to respond optimally to any challenge is ultimately what separates the champions from the also rans. Mental imagery takes the process beyond ordinary worrying. It lays down the blueprint for how to best respond to anything that may go wrong — to ensure the best possible outcomes occur. Having a contingency plan will enhance confidence that nothing is left to chance. Practising all contingencies in your mental imagery will reinforce such confidence.

When you catch yourself fretting, ask yourself whether you are worrying or are you praying/planning/imagining. If the former, then refocus on the latter. You will likely experience a noticeable drop in anxiety, as you begin to imagine coping better.

Recent research has found that the number one stress management strategy is having a well-developed plan for facing stressful challenges (the second was practising relaxation). Planning, in effect, is the antidote to worrying, and about virtually imagining how you would like a situation to unfold. The first step is to identify your stressor triggers, and then your optimal response. By practising executing your plan in your imagery — you will then be more likely to respond effectively rather than react negatively. See the blissor/stressor monitoring guide in the *Appendix C*, which provides a template for increasing awareness, leading to better practice of the above.

The importance of contingency planning is integral to all high risk professions that can make the difference not only between success and failure, but between life and death. For example, astronauts undergo simulation training for every potential eventuality. They are also trained in mentally rehearsing their response, to ensure that reactions are smooth and automatic, for there is no room or time for errors. There are no 'do-overs' in space. Airline pilots undergo regular simulation training for events that no one ever wants to experience, but hopes they will respond effectively to.

It is also important to anticipate what might simply distract you in an upcoming event or encounter. For example, if you find people chatting, or worse chuckling, in the back of the room during an important presentation distracting and unnerving, then include such an image in your imagery along with maintaining your composure and best focus (and humour?), and staying on track with your purpose.

If and when the distraction does occur, you will then be able to ride it out with ease, maintaining your optimal focus. Others might not find the example above distracting, but may get unnerved with a delay to their presentation. You might have felt well prepared and confident to begin your presentation, but a delay might allow room for doubts and fears to begin to creep back in. Having a mental plan and imagining executing your plan will put you in good stead in the event you do encounter a delay.

What If ...?

What separates champions from the rest of the field is their ability to get back on track quickly when faced with obstacles and distractions. They anticipate and prepare for all such eventualities. A highly successful Australian sporting team routinely practice a *What if...* exercise that involves brainstorming all that could go wrong, in the lead up to and during their events. For example, what if the team bus is late or gets a flat tire? What if the top scorer gets injured? What if there's a bad call from the referee?

Once the list is complete, the team then sets about planning an ideal response to each circumstance, called a *Refocus Plan*, and then rehearse this plan in their mental imagery. If you want to increase your chances of success, you need to be aware of, and prepared for, all potential challenges that you may face, and how you might best respond to your advantage. Most people develop this capacity after years of experience, but you can fast track such learning by practising refocusing in your mental imagery.

Coping With and Adjusting to Change

Speaking of change, it is among the top sources of stress in the workplace, and it is one of the few things you can count on with certainty. Most people get uncomfortable when thrust out of their comfort zone. Playing out the required adjustments in your mental imagery can smooth out your transition, creating a more comfortable workplace for you again.

Even though some changes may be welcome, they may nevertheless require changes that make you uncomfortable, e.g. being promoted. This may mean more responsibility and new pressures. It could also mean a change in dynamics with your co-workers that can be unsettling. Mental imagery will help increase your readiness and comfort with your new role and responsibilities.

Making Decisions

The great advantage of applying mental imagery to decision making is that you get to avoid 'cost of real-life trial and error'[83]

Improving our decision-making begins with the simple act of becoming more aware of the choices we make while we're making them, and then more consciously making better choices each and every moment of each and every day — that are in alignment with our best interests. Mental imagery can assist with improving our fortitude to follow through on making better choices in face of bad habits and temptations that take us off our best path.

We make thousands of decisions each and every day. Some are minor and routine, and others are life altering and out of the blue; and many more in between. Much of how we decide is reflexive and dictated by our unconscious mind. This is actually a good thing for the most part, as creates greater efficiency in how we get through the day. Can you imagine having to decide whether to stop at a red light or not every day on your way to work? It is virtually automatic and of course desirable. There are many decisions we make on a regular basis, however, that might be all too automatic — that are undesirable with reference to our goals and best interests.

Research has shown that even when we think we're making fully conscious decisions there is much in play that remains below our awareness, which influences our perceptions and choices dramatically.[84] Much of this emerges as a result of subtle emotional reactions, associations, and images hard wired in our brains (based on our predispositions, and learning history and habits). Without having clearly defined criteria for the basis of our decisions going forward, we are left at the mercy of this unconscious process, and destined to continue with old outmoded patterns ingrained from our past. And remember, we often also have competing inner agendas to contend with as well.

One of the most stressful aspects of high performers in the workplace is the pressure to make the right decisions in quick time with limited information. Playing out the options in your mental imagery can help you access the wisdom of your mind (intuition) more efficiently than pros and cons lists. By utilising the mental process of mental imagery you may more directly ascertain the best course of action for the best outcome.

For example: Finding Ms/Mr Right. Most of us are far better at knowing what we do not want in a partner. It is a bit more challenging to delineate what it is we do want. Many seeking love engage in creating lists of their ideal partner in order to recognise and choose the right one. While this has merit, it might actually steer you in the wrong direction of what might actually make you happy. Do you want to be right or do you want to be happy? What is ultimately most important is how you feel in relation to your partner. (Notice I didn't say how they make you feel.) For example, how comfortable, stimulated, challenged, supported you feel. What kind of dynamic would most appeal to you? How do you feel about yourself with this person? Do you enjoy yourself? Are you able to be fully yourself? Having a clear image of how you would best like to feel is far better criteria than what may turn out to be highly irrelevant details.

What do you most want to be loved and accepted for? This is often a missed step in the vetting process. What attributes might your ideal partner be seeking in you? What kind of partner do you aspire to being? This is ultimately more within your control to cultivate and demonstrate as long as authentic to your true self. Remember, we need to be prepared to give what it is we wish to get. So, if we value honesty and trust in another, then we need to be ready to reveal our true selves. As I like to say: you can only be loved to the extent to which you are open to being vulnerable to love.

Love Boosts Your Self-Image

My theory of the bliss we experience when we fall in love is that it's a result of the boost to our self-image. Seeing ourselves reflected in our loved one's eyes in a way that we may not have believed possible previously. We *rise in love*. This is also a key factor in the difficulty letting go when things go sour. In losing this person, there's a sense we are losing this cherished part ourselves as well. And who would want to let go of that? But you get to keep all those wonderful attributes and images that you have come to love about yourself; and can be grateful to the other for waking you up to this boosted self-image. You do not have to remain attached to them in order to retain the positive images.

One very basic technique for using mental imagery in decision-making is to sift through an array of options, whether they have to do with a job, partner, home, etc. and tune into your sensory impressions as you imagine each one. How do you feel? What bodily sensations are you aware of? Every one of us has our own unique signal that indicates our best option based on the information before you. Drawing upon your imaginal circuits to determine the best decision bypasses the mind-chatter or fear factor that clouds accessing your best judgement. For me, the signal is as simple as being able to imagine an option or not; and whether dark or light.

For example, if you are deciding between two job offers, and can picture option A more clearly and vividly than the option B, that's a good sign for A. Pay attention to how images register in your body as well. If you find yourself tightening up when considering working with someone, this is a bad sign. If you feel more energised, this is a good sign. Your body is constantly sending you signals that too often go ignored. First we get a whisper in our ear. If unheeded, we get a tap on the shoulder. If still unheeded, we get a knock on the head. We can save ourselves a lot of pain and grief if we were to just listen and heed those whispers.

Sometimes it is hard to determine what an image is and what a premonition is. Could it be that we're better at imagining that which is predestined? Or does the practice of imagery bring us closer to such a destination? There is even the suggestion that if what you are attempting to achieve and imagine is not in the cards for you than not only will the imagery fail (if it doesn't already elude you), but it will hasten driving away (or driving you away) from what is imagined.

While most of this book is about generating images, drawing upon mental images for decision making can be a more intuitive process of *receiving* rather than *directing* images. It can seem a very subtle process at first, but with practice it will come through louder and clearer for you.

Use it or lose it!

The key is to discern between what is wishful thinking and what is fear versus what is truth and intuition. The more there is at stake, the more clouded our discernment. With practice, however, you can develop a more and more reliable source of inner wisdom that will guide you through life, and keep you on track.

Jogging Your Memory: Storing and Retrieving Information

Using images to store information will make it easier to retrieve when you need it. This is similar to the exam situation mentioned previously — how you might not remember the answer, but you can remember where it appeared on a page, e.g. bottom of right page. If you stick with the image, the material will likely also come up for you if you allow it. As mentioned above in the decision-making section, this is a process of receiving the image rather than directing it. This cannot be forced, but only invited and welcomed. When you try to force it, it will elude you. Not unlike falling asleep. The more you try to fall asleep, sleep eludes you. You can only allow the process to unfold naturally.

To improve your memory, the first step is to imagine yourself using information as you are taking it in. The more specific you can be with the future occasion that you might use the information the better. And then at that later date and occasion it is more likely to come up naturally, as you will have programmed it to. When you can imagine applying the information it strengthens consolidation into your memory bank of experience, which goes beyond simply remembering a theory, concept, practice or detail. This explains why those who retain more information than others also tend to be slower readers. By taking their time (consciously or unconsciously) they are allowing their brains to process and store the information more readily rather than rushing through the material in haste (and avoid 'haste making waste'). They then do not need to go over the same material as many times as those who are speed readers.

Linking imaginal devices that are not necessarily related to the information to be retrieved can also be helpful. For example, associating colours with certain information you are studying will help. Such that, all you will need to do is run through your array of colours and the information linked to each colour will appear. For example, I find that my best ideas come while I'm out in nature, and far away from notes and computer. This is typical of the creative process, but also annoying when you have no recording device handy (and I'm not one to bring notebooks with me when trekking), and don't want to spoil the walk/ run by being preoccupied with remembering an idea.

Remembering in Technicolour

I'll never forget one time being out on my beloved Greenbelt in Nepean Ontario, when great ideas kept coming and coming about my Master's thesis research. When the first idea came along I assigned it a colour. Then another great idea came along, and so I assigned it another colour. Then another with yet another colour. At which point I then declared a time out and requested no more! I also imagined that the colours (linked to the ideas) would then come back to my attention while I sat on the couch upon my return home. This last point is important for jogging your memory. You need to develop both a storing device as well as retrieving prompt. In this case, it was sitting on the living room couch. Sure enough, while I was sitting on the couch, the colours came to mind followed by the ideas one by one. It felt like magic! You might not need the colours for this system to work, but the way the brain is designed, images such as colours seem to work far better than words for memory storage and then retrieval. This has to do with the fact that language came much later in our evolution.

Just as imagery can be useful in storing information in your memory banks, you can draw on imaginal processes to remember or find something that may have inadvertently gone missing. For example, you may have misplaced an object that you need, and cannot remember where. Trying to think your way logically to finding it is much less efficient than trying to imagine your way. Try instead to just hold an image of the item and then notice what comes to mind or body next, and simply follow those inclinations. This is similar to how intuition works; that by holding your intention in mind your brain sends out search parties (aka spindle neurons) scanning your brain to find the solution and retrieve the information, or locate the item you are searching for.

A personal example occurred for me one day as I prepared to take my dog out for a walk. I wanted to wear my favourite green paisley bandana, but it wasn't where it was supposed to be. So, I called it up in my imagery and immediately got an image of my bookcase — a specific back corner of a shelf that was not visible simply passing by. I just went with the image, and low and behold, there it was tucked back in the corner. I do not remember putting it there, and it is certainly not a place I ever put my bandanas (and anyone who knows me, knows that I have a vast collection of them that I keep hanging on racks). I must have put it there while preoccupied with doing something else; that is, unconsciously. But the position quickly came to mind when I bid it to. It had registered with my sense of sight, and stored in my unconscious mind.

This is akin to the automatic/reflexive thinking that Kahneman writes about in *Thinking Fast and Slow*.[85] He also refers to this as the intuitive mind. This is a technique that I now use regularly whenever I am looking for something. I hold the image of the object, and then follow my next inclinations without questioning.

While the above example depicts a relatively minor issue, it was stepped up a few notches since I first wrote this — when I noticed my diamond ring was missing! This ring is very special to me, way beyond its material value (as it was given to me by mother who found it in the snow shortly before giving birth to me). I straightaway went into a panic, catastrophising the loss, but quickly caught myself, took a few deep breaths and just followed my own advice to picture the ring lovingly/ beckoningly. I let go of all the angst … and just trusted the image to lead me to it (rather than using my logic and process of elimination).

I was stunned by how quickly I found it! It was like my eyes remembered and directed themselves immediately to the spot where I had mindlessly taken it off and left it. It was in a place I would never consciously have left it, amidst clutter on the kitchen counter. I actually found myself looking at the ring an instant before I registered what I was seeing. This is related to research on premonitions, where it has been demonstrated that the body registers upcoming information before it is consciously available. In the case of this missing ring, my eyes found the ring before I even realised.

Another poignant personal example had to do with remembering to bring my lunch to work. So many times I would go to the effort to make a lunch I could look forward to (other than the lousy canteen food that we had available at the time), but would then forget it in the fridge in my haste to leave the house! Anyone else out there have this problem? Someone suggested that I put my car keys on top of my lunch in the fridge. Well, one day I was getting ready to leave the house and couldn't find my car keys. They weren't hanging in their usual spot.

I couldn't for the life of me figure out where they might be, and so I decided to just let my intuition (aka image of the keys) lead me. I found myself wandering from the door until I stood in front of the fridge, but I did not open it. I felt stupid standing there! What was I doing standing in front of the fridge? Made no sense to me at the time. In my frustration, I started the process over, and again found myself standing in front of the fridge. I thought, This isn't working. I just grabbed my spare car keys (which did not include my office key, but I knew I could get security to open my door for me), and left. It was only when I was halfway to work that I realised why I was standing in front of the fridge! I must have been thinking about what I'd have for lunch when my memory got jogged. This is a clear demonstration that our intuition can be a lot smarter and more efficient than our conscious/rational mind.

Now, my examples were of relatively minor consequence. I had (many) other bandanas, and even though this one was my favourite, I knew it would turn up eventually. Same goes for the keys. I would have eventually discovered them in the fridge, and luckily had a spare set. The missing ring stepped up the challenge because of my attachment to it. Nevertheless, the same process works regardless of the importance.

As the stakes go up, however, so does our level of anxiety that interferes with the process. So, the trick is to practise with the little things and train ourselves to identify that state of mind that answers our bidding, and develop the ability to bring it up at will when needed. There have been more serious examples where holding an image of the desired result or item saved lives and averted disasters. Jonah Lehrer recounts a few in his book on the creative process (also named *Imagine*), though he only refers to imagery in passing.[86]

One such example cited is the case of a pilot landing safely despite serious malfunction on the plane. As pilots undergo plenty of simulation training of managing disasters, their minds are trained to remain calm under pressure. In the case that Lehrer recounts, the pilot reports keeping an image of landing the plane safely in mind while urgently problem solving how he was going to be able to make this happen considering the malfunction. By holding the positive image, the brain then is able to source the relevant information from his memory (via spindle neurons that scanned the brain like a search party) that led to the right decision. The brain operated consistent with the desired image of landing the plane safely. If, on the other hand, the dominant image was of the plane crashing, there might have been a different result.

The plane landing on the Hudson River in New York City is a similar story. The pilot was merely following his training, and focused on an image of landing safely; the rest, as they say, is history, and now a major motion picture.

The moral of the story is to keep your eyes (if only your mind's eye) on the prize.

Breaking Bad Habits and Changing Behaviour

When attempting to break a bad habit, you need to contend with extinguishing the hold of the old. But history need not be your destiny! Mental imagery of the new behaviour will help shake off and override images and habits of the old. It gives you the extra practice to consolidate changes more rapidly, especially for when under pressure as this is when most people tend to revert back to old (bad) habits.

A tip to keep in mind is to not focus on what you are trying to stop or change, but to focus on the new behaviour. For example, if you're trying to cut back on coffee, focusing on not drinking coffee during work breaks tends to bring up the image of coffee during work breaks. You might even be able to conjure up the scent of fresh brewed coffee. On the other hand, if you picture taking a couple deep breaths and enjoying a glass of water instead, then you are more likely to be successful. It takes an extra conscious effort to practise the new habit or behaviour in order to eliminate the old (bad) habit. Mental imagery will accelerate this process.

Common behaviours people seek to change are related to healthier lifestyle, and the ones that so many so often fail at. Building stronger images of the desired behaviours going forward will help you to leave behind the bad habits of old. It will strengthen your resolve as well as your chance of sustainable changes.

Acting in your best interests

Acting in your best interests is frequently also best for all concerned. It can often require shifting from a habit of putting others needs first to your own detriment. Putting yourself first can often be quite challenging after a pattern of always putting others needs and wants first. This can often lead to resentment and worse. Making a change to acting in your best interests involves a two pronged attack. First you must decide to act more in accordance with your best interests, and second feel good about it. The first is usually much easier to arrive at than the second. If you have overriding feelings of guilt or lack of deservedness, this will interfere with your willingness and capacity to follow through on your decision. So, even if you can picture pulling off assertive behaviour and ultimate reward, you might still have residual feelings related to fear and misgivings that can be punishing. This can play out similarly to being able to shake off the negative images covered above.

A classic example is telling someone 'No' when being asked for a favour that would significantly inconvenience or compromise you. Picturing yourself kindly communicating some variation of 'Sorry ...' or 'No ...' and feeling fine and unapologetic (and without the need to go into a lengthy explanation) will enhance your capacity and comfort with pulling it off for real. Maybe even include a mental pat on the back for following through on your best interests.

The same goes for resisting temptation (e.g. a drink, cigarette, drug, sweet), which may require a simple and gracious 'No thank you' and perhaps a brief explanation if this is a major change such as: 'I'm cutting back/I've quit/I'm giving it up/I'm on a diet'. Picturing yourself pulling this off with grace and poise will increase the likelihood that you will follow through. You might need to reinforce the imagery for when added pressure is applied, tempting you off course. Imagine firmly and calmly staying the course — in line with your best interests without having to justify your self-commitment. If others fail to understand, then you might have a bigger decision before you, and consider changing your social influences and environment. In many cases, however, you will likely get admiration. Maybe picture that too. Remember: self-fulfilling prophesies work!

Breaking out of the norm at work

Acting in our best interests can be challenging in the workplace if what you need or prefer is against the norm in your work environment/culture. Many work norms are overt and transparent, and in place for good reasons, e.g. to ensure compliance with policy, standards and productivity. Many norms are covert and implied, such as not taking breaks or working late, which are not necessarily conducive to achieving high standards and productivity. Breaking out of such outmoded norms in the workplace can be challenging.

Your own self-improvement may be what is most within your control, though I'm sure you can also imagine where there is room for improvement in your work environment or culture as well. All too often, however, you'll find your workmates prefer to engage in complaining among themselves (e.g. about office politics, work norms, etc.) which can become infectious and toxic, rather than step up and do something about it. Too often people will wait for someone else to instigate change, rather than recognise their potential for being an agent of change. Could such change begin with you? What would it take for you to step up to create a positive change? Can you imagine it?

What often prevents us from stepping up is often the fear of ruffling feathers (negative image). Meanwhile you and your workmates may already be tolerating negative conditions unnecessarily. That will ultimately undermine morale and productivity. So, you wouldn't be doing anyone any favours by sitting on your hands.

It can be as simple as taking breaks for a cup of tea in a workplace, or leaving the office for lunch break, where everyone fears appearing like they're slacking off. Ironically, no one questions the smokers needing a smoke break. They have an in-built cue for taking breaks — the craving. Non-smokers also have cues that too frequently go ignored until it knocks them over the head with a flu or worse.

A client of mine who was new in her office was too self-conscious to get up for a cup of tea. She was concerned with everyone noticing, and then what they'd be thinking. I suggested that instead of them inwardly deriding her, they may actually be applauding her. By having the courage to take the first step, she would likely be rewarded by others following. Just like the classic case of the dance floor. Few want to be the first to step onto the dance floor even though they really want to dance, but once one pair does, many quickly follow. After practising getting up for a cup of tea in her imagery and feeling good about it, the client then tried it out in the office. And sure enough, others did get up and follow her to the kitchenette, and enjoyed a lively conversation. The boss included!

Sometimes it is only our misguided fears and perceptions that dictate our behaviour and thereby our wellbeing and performance. We need to remember that these are only images that may or may not be accurate or long outmoded. Rather than passively reacting according to them, we can create new images aligned with our best values that lead to new practices and norms.

Health and Healing

Nothing is more important than our health, upon which everything else hinges in our lives. Mental imagery applications for health and healing is a well-developed area of great relevance. Imagery can be applied to basic health and lifestyle behaviour — imagining yourself making healthy choices and engaging in healthy behaviour generally. It is also widely applied to recovery from injury and illness. This is covered in greater length on *Inner Spa: Supplement* where I provide an overview of mental skills applied to recovery from injury and illness, and highlighted below.[87] The material also appears in a chapter I coauthored that appears in a medical textbook.[88] There are also several highly regarded reference books on the topic.[89]

Your body has healing processes already in motion whether you apply your mental imagery or not, but fully participating in your healing with your imagination mobilises your healing processes to the fullest. There are several ways you can use your imagery to facilitate the recovery process. First, you can picture yourself fully recovered and functioning well again at your favourite activities and feeling good about yourself and your body (aka end result imagery).

Second, you can picture the healing processes at work/seeing and feeling the healing deep within your body. It helps to have a full understanding and picture of what the healing process would actually look like, so ask your health practitioner for help with this. For example, you could picture a fractured bone mending and knitting together, or your white blood cells being much larger and more powerful than the disease or virus you are fighting, engulfing and carrying them away.

Using colours may enhance your imagery effectiveness. Colours such as emerald or amethyst hues are traditionally considered healing colours. Try imagining the healing colours coursing throughout your body and especially surrounding and enveloping and infusing the area of your body you are focused on healing and mending.

Another good application for imagery during any treatment you are undergoing is imagining your body receiving maximal benefits from it. For example, if you are receiving ultrasound treatment, imagine your body maximally breaking down scar tissue and efficiently washing it away. If chemotherapy, imagine the cancer being dissolved and leaving only healthy tissue in its wake. In addition, given the ravaging effects of radiation and chemotherapy, you might also add being able to keep your food down afterwards — taking in full nourishment that enhances your body's defences and healing power.

Imagery can also be very helpful in managing any pain you may be experiencing. Try picturing cool blues or aqua running through your body to the area needing relief. Alternatively, you could picture an ice pack cooling the area or imagine being immersed in cooling and soothing water. Simply breathing deep and imagining sending soothing and cleansing oxygen to the source of pain can also bring relief.

See *Appendix D* for the Inner Healing Guided Imagery Script, which is designed to promote recovery and healing from injury or illness.[90]

Other People Matter

Chris Peterson, one of the founders of the positive psychology movement who died recently, is most fondly remembered for his motto: 'Other people matter'. Our connections with others have a huge impact on our health and our wellbeing. How we relate to others can be among the most hard-wired patterns of feeling and acting there is; and therefore among the most challenging to override. In many cases this is to our benefit. Often-times, however, it is something we need to transcend in order to better flourish and reach our potential. We cannot go back and change the conditions that shaped us, but we can as adults acknowledge our strengths, and create better conditions to heal old wounds and fill in any gaps.

Relationships can be one of the most powerful triggers for self-growth and development. They hold up a mirror to both see ourselves more clearly as well as highlight what is best and worst in us. And while they can be our greatest source of fulfilment, few of us have role models or training for mastering relationship skills. Comedians joke that if marriage were anything else it would be outlawed by now, given the dismal failure rate. So, clearly there's plenty of room for improvement, and therefore plenty of scope for practising changes required in our mental imagery. This usually involves getting better at expressing oneself in a way that can be heard and understood as intended, which often means being able to better manage one's emotions in the process (both as sender and receiver).

Because so much of what gets in the way of successful relationships is hard-wired from your childhood, it can be especially challenging to break out of such patterns and create new more adaptive ones. When the new preferred pattern is identified in couples counselling, I always encourage my clients to first engage in mental imagery, before trying it out in person. See *Chapter 8* on rewriting history, which further elaborates on the rewiring process.

While relationship advice is beyond the scope of this book, and there are endless possibilities for applying mental imagery to relating, it's safe to say that any change you are interested in making in your relationship skills can be improved with the practice of mental imagery. This will accelerate your progress immeasurably. You are already engaging in imagery so it's best to be in charge of what those images are, and switch to the preferred positive version or script when you catch yourself sliding back to reviewing past negative versions or scripts.

Our families obviously play/ed a huge role in who we are and become as adults. These days, it is our work mates who have also become like family. While you may have chosen and enjoy your job, you likely didn't get to choose the people you work with. Think about it! These are people with whom you spend more time with than your real family! And many people bring their (unresolved) family issues with them into the office. Learning to adapt and optimally manage such scenarios is facilitated by imagery practice. This might mean learning to be more assertive; or dealing with difficult clients, customers and colleagues; maintaining appropriate boundaries, and more.

An extreme example is of a space mission. The team is selected on the basis of their individual expertise and need for a mission, and NOT for how well they get along. Yet get along they must to succeed and withstand a mission in such a small and confined space with no escape for days on end! Not even to sleep — for they take shifts, and sleepers are strapped into the wall in the same space where others will be continuing to conduct their mission. You might feel like you are trapped yourself without any escape in certain circumstances at your job. But you can escape mentally, or better still, have a 'go-to' place mentally that fosters the mental condition conducive to best managing the situation before you. Being able to pull this off would take practice, and mental imagery offers the opportunity to practise such incidents as many times as you wish until it feels natural to you.

Personal Best Imagery Guide

Below is a basic step-by-step guide for engaging in your personal best imagery. It might help to first take some time to write out how each item could apply to your goal or pursuit. The more details you can include specific to your case the better. Remember to keep in mind mental imagery guidelines from *Chapter 5*. See also *Appendix D* for the full Personal Best Guided Imagery Script which is also available as a recording at www.bigskypublishing.com.au.

1. Imagine your dream goal — achieving highest success possible.

2. Imagine an immediate success — for upcoming event, opportunity, or within a certain time frame.

3. Recall a previous achievement, success, or personal best and flash forward to upcoming event or opportunity. Review your list of strengths and what you most enjoy. Replay how great it felt and went, e.g. feeling confident and focused; in a great mood; strong and effectual; moving fluidly; transitioning smoothly; responding well; doing what you most love to do, and in the *FLOW*.

4. Review the key elements of what it will take, and being super effective. It's best to start with what you feel most confident about, or your favourite, and work your way to least favourite.

5. If your event or opportunity involves making decisions imagine making the best choices that keep you on track (and resisting temptations that take you off track with ease and confidence).

6. Practice refocusing and distraction control. Practice managing all contingencies with great aplomb, and with great ease.

7. String together your event or performance in a reality sequence. Imagine from pre-start to post-finish.

8. Imagine a strong finish or positive outcome.

9. Imagine congratulations and relevant accolades! And allow yourself a moment of self-congratulations, savouring your well-earned success.

10. Focus on the *next step/s* you need to take to reach the desired goal. Imagine putting in the time and effort that is immediately before you, and feeling great about it.

Summary

By now you realise how mental imagery can improve many different aspects of your life. In any area that you would like to do better and be better at mental imagery practice will accelerate your progress leading to greater wellbeing and success.

Appendices

Appendix A
Positive Psychology Interventions Sampler

Chapter 2 highlighted the links between the most popular positive psychology interventions and mental imagery. This Appendix contains a selection of those intervention strategies that you can apply to enhance your wellbeing — keeping in mind that you can augment the benefits of these exercises by more consciously engaging in the mental imagery component that naturally occurs in the process. These are:

- Signature Strengths
- A Beautiful Day
- Writing Your Eulogy
- Cultivating Gratitude
- Loving Kindness Meditation

Signature Strengths

The purpose of this exercise is to encourage you to own your signature strengths by finding new and more frequent uses for them. According to Seligman, a signature strength has the following hallmarks:

- A sense of ownership and authenticity ('this is the real me')
- A feeling of excitement while displaying it, particularly at first
- A rapid learning curve as the strength is first practised
- A sense of yearning to find new ways to use it
- A feeling of inevitability in using the strength ('Try to stop me')
- Invigoration rather than exhaustion while using the strength
- The creation and pursuit of personal projects that revolve around it
- Joy, zest, enthusiasm, even ecstasy while using it.[91]

Instructions

1. **Signature strengths:** What are your signature strengths x 5 (i.e. VIA Q results)?

   - Go to www.authentichappiness.org to complete the VIA Survey of Character Strengths.

   - How do these compare to what you might have predicted? This could be according to the list of 24 possible strengths and/or based on your own subjective assessment, and/or those of others who know you well.

You may wish to concentrate on a single strength or cluster of (related) strengths, as well as on a single or certain area/s of your life for the following questions.

2. **Strengths manifestation:** How do your strengths manifest in your life?

3. **Upsides and downsides:** What are the upsides and downsides of your strength/s? That is:

   - What are the positive impacts of your strength/s in your life? e.g. on health, profession, education, relationships, etc..

   - What are the potential downsides of your strength/s (aka weaknesses as overuse of strength)?

4. **Conditions:** What conditions and practice are conducive to the expression and development of your strength/s?

5. **Strength/s in action:** Attempt to use your strength/s in a least one new way this week, and reflect on your experience:

   - How did you feel before, during and afterwards?

   - How challenging or easy was the activity?

   - Did you notice how quickly time passed?

   - What was your sense of self-consciousness?

   - Is this worth repeating?

6. **Strength/s and Success Link:** Notice any successes throughout the week, and reflect on the extent to which they might be related to the expression of a strength/s.

A Beautiful Day:
Creating versus Reacting

Notice how the words 'creating' and 'reacting' are identical. Take the
'c' out of the middle of reacting and you get creating, which is where
more happiness is at — by taking charge of creating your own reality,
rather than merely reacting to the forces around you, and taking
greater control over your destiny.

Calvin and Hobbes

Source: Watterson, William, 'Calvin and Hobbes', Cartoon, 1995, Andrews McMeel Publishing, Kansas City.

As mentioned in the first chapter of this book, I love to show the
attached Calvin and Hobbes comic strip to my clients, and inserting
the word 'NEW' at the end 'I gotta get my life some (NEW) writers.'

Have a go at creating *A Beautiful Day* according to Seligman's
instructions below. Remember, it is not about creating a perfect day,
but one that is well within your control. You may wish to consider
including all elements of the PERMA[92] model.

A Beautiful Day

Design a beautiful day (a 24-hour clock day) that is possible for you to
live currently. Explain why you chose each element.

Try to live that day and record your feelings while including the
following questions:

Part 1: Were you successful in living that day? Why or why not? Were all
of the qualities of your beautiful day truly beautiful? Why or why not?
What would you now change about your perception of a beautiful day?

Part 2: Is there any action you might take to move toward achieving a 'beautiful day' on a more regular basis? How does your conception of a 'beautiful day' fit in with your life goals?

Source: Seligman, M. (2007). *A beautiful day: Applying principles of positive psychology.* Retrieved April 14, 2009, from http://www.ppc.sas.upenn.edu/beautifuldayactivity.htm

Writing Your Eulogy[93]

Happiness means different things to different people and most people don't actually know what makes them happy. Visualising your own funeral may seem like a strange way to find out, but it's a powerful way to identify your 'core values', or the things that really matter to you most.

Values are similar to goals. Where goals are often quite specific concrete descriptions of things we would like to achieve, values are more conceptual. To 'go to the gym three times a week' is quite a specific goal. To 'be fit, active and healthy' is a value. To 'get married' is a goal, whereas to 'have loving relationships' is a value. Other values include honesty, compassion, justice, creativity, community, adventure, etc.

So while you may succeed or fail at reaching goals, your values remain constant. Identifying and staying true to your values will keep you on track for a happy and more meaningful life.

Steps

1. Imagine that you are at your own funeral. You're listening to what your loved ones are saying about you: the good stuff (and the not so good), the dreams, the aspirations, the things that you were connected to, the things that meant a lot to you. Perhaps they mention the things that you didn't get to do, or the opportunities that were lost.

2. Take 15 minutes to write up your eulogy. Be honest. What are the core values and the achievements that you would like to be remembered for? If you are finding this process difficult, you can spend time on it.

3. Sometime after you have completed the eulogy, reflect on your experience of the exercise. Ask yourself what you learnt from writing it.

4. Consider whether the values you listed are really yours and not someone else's (e.g. what you think they should be). Settle on the values that feel most real to you.

5. Finally, think about how you can turn your core values into goals. They may be small things, like coming home from work earlier, or bigger things that you've been wanting to do for a while.

Whatever these steps are, write them down, make sure they reflect your authentic values and do them!

Cultivating Gratitude

PART 1: Gratitude journal and letter

1. Daily gratitude journal: Maintain a list of highlights daily (minimum 3–5 per day over 5 days). Typically, such a habit begins with an end of day review (list) of that for which you are grateful.

2. Gratitude letter:
    *   Write a gratitude letter to someone in your past who played a significant role in your life; or who did something that meant a lot to you (who you may not have properly thanked up until now). Express thanks along with specifying what you are thankful for, what impact it has had on you and/or your life, what it meant to you, how it changed you, etc.
    *   Optional: Deliver (optimal) or send the letter. Describe and reflect on the response (both ways).

PART 2: General attitude of gratitude

1. Notice and express appreciation or thanks as much as possible. Don't wait until doing a highlight review (hopefully this list will grow by leaps and bounds with practice). Try to catch that for which you are grateful for sooner and more immediately, and express thanks (if even only acknowledging to yourself) in the moment.

2. When feeling negative and aware of what is not going well try to refocus to all that is going well. All that you have to be thankful for (aka count your blessings instead). You can even be thankful

for the lesson the negative situation presented you! And other opportunities before you to improve the situation. Even if only just your specific capacities for improving the situation. Obviously, there are times when it is natural and appropriate to feel negative emotions, and when attempting to turn them around precipitously is ill advised. The purpose here, however, is to apply the instruction to those cases of gratuitous negativity or complaint.

3. You might also notice that you become sensitised to when thanks are called for but lacking in those around you (or worse, excessive complaining without taking responsibility or steps to resolve; and poor balance of expressions of appreciation). Contrast with expression of appreciation and thanks — whether by you or others.

Gratitude buddy

Recruit a 'gratitude buddy' — someone with whom you share your highlights, observations of thanks, and subsequent impacts. This might be over a specified and contained period of time or might go on for days, weeks, lifetime. Ideally, you would also include expressions of appreciation for one another, but keep it real and genuine, and the more specific the better.

Loving kindness meditation

Regular practice of the LKM is beneficial in cultivating the attitude of kindness and compassion (versus the act of kindness). The flow-on impact is likely to naturally lead to increased awareness of, and opportunity for, acts of kindness. It is also a method by which a person may become more open to receiving kindness.

Instructions[94]

Get yourself into a comfortable position and close your eyes ... sit upright and focus your attention on your breathing ... inhaling deeply ... and exhaling fully ...

Focus your attention on your heart centre/chakra ... imagine breathing in divine love from behind your heart (through mid-thoracic centre) ... and blowing it out through the front of your heart centre ... Fill your heart with divine loving kindness with every in breath ... and releasing (and sharing) with every out breath ...

Reflect on a person for whom you already feel warm, compassionate and loving feelings towards ... This could be your child or spouse, or even a pet ... allow the warm and tender feelings to rise up within you ... tune into these feelings more and more ... and once they have taken hold, gently let go of the image of your loved one ... and simply hold the feeling ... allowing the feelings to flow through your heart centre and filling the space within your entire body ... Now, extend the warm loving feelings to yourself ... cherish yourself as deeply and as purely as you would cherish your own newborn child ...

Keep breathing consciously through your chest area ... letting the sensations fill your entire body as you manifest the following thoughts ...

May I be peaceful ... May I be free from all negativity and fear ... May I experience real serenity and harmony in my life ... May I develop love and kindness for myself ... patience and acceptance towards myself ... May I be kind to myself ... May I be happy and content.

Option A: Next, radiate your warm, tender, and compassionate feelings to others ... first to a person you know well ... then gradually calling to mind all your friends and family ... to your neighbours ... and then all the people with whom you have a connection or encounter in daily life ... even if remote, like the checkout clerk or taxi driver ...

Ultimately, extend your feelings of love and kindness to all people and creatures of the earth. To do this, you might visualise your community, your city, your region, your country, your part of the world, to parts of the world facing natural disasters and conflict ... and finally to the whole earth and galaxy.

Option B: Now, start visualising people you know and love ... who you care for ... and share your merits with them ... allow the loving sensations to flow out of your body via your heart centre ... sharing your merits and good qualities with them ... you may visualise the sensations or simply feel them .... But make sure you *feel* them ... May I develop equanimity, peace, tranquillity ... May I share my merits with loved ones ...

Now extend these feelings towards people who are not so close, maybe even those with whom you have had conflict, or may potentially experience difficulties with in future ...

Send your good vibrations and good will to those who need it. May they develop a deeper awareness of themselves; May they develop equanimity, peace, and tranquillity. May I share my merits with them, my equanimity with them ...

And now share your good will and good thoughts with all beings ... all beings, no exception ... near or far. May all beings be peaceful; may all beings be happy ... all beings.

Amen ('so it is').

Appendix B
Relax to Max

The following text is an (updated) excerpt about relaxation from *Inner Sports: Mental Skills for Peak Performance*[95]; re-released in 2011 in *Inner Spa: Supplement.*[96]

Relaxation is a major skill and asset towards fostering the mental fitness necessary to reach our greatest potential and maximise well-being. If you try to remember a peak experience or peak performance from your past, you'll probably recall a sense of feeling loose and relaxed, yet sharp, focused and in control, which is characteristic of the experience of 'flow'. Practising relaxation helps cultivate our ability to more consistently and efficiently achieve the flow state.

Applications

There are many applications for the practice of relaxation, the most common being:

- For stress reduction
- Enhance quality of sleep
- Enhance recovery from training and competition
- Enhance recovery from injury or illness
- Enhance imagery skill
- Enhance performance in general
- Enhance focus and learning capacity
- Enhance fluid performance

It is easy to relax when there are no pressures, no meetings, no major competitions, deadlines, quick decisions to be made, traffic, family crises, etc. Staying calm, cool, and collected under pressure, however, takes deliberate practice and awareness.

Have you ever noticed how some of your best ideas occur just as you're falling asleep, or walking in nature, in the shower or in the car on a long road trip? These are times when we are tapping into our alpha state, which is a state of mind when we are most relaxed as well as creative. It is also the mental state most closely associated with the experience of 'flow', of being 'in the zone', etc. Contrast this with when you are in a hurry and rushing around.

For example, trying to hurriedly get a key in the door (and dropping the keys in the process!); or forgetting something important in our rush to get out the door, and having to double back; or having to re-read the same paragraph a second and third time in our hurry to get through the material, and still not absorbing the information. Do you recognise yourself in any of these scenarios? Inevitably, by rushing, we become less efficient and focused, and whatever we were trying to accomplish, ends up taking either twice as long, or leads so sub-par performance. Much of the time, this is because we are so anxious about where we are going, about results or outcome, that we don't pay enough attention to where we are now — to the 'here and now', which is critical to peak performance in sport and any meaningful life pursuit, as well as our wellbeing.

The key is to catch ourselves during these moments, and slow down, and relax, rather than succumbing to the temptation of trying even harder, or pressing. You may have noticed that when playing a sport and things are not going so well, there is the tendency to try harder, which often yields even worse results. For example, trying too hard in tennis, often translates into hitting the ball in the net or way outside the lines. When you catch yourself in the downward spiral of trying harder and harder, with worse and worse results, use this as a cue to 'try softer', as Jim Loehr, who has done a lot of work in professional tennis, suggests.

Often it is our concept of success that interferes with being able to let go and relax. Many associate the relentless pursuit and drive to achieve with success and excellence, and equate 'discipline' with hard work only. It is because of this that it has been suggested that maybe we should refer to humans as 'human doings' rather than 'human beings', for we seem to define and value ourselves more by what we 'DO' rather than based on our 'being'.

Often, for optimal wellbeing and peak performance, the principle of 'less is more' becomes more effective. The discipline for balance, for quality rest and letting go of pressure and concerns, becomes of greater importance to continued success and fulfilment, as well as maintaining optimal health and wellbeing.

Maintaining balance between work, rest and play is the key to reaching our highest potential and staying healthy and well. It's about maintaining balance between nurturing our Being as much as our Doings; and recognising that the quality of our training and performance (whether in sports or other careers) depends on the quality of our R&R time (which includes: rest and relaxation, as well as recreation).

Relaxation training allows us to be more efficient and effective in our endeavours, as well as helps us to cope better with any obstacles and setbacks we may face. With practice, we enhance our ability to weather any storm in life, and therefore more readily reach the rainbow(s) (as well as the proverbial pot of gold). Being relaxed allows us the space to find the inner calm and clarity necessary for ideas and resolutions to flow naturally and easily — to see the opportunities and positives in every situation, and to draw on our inner resources of strength and insight.

It is said that 'if you do not go within, you go without'. This is important for offsetting preoccupation about past mistakes and regrets, and worries about the future, as well as dependence on external factors for our happiness and well-being, rather than being connected to the present moment (the only moment in which we have any power and control), and our current inner being and strengths.

Relaxation training also enhances our mind/body connection which can be so important in sports and when facing health challenges. In addition, the more in tune we are with our bodies, the better we tend to treat it, such as eating less junk food, and drinking less coffee and alcohol, etc.

Unfortunately, some people equate practising relaxation and meditation techniques with 'doing nothing', or being too mystical or alternative. But what could be more natural and normal than drawing upon our body's innate ability to produce a deeply restful and peaceful state of being? Much better than reaching for chemical relief for the many stress-related ailments plaguing us nowadays, such as medication for the pain of tension headaches and migraines, ulcers, digestive disorders, hypertension, asthma, etc. All of these are known to respond well to regular practice of relaxation or meditation, and without the added cost and side effects.

Relaxation benefits

There are many well-documented health benefits attributed to relaxation practice. Basically, regular practice of relaxation techniques reverses many of the ill effects caused by stress.

Physically, some of the benefits are:

- Decreased metabolic rate
- Decreased heart rate
- Decreased respiration rate
- Decreased oxygen consumption — Deep abdominal breathing optimises our oxygen consumption — allowing more oxygen to reach our muscles and our brain more efficiently
- Reduced muscle tension
- Reduced blood pressure and hypertension
- Decreased lactate
- Decreased cholesterol
- Decreased cortisol (a major stress hormone)
- Improved blood circulation
- Increased alpha brain waves (which is associated with creativity and the flow state)
- Improved reactivity to stress (both physiologically and psychologically). What this means is that we react more rapidly to a stressor, followed by a rapid recovery; whereas when tense, we would be slower to react, as well as much slower to recover from a stressor. For example, a relaxed person would react more quickly to a shockingly loud noise, and recover almost instantly, whereas a tense person would be slower to react, and would take a lot longer to recover from the shock.
- Relaxation has also been shown to increase immunocompetence, which means our immune systems are stronger and more resistant to viruses or disease.

Some of the psychological benefits to relaxation training include:

- Greater mental clarity and calm
- Improved concentration
- Greater emotional control
- Increased creativity
- Better sense of humour (have you ever met an uptight person with a sense of humour? And if they do joke, it's more likely at someone else's expense).
- Relaxation produces greater mental readiness. We are more open-minded and receptive to new ideas and solutions when relaxed. An open mind is like a parachute; it works best when open. It is by maintaining an open mind and sense of humour that we avoid getting, what Ashley Montague, refers to as psychosclerosis (i.e. hardening of the mind), which produces rigid and negative thinking.

All of these benefits have obvious implications for performance enhancement and wellness!

Some people say they relax only when they sleep. But sleep is not always as restful as it can be, and if you know of anyone who grinds their teeth during their sleep, you know what I mean! Practising relaxation enhances the quality of rest that is achieved during sleep. Many report having one of the best night's sleep ever after practising a relaxation exercise. In addition, it has been demonstrated that with practice, one can arrive at a stage of deep physiological rest within 10 minutes of relaxation, which can take up to 4–6 hours to get to by sleeping. Relaxation training, therefore, provides a much more efficient and restful alternative to napping.

Diaphragmatic Breathing

Central to all relaxation and meditation techniques is diaphragmatic breathing, otherwise known as deep abdominal breathing. What this means is, inhaling slowly and deeply expanding your belly before filling your chest; and exhaling fully and steadily, taking a little bit longer on the out breath than the in breath — completely expelling all the used oxygen and freeing up more space for each fresh new breath you take. Sometimes it is easier to focus on exhaling fully, than to concentrate on inhaling abdominally. This has two advantages, first because your body will automatically respond to a full exhale with an abdominal breath — it is a reflex reaction, and the second advantage is that you can only fill your lungs to the extent that they have been emptied by the previous out breath.

So, by focusing on a full exhale, you are ensuring that you have cleared your lungs of all the used oxygen, leaving more room for fresh oxygen to fill your lungs. This can be especially important during stressful conditions, for we tend to hoard our breath then, and not exhale as fully as we might, which creates a situation where we are trying to get more and more oxygen into less and less space in our lungs. This is also one of the main causes of side stitches when running.

Take a moment now to notice your breathing. Is your chest alone expanding, or is your belly involved too? Now try focusing only on the exhale — completely emptying out your lungs, perhaps even exaggerating it at first by compressing your diaphragm area, and then see what happens to your abdomen on your next in breath. You will have noticed that your body takes an abdominal breath without you even having to think about it!

A special nature of breathing is that it is both voluntary and involuntary, i.e. we can consciously control it, yet keep breathing whether we are thinking about it or not. Also, the same part of the brain which controls our breathing also plays a large role in our emotions — the Limbic System. Our brains are wired such that our emotions will affect our breathing patterns, and likewise our breathing can affect our emotions. When angry, tense or upset our breathing tends to become very rapid and shallow, or we might even hold our breath. Whereas, by controlling our breathing, by taking a few slow deep breaths, we are able to gain greater control over our emotions. Our mental/emotional state, therefore, is reflected in our breathing, and vice versa — our breathing impacts our mental/emotional state.

Eastern traditions have long considered the breath to be the junction between mind, body, and spirit, the bridge between the conscious and unconscious. Breath, therefore, plays a central role in Eastern Spiritual practices, and evolution of consciousness.

We can liken our minds to the sea — when anxious and upset our minds become like the turbulence experienced during a storm. By focusing on deepening our breathing, however, we can reach to deeper and deeper levels within ourselves, far below the turbulent surface, to where it is calm and peaceful. (Being an avid diver myself, I like to also imagine a coral reef — where it is not only calm and peaceful, but glorious and beautiful as well!). A calmer place from which we are able to respond more effectively, with greater composure, to the demands we face.

Fitting in attention to breath throughout our day is a first step towards cultivating the relaxation skill. There are many cues during our daily lives which we can use to remind us to attend to our breathing — to deepen it and slow it down. Here are a few examples:

- Any time you catch yourself 'clock watching' is a good cue, because if you are anxious about time or wishing you were somewhere else, then you are probably not as relaxed and effective as you could be.
- While on the phone is another good cue. Take a moment for a deep breath before picking up; or focus on deep slow breaths while you are listening (rather than waiting impatiently for what you have to say next). You may be surprised at how much better a listener you become!
- Any time you are kept waiting, whether in traffic, at work or at training, on hold on the phone, etc. you can use this as an opportunity for a little 'time-out', as a 'breather', rather than waiting impatiently, and probably even holding your breath, for the green at the lights.
- Focusing on the breath is also a great 'refocusing' tool. It's a tool for getting our mind back in focus after an upset or distraction. Focusing on the breath achieves four benefits for refocusing:
  - It helps to relax our mind and body
  - It provides a neutral focus from that which upset or distracted us
  - It gets us back into the present, the 'here and now'
  - It leads to a greater sense of control
  - It leads to a positive frame of mind

Meditation techniques

There are many different forms of meditation techniques. What they have in common is:

- Focus on abdominal breathing
- Inhaling slowly and deeply
- Exhaling fully and steadily
- Extending the out breath relative to the in breath

How they vary is according to:

- Whether attention is directed to the breath alone (i.e. just attending to our breathing wherever our breath passes through our bodies, e.g. through the nostrils, down our throats, into our chest, the rise and fall of our abdomen) (Mindfulness Meditation).
- Whether there is use of what is called a 'mental device', which is simply a word or phrase that is silently repeated and paired with the breath, some examples might be focusing on a Sanskrit word (Transcendental Meditation), or 'Letting Go,' and 'Releasing' with every out breath, and imagining pure/healing/divine/energy in with every in breath.
- Or one can use counting as a mental device, such as counting breaths from 1–100 (Zen meditation). The idea here is to count breaths, and when you lose count you have to start over. It is OK if your mind strays to other thoughts, as long as you are able to keep count of your breaths. This type of exercise helps train both relaxation and concentration.

For beginners, I recommend a 'mini meditation'; a 10–1 breath countdown, which combines all of the elements just mentioned. All that you need to do is focus on inhaling slowly and deeply, and exhaling fully and steadily, and count your breaths from 10 to 1. You may want to add some self-suggestions such a mentioned earlier, such as 'Letting Go' or 'Releasing all cares' with every out breath, and breathing in purifying, refreshing, and healing oxygen with every in-breath.

When you reach 1, you might also want to try adding a little imagery of a favourite place or scene where you feel most at home and serene — a special or sacred time and place. For many this means somewhere in nature, on a beach, or high up on the bluffs watching the waves crashing up against the rocks, and feeling the sea breezes and the warmth of the sun. Or it could be imagining watching a sunset or sunrise over the ocean. You can include loved ones and beloved pets for company if you wish — anything that makes you feel 'warm and fuzzy', wherever at peace and feeling warm and loving, and then when you are ready, you might want to count your way back up to 10 again, and notice how you feel. This is a relatively easy and short exercise that can be practised several times throughout the day and only takes a couple of minutes to complete. You might want to take a few moments now to stop reading, and try out this mini-meditation before continuing.

Body relaxation techniques

While meditation techniques tend to focus predominantly on the breath, other relaxation techniques tend to focus on the body as well. The advantages are that the body provides a mental focus to keep the mind from wandering, and it also fosters the mind/body awareness and control that is important for athletes as well as healing.

'Progressive relaxation' is a major form of body focused relaxation. This involves the contraction and release of the major muscle groups of the body, starting from the head, and finishing with the feet; or beginning with the feet and working up to the head. The contraction/relaxation action serves two purposes, 1) to demonstrate and heighten awareness of the difference between tension and relaxation, and 2) the muscle returns to a more relaxed state following the contraction. Try it now — hold your hand in a fist as tight as you can for about six seconds, and notice how the tension feels (remember your breathing!) … hold it … and then release — again noticing how it feels, warmer and more relaxed.

Progressive relaxation may also be practised without the contraction phase, by simply progressively passing one's attention from one muscle group to another, focusing on relaxing the muscles and releasing any tension. One can imagine sending relaxing breaths throughout the body to the various muscles.

Another quick and easy way to induce relaxation is to turn one's eyes upwards. This can be done with either your eyes open or shut. What this does is sets up a neurophysiological response producing the alpha state associated with relaxation. This technique is employed in the work of the 'Mind Switch' researchers, who have trained disabled people to control their environment by switching to the alpha state. Ashley Craig and colleagues have developed a special cap fitted with electrodes linked to light switches, the phone, door locks, etc. that respond to the shift in brain waves (i.e. light goes on or off, phone is answered, door is locked or unlocked). Try it now, while remembering your abdominal breathing — focus your eyes upwards as you breath slowly and deeply, and hold it, and then notice how if feels when you release your eyes. Simply unfocusing your vision will also produce similar results, i.e. with your eyes open, try to unfocus or blur your vision, while remembering your breathing. This too, can be mentally relaxing and produce the alpha state within a couple of minutes.

'Inner Massage' is a yoga based body relaxation exercise that differs from the progressive relaxation format. Inner Massage follows a more circuitous route to when passing through the body, which is much more like how our nervous and circulatory systems travel throughout our bodies. It also focuses more on the joints of the body, rather than muscle groups. This can be effective for there is greater nerve ennervation at the joints. There are also greater amounts of electromagnetic energy and tension stored in the joints. The pathways of inner massage are also very similar to the chakras in yoga and the meridian pathways associated with acupressure and acupuncture.

Recommendations for practice

- Take a few moments throughout your day to focus on relaxation.
- Start off relaxation practice on your own with 5–10 minutes per day, and gradually build up to 20–30 minutes per day.
- Be sure to be in a comfortable position with good posture. Do not slouch if you are sitting — keep your spine straight. If you are lying down, you may want to use a few props such as a pillow under your knees to take the pressure off your back, and a rolled up towel under your neck to support the neck.
- Be in a quiet place where you are not likely to be disturbed (you may notice, however, that pets will be very attracted to joining you).

- For some, it helps to keep a routine time and place for relaxation or meditation. This helps foster the habit.
- Also, transitions during the day are a good time for practice.
- Finally, it is best to practise on an empty stomach, for the same reason we do not exercise on a full stomach — as the blood is redistributed to the periphery, and away from the organs.

As happens with exercise, with greater relaxation practice, you may find that you begin to crave relaxation more and more often and for longer periods of time. Listen to your body's messages and urgings — these are the signposts to being in the Flow, and towards achieving peak performance, health and well-being!

Appendix C

Blissor Versus Stressor Monitoring Guide

Stressor/Complaint Reflection	
Source	Perception
1. Date?	8. Where was my attention focused?
2. Time?	9. What images or memories were brought into focus?
3. Place?	10. How was I feeling? Physically/emotionally. What
4. What was I doing?	concerns, doubts, or worries came to mind?
5. Who was with me?	11. What was I saying to myself?
6. Stressor? Situation or event?	12. Beliefs or values that were relevant?
7. Checklist item #?	

Blissor/Highlight Reflection	
Source	Perception
1. Date?	8. Where was my attention focused?
2. Time?	9. What images or memories were brought into focus?
3. Place?	10. How was I feeling? Physically/emotionally. What
4. What was I doing?	concerns, doubts, or worries came to mind?
5. Who was with me?	11. What was I saying to myself?
6. Blissor? Situation or event?	12. Beliefs or values that were relevant?
7. Checklist item #?	

Highlight/Blissor Sources/Checklist*

1. Positive human interaction
2. Positive interaction with nature
3. Positive connection through play, games, sport, physical activity
4. Positive personal accomplishments
5. Positive personal discovery or creativity
6. Positive physical sensations (i.e. pleasure)
7. Pure relaxation
8. Positive amusement and/or entertainment.

*Adapted from *Positive Living Skills* by Terry Orlick[97]

Reaction	Consequences	Insight/Reflection
13. How did I react? 14. What words best describe the sensations I felt?	15. How severe were the feelings or sensations that I felt? (0-5 scale) 16. Were there delayed after-effects? 17. How long did it take to recover?	18. What would be your ideal or preferred response? 19. Can you imagine responding better next time to a similar trigger?

Reaction	Consequences	Insight/Reflection
13. How did I react? 14. What words best describe the sensations I felt?	15. How intense were the feelings or sensations that I felt? (0-5) 16. How long did the feelings last? 17. Any flow-on effects?	18. What lessons, insights or benefits did you gain from this experience? 19. Can you imagine re-creating this experience

Complaint/Stressor Sources/Checklist*

1. Negative or absence of human interaction
2. Negative or absences of interaction with nature
3. Negative or absence of positive play, games, sport or physical activity
4. Negative or absence of experiencing positive personal accomplishments
5. Negative or absence of experiencing positive personal discoveries or creativity
6. Negative or absence of positive physical sensations
7. Negative stress and .or absence of pure relaxation
8. Negative or no positive entertainment.

Appendix D
Guided Imagery Scripts

This Appendix includes a copy of the guided imagery scripts and vision buddy guidelines covered in the book. The scripts have been recorded and are available via www.bigskypublishing.com.au.

Relaxation Prelude

Below is a basic relaxation prelude for the practice of mental imagery. It stems from a standard hypnotic induction protocol. Follow these steps to relax your mind and body before practising mental imagery. Ellipses ('…') have been used to indicate when to pause — to allow the image to take shape before moving on to the next step.

1. **Find yourself a comfortable position in a quiet space.**

   Close your eyes and focus on your breathing. Inhaling slowly and deeply, and exhaling fully and steadily — completely expelling all the used oxygen to maximise space in your lungs for each fresh new breath you take.

2. **Once you find yourself in a comfortable rhythm of slow deep breathing begin a countdown from ten to one (10–1) with every cycle of breath.**

   Imagine you are descending a staircase (or an elevator if you prefer) as you do so. With every exhale, imagine you are descending deeper and deeper into your subconscious mind … releasing and letting go … leaving all mental turbulence on the surface of your mind as you descend into the more peaceful realms of your inner self … Ten … breathing slowly and deeply, and exhaling fully and steadily … Nine … releasing and letting go … Eight … Seven … Six … Five … descending deeper and deeper within yourself … Four … Three … Two … And when you reach One, you are ready to commence your mental imagery …

Peak Experiences and Performances Imagery Guides

This section covers how to practise recalling peak experiences and performances. First, take a moment to carefully consider what experiences you want to recall. You might wish to choose parts of different experiences and performances, or stick to one at a time.

As discussed in *Chapter 5*, the first step to practising mental imagery is to get into a relaxed or hypnotic state. Research has shown that the mind is more open and receptive when in this state. Positive suggestions and imagery are more likely to take hold.

Refer to the steps to relax then follow the guides for recalling either a peak performance or a peak experience. I've used generic instructions here that you can adapt to your own imagery. The more you can personalise the guides, the better your images will be. Take a moment to reflect on your own personal experiences, and how they might compare or differ. Remember, your experiences are the ones that count.

Ellipses ('...') have been inserted to indicate when to pause — to allow the image to take shape before moving on to the next step.

Peak experience recall imagery guide

Once you've relaxed (see the *Relaxation Prelude*), follow these steps to practise a peak experience recall.

1. **Imagine that you have arrived at a door or gateway to the time and place where you experienced your all-time peak experience.**

   A place where you felt at your very best ... most serene ... most happy ... most joy ... most blessed ... could be what some consider a 'holy moment' ... take in the sights and sounds of this time and place ... what do you notice? What do you see? What do you hear? What do you feel? What do you taste? What other sensations are you aware of? Totally immerse yourself back into this wonderful experience of your life ... savour and immerse yourself ... feeling great appreciation and gratitude as you do so ... savouring this peak experience of your life ... there is great power in recalling all of the details and sensations of this wonderful moment in time ... when time seems to stand still ... and all is well in your inner world ... Continue to savour and enjoy recalling this experience ... remembering your breathing as you do so ... slowly and deeply ... exhaling fully and steadily ... as you continue to immerse yourself more deeply and intensely into the experience ... What are you feeling? What are you thinking? Is anyone joining in with you? What are they doing or saying? As you continue to focus on this image ... try to gradually strengthen and intensify it ... strengthening and intensifying.

2. **When you feel you have fully re-created the experience, give it a name.**

    Think of this as a kind of file name ... to file away in your mind to be recalled at any time you wish to feel this way again. Repeat your file name to yourself as you continue to engage in your imagery.

3. **Picture feeling this way in an upcoming situation, challenge or event where you would like to feel this way again.**

    Once you have practised a strong image of this experience, you will be able to merely repeat the file name to generate this wonderful feeling of wellbeing again — on cue. Promise yourself that you will revisit this experience often.

4. **When you are ready to close the file on this image, and to return back to the here and now begin your ascent back up from one to ten.**

    Count back up the steps the way you came ... taking your time back up to full consciousness ... remembering your breathing ... as you count back up from one to ten ... Open your eyes gently before refocusing on the here and now.

Once you have practised a strong image of this experience, you can just repeat the file name to generate this wonderful feeling of wellbeing again — on cue. Promise yourself that you'll revisit this experience often.

Peak performance recall imagery guide

Once you've relaxed (as per the *Relaxation Prelude*) follow these steps
to practise a peak performance recall.

1. **Imagine that you have arrived at a door or gateway to the
   time and place where you experienced your all-time peak
   performance.**

   The time where you performed at your very best ... a time
   when you felt optimally ready and prepared ... feeling
   confident and self-assured ... relishing the challenge before
   you ... Take in all the sights and sounds as you (try to) recall
   all the thoughts and feelings as you approached the event of
   this great performance ... what were you thinking? ... What
   were you feeling? What do you notice? What do you see?
   What do you hear? What do you feel? What do you taste?
   What other sensations are you aware of? Who, if anyone, are
   you aware of?

2. **Now take yourself back to a peak moment of this event.**

   Choose one that epitomises the experience for you ... bring
   up all the feelings and sensations ....Totally immerse yourself
   back into this great performance of your life ... where is your
   attention focused? ... what are you doing? What sights and
   sounds are you aware of? Who else is in the picture (if anyone)?
   What are they doing and saying? ... Fully immerse yourself
   back in the key moments of this all-time great performance
   ... when you were in the flow ... feeling strong and flexible ...
   totally engaged in what you are doing and performing at your
   very best ...

3. **Now recall what it was like afterwards.**

   How did it feel? Imagine any applause or congratulations ...
   imagine the celebrations ... What are you thinking and saying
   to yourself? What are others saying and doing? Savour this peak
   performance of your life ... there is great power in recalling all
   of the details and sensations of this excellent moment in time
   ... this great memory ... recalling all of your strengths and

capacities … your skill and talent… Continue to savour and enjoy recalling this experience … remembering your breathing as you do so … slowly and deeply … exhaling fully and steadily … as you continue to immerse yourself more deeply and intensely into the experience … what are you feeling? What are you thinking? Is anyone joining in with you? What are they doing or saying? As you continue to focus on this image … try to gradually strengthen and intensify it … strengthening and intensifying … and when you feel you have fully re-created the experience, give it a name … a file name so-to-speak … to file away in your mind to be recalled at any time you wish to feel this way again. Repeat your file name to yourself as you continue to engage in your imagery.

4. **Once you can fully re-experience this peak performance in your mind — you can project it to a future event where you would like to feel and perform the same way again.**

   Bring up the scene of an upcoming event … and picture yourself feeling and performing at your very best again … Imagine approaching the event the same way … performing the same way … and finishing strong and with a flourish at the upcoming event. Continue the image with what you expect and hope to occur after the event. Clearly imagine the aftermath with the applause and congratulations … And congratulate yourself on creating yet another experience and performance … of fulfilling your potential.

5. **When you are ready to close the file on this image, and to return back to the here and now begin your ascent back up from one to ten.**

   Count back up the way you came … taking your time back up to full consciousness … remembering your breathing … One … Two … Three … Four … Five … Rising back up to the here and now … Six … Seven … Eight … Nine … Ten — back to the here and now. Open your eyes gently before refocusing on the here and now.

Peak experience and peak performance recall sample scripts

The following sample imagery guides give you an idea of the kind of detail to include in your recall and mental imagery practice. Include all your senses and really try to be back in that moment. Remember to first reach a state of total relaxation before you begin.

Peak experience recall

The steps below show you a specific example of how a peak experience recall can become a powerful mental image for you to draw on and use.

1. **Imagine that you have arrived at a door or gateway to the time and place where you experienced your all-time peak experience.**

   I am on a cliff-top rock overlooking the ocean. This is a place where I felt at my very best … most serene … most happy … most joyful … most blessed … I consider this a 'holy moment …

2. **Take in the sights of this special place.**

   I can see far out to the horizon … the ocean is slightly choppy with whitecaps … there are a few sailing boats … I am thrilled to see a pod of dolphins as they frolic along the coast.

3. **Recall the sounds you heard.**

   I hear the sound of the waves and the calls of seabirds … the sea breeze rustling the bushes and trees around me.

4. **Remember the tastes and smells you experienced.**

   I can smell the saltbush around me and smell and taste the salt in the air.

5. **Recall other sensations you were aware of.**

   I love the sun on my face and the cool sea breeze gently blowing my hair.

6. **Totally immerse yourself in the experience and fully appreciate its value to your life.**

   I feel so lucky to have made my way up here this time. I can't wait to share this place with others, but in the meantime I am savouring this experience all for myself. I feel like nothing else exists except me and the dolphins playing below.

7. **Remember how you felt.**

I am feeling whole and fully alive.

8. **Remember what you were thinking at the time.**

There's nowhere else I'd rather be right now.

9. **Strengthen and intensify the image and sensations.**

I can feel the breeze as I gaze out to sea … wishing I could join the dolphins below, but happy to watch them from my perch above.

10. **Create a file name that depicts this experience to file away in your mind to be recalled at any time you wish to feel this way again. Repeat your file name to yourself as you continue to engage in your imagery.**

I am going to name this recall 'The Rock'.

11. **Picture feeling this way in an upcoming situation, challenge or event where you would like to feel this way again.**

I find that it really helps me to imagine 'The Rock' whenever I am feeling overwhelmed by life. It automatically puts me in a better mood and mindset.

12. **When you're ready to close the file on this image, and to return back to the here and now, begin your ascent back up from one to ten.**

Count back up the steps the way you came … taking your time back up to full consciousness … remembering your breathing … as you count back up from one to ten … Open your eyes gently before refocusing on the here and now.

Peak performance recall

The steps below show you a specific example of how a peak performance recall can become a powerful mental image for you to draw on and use.

1. **Imagine that you have arrived at a door or gateway to the time and place where you experienced your all-time peak performance.**

   I am playing my rival in a tennis match. I will perform at my very best ... I am totally ready and prepared ... feeling confident and self-assured ... relishing the challenge before me ...

2. **Review all the sights and sounds, thoughts, feelings and sensations of the game.**

   I look out to see the crowd waiting in anticipation as I walk out onto the court. I can hear them murmuring. I focus on my pre-match ritual and warm-up ... I'm so excited and ready to play. The game starts and I perform better than I ever have. I'm aware of my opponent but I focus only on hitting the ball. I think of nothing but playing tennis. I feel fit and full of energy.

3. **Now take yourself back to a peak moment of this event. Choose one that epitomises the experience for you ... bring up all the feelings and sensations ....Totally immerse yourself in this great performance of your life.**

   The match is at break point; I can win from here. I am on my toes ... I am taking deep breaths and just let my instincts take over ... here it comes! I make a clean hit with a big grunt and the ball slams down the line for a clean win! I hear the cheers and I grin at the crowd.

4. **Now recall the applause and celebrations afterwards. What are you thinking and saying to yourself? What are others saying and doing? Savour this peak performance of your life ...**

   The aftermath is like a dream ... Everyone is congratulating me. I've seen so many others win, but this time it is me accepting the trophy and making a speech. I am gracious and grateful, while also acknowledging my great opponent. I am so proud of myself and feel my win is well deserved as I have trained and prepared for this moment all my life.

5. **When you feel you have fully re-created the experience, give it a file name.**

   File it away in your mind to be recalled at any time you wish to feel this way again. Repeat your file name to yourself as you continue to engage in your imagery. For example: 'The trophy is mine'.

6. **Once you can fully re-experience this peak performance in your mind you can project it to a future event where you would like to feel and perform the same way again.**

   Next time I face such an opponent again, I can remember this match, and this helps me to believe in myself for the next time I meet up with this particular rival, or anyone else I have yet to beat. For example, I can picture playing and feeling this same way again at the next tournament ...

7. **When you're ready to close the file on this image, and to return back to the here and now, begin your ascent back up from one to ten.**

   Count back up the way you came ... taking your time back up to full consciousness ... remembering your breathing ... One ... Two ... Three ... Four ... Five ... Rising back up to the here and now ... Six ... Seven ... Eight ... Nine ... Ten — back to the here and now. Open your eyes gently before refocusing on the here and now.

Applying Mental Imagery for Creating Your Best Self

Quantum leaping to your best future self

Imagine yourself as your best self possible at some point in the future, after all has gone as well as you'd hoped. You are living your dream life, having accomplished your dream goals. You have fully capitalised on your talents, skills and knowledge ... fulfilled your potential ... Living your life as you ideally imagined it ... It is probably best to write it out first — to generate the picture as fully as possible. Then spend time imagining yourself as this person.

What is it like? What do you notice? How does it feel? And probably most importantly, what did it take to get here? By practising this image you will more likely act in accordance with it — in alignment with the values it represents. This will facilitate overriding negative images that prevent you from taking your best courses of action and achieving your best life.

Conversations with your best future self

Imagine this older and wiser version of yourself; one who is more accomplished; with your fondest hopes and dreams fulfilled. Wouldn't you love to have a conversation with him or her? Who better to support you and to count on than your inner best future self? While external supports are always wonderful to have, nothing builds confidence and security like being able to rely on your own internal resources. Making a direct connection with your BFS can short circuit any inner saboteur that may exist within. It can also fast track making the choices that are more closely aligned with your BF. Some questions you might want to ask are: What are their impressions looking back at you now? What are they proud of? Grateful for? Sympathetic about?

Do they have any advice for you? Any words of encouragement? Don't forget that they are also relying on your present self to be and do what leads to getting to enjoy being them. What do they think of your current options? Ask them to show you how life can be ... how to smooth the pathway to a better future ...

A variation on the above theme is to write a letter from the BFS. Try to focus on receiving the message without thinking too much about it. Just write what first comes to mind ... Remembering that intuitive impressions often don't come in words, but in more sensory impressions. Allow them to speak to you ...

Best future self imagery guide

1. Get yourself into a comfortable position ready to relax and tune in to the inner calm within yourself ...

2. Focus your attention on your breathing ... taking in slow deep abdominal breaths, and exhaling fully and steadily ... fully

expelling all the used oxygen in your lungs ... releasing and letting go with every out breath ... releasing and letting go of all cares and concerns with every out breath ... detoxing with every out breath ...

3. And once you have cleared and refreshed your lungs ... focus on breathing in purifying energy with every in breath ... oxygenating your body and mind ... washing away any residual tension in your body and mind ... clearing space for your mental imagery ...

4. Now take yourself to a certain point in your future — this could be one year, five years, to the end of your years in this lifetime, but decide this before you settle in to your imagery.

5. Imagine yourself at this future date, being and having accomplished all that you'd dreamed possible ... having accomplished your best at whatever endeavours ... feeling and being as you would wish to become by this stage of your life.

6. Imagine having overcome all obstacles in your path with great aplomb ...

7. Imagine the kind of attention you are now receiving from others ... in your professional life ... and personal life ... who are you biggest supporters? ... who is closest to you? ... imagine what it feels like to be surrounded by such support and love ... who believed in you most ... and likely new players in your life as well (and while you might not be able to imagine them specifically — you can imagine what it feels like to have them in your life).

8. Imagine having fully capitalised on your potential to this point ... and maybe even discovering new talents and endeavours to apply them to ... how your achievements have opened up new doors to great new opportunities and adventures ...

9. You are living your life as you ideally imagined ... and with ideal companions along the way ...

10. Spend time fully imagining yourself as this person ... how it feels ... emotionally ... energetically ... what you see ... and hear ... and any other sensations ...

11. What is it like being here? And probably more importantly, what did it take to get here? Fully explore looking back at how you got here ... the paths you took ... the choices you made ... the strengths and talents you developed and built upon ... the new skills and abilities you developed ... the changes you made ...

12. Once you've made a good connection with your BFS (your best future self and your new best friend), you might like to ask a few questions so that you can benefit from their wisdom. What are their impressions looking back at you now? What are they proud of? Grateful for? Sympathetic about? Do they have any advice for you? Any guidance for how to overcome any perceived challenges? Any words of encouragement? Words of wisdom? What do you need to let go of? And what do you need to build on? What are the small steps that you can enact today towards reaching this brilliant future self? Ask them to show you the best way forward ...

13. Ask your BFS to stay accessible always ... to nudge you when you need nudging ... to draw courage and strength when you need it ... to direct you to soothing and comfort and when you need it ... and to take time for self-care and rest when you need it ... promise to heed their guidance and advice ... and to rest easy in the knowledge that their newfound and well earned wisdom and confidence is yours ... be receptive to it, and willing and committed to move towards it and all that entails ... to move towards greater good fortune ... and flourishing wellbeing ...

14. Take a few deep breaths, and with every out breath/exhale, release whatever no longer serves you towards this path to your best future self ... and with the next few in-breaths embrace this new and better you with every inhale ... and conclude with thanking your BFS. Then move on with your day enacting whatever next steps are on the course of your best future self.

After completing this exercise, be on the lookout for any impressions that come to mind connected to your BFS ... they may arise as memories, but of the future (and not from the past) ... When you bid such information you are on the verge of tapping into your more intuitive self, your clairvoyant self ... you are drawing upon the reservoir of (potential) information that is yet to be fully explained though confirmed by science, and considered another dimension that is information. By bringing more conscious awareness to this process, and actively engaging with it, you can take better advantage of the opportunity to create a better future for yourself.

Vision Buddy Guidelines

This exercise is based on imagining goals being achieved. It is, therefore, recommended that you keep the goal setting guidelines in mind as you embark on your vision buddy practice (see *Chapter 4*). As with goals, daily practice will yield best results. This is gratifying in so many ways, as the simple practice generates an array of positive emotions conducive to wellbeing, health and performance in general.

The exercise can be conducted in pairs or groups. You get the benefit of increasing synergy with increasing numbers, but only up to a point — probably five people at a maximum (beyond five may get tedious as each person must wait their turn). The advantage of groups is that greater numbers takes the pressure off individuals to come up with what is called for.

Vision buddy steps

Remember to keep in mind the guidelines for practising mental imagery, which begins with relaxation and clearing our minds.

Step 1: Choose a vision buddy or group carefully from among people or community you know you can trust. While your closest friends or relatives might seem a best choice, it is sometimes more beneficial to practise with someone who is not so close, yet of like-minded values and commitment to the process. Groups may form around the practice, while not necessarily maintaining personal relationships outside the group.

Step 2: Each individual takes a turn at stating their goals that they would like support for. Generally, and especially after dream and long-term goals are established, it is best to focus on what is within immediate control; and immediately achievable by next meeting of the pair or group. It would be appropriate to ask questions to gain greater clarity and specificity to enable the buddy's conceptualisation of the goal (refer to goal setting guidelines in *Chapter 4*). But do resist the temptation to offer advice.

Step 3: Once the goal information has been articulated and received by everyone, each vision buddy will wait for a positive image to emerge in their mind relevant to the goal in question. It is important that you do not force this image to appear, but to engage in the spirit of allowing an image to form naturally.

If you draw a blank (or recognise mental interference), then it is best to pass, and not offer up what might be an inappropriate and useless image. While this might seem a bit disconcerting, it is the respectful thing to do. This requires an element of trust that while your best intentions may well be in play, the images are not. The focus is on quality and not quantity. Having said this, this is less likely to be an issue among the more skilled and practised among you. But the only way to get better is to keep trying.

Step 4: Each vision buddy expresses and the image that came to mind of the goal being achieved. A suggested sentence stem would be: 'I hold the image of you ... ' fill in the blank with specific images regarding goal success and how it would feel. The intention by the word 'hold' is that you will not only share the image, but also commit to holding that image for an agreed period of time. The idea is to not only express the image directly to your partner when gathered together, but to also take time throughout the near future to hold the image (to imagine for another — just as you might pray for another) until you next meet up again. The prescribed or agreed amount of time depends on what suits your partnership or group. This could be once/day or more over a period of a week or longer. Obviously this requires a strong level of commitment and trust. The synergist impact well fuels the effort though.

Step 5: Seek feedback for how well the image shared by your partner/s resonated. And return the favour, until everyone's goal has been attended to.

The emphasis is on *allowing* an impression to take shape as this engages your more intuitive mind, and you will therefore be likely to come up with more appropriate image that will resonate with your partner (see the section on intuition in *Chapter 9*). Sometimes these images will make no sense to you, but it is not up to you to decide, but simply to express. The image or information you provide may be more on target than you realise, and you may be pleasantly surprised! This is where the process can seem quite magical.

Rewriting History

1. Get yourself into a comfortable position ready to relax and tune in to the inner calm within yourself ...

2. Focus your attention on your breathing ... taking in slow deep abdominal breaths, and exhaling fully and steadily ... fully expelling all the used oxygen in your lungs ... releasing and letting go with every out breath ... releasing and letting go of all cares and concerns with every out breath ... detoxing with every out breath ...

3. And once you have cleared and refreshed your lungs ... focus on breathing in purifying energy with every in-breath ... oxygenating your body and mind ... washing away any residual tension in your body and mind ... clearing space for your mental imagery ...

4. You might like to go to that special place from the peak experience recall imagery where you feel at your very best — most at peace, alive, confident, loving and beloved ... most calm and focused ... with each breath bring yourself to this deep well of strength within yourself ... breathing slowly and deeply ... and exhaling fully and steadily ...

5. And when you are ready, take yourself back to the time and place where you experienced your most recent challenge ... when you might not have reacted as you'd wish ... the one that you'd like to do over ... take this opportunity to recreate the images of that time and place ... entering it with a state of calm and positive focus ... reconnect with the moment just prior to the event ... remembering your breathing as you do so ... and then picture

it unfolding better this time ... imagine yourself responding better ... with greater equanimity and positive focus ... expressing yourself as you'd prefer ... acting and responding as you'd prefer ... making better choices ... Run through your preferred scenario and your more positive response ... taking your time as you do so ... you might need to slow it down, or press 'PAUSE', to feel more in control ... take a few breaths and try again ... and once you've become comfortable with your better response ... imagine it again in real time ... Replay the scene in real time — unfolding as you would prefer ... imagine the satisfaction of meeting the challenge well and the flow-on benefits ... and how good that feels? You might want to even congratulate yourself? Or imagine someone congratulating you?

6. When you have completed replaying this scene ... think of an upcoming situation where you might likely encounter such an opportunity again ... Flash forward to such a scenario, and practice responding well again ... allowing your best self to shine ... Imagine how good it feels knowing you can meet this challenge well ... and to greater benefit for all concerned ... and allow yourself an inner smile as you connect to your best self in action.

7. When you have completed running these images through your mind thank yourself for engaging in such positive programming ... and then take your time coming back to the here and now. With every breath commit yourself to maintain this connection with your best self ... to feel and do better ... as you bring yourself back to the here and now.

8. Breathing slowly and deeply bring yourself back to the here and now, and open your eyes and reflect on this experience.

Inner Healing Guided Imagery Script

Before beginning your inner healing imagery take a moment to get into a comfortable position and relax ... close your eyes and take a few slow deep abdominal breaths ... inhaling slowly and deeply ...

exhaling fully and steadily — completely emptying out your lungs before each fresh new breath you take … Focus your attention on you breathing throughout this exercise … slowly and deeply … as you focus on your breathing feel your whole body relaxing … With every breath, allowing yourself to become more and more relaxed …

Inhaling slowly and deeply … exhaling fully and steadily … As you exhale, imagine any tension, pain or discomfort flowing out of your body … releasing and letting go with every out breath …And breathing in soothing and healing oxygen with every in-breath … Inhaling slowly and deeply … exhaling fully and steadily … and with each breath — becoming more and more relaxed … Just continue with your breathing for a moment … relaxing your body and mind …. Inhaling slowly and deeply … exhaling fully and steadily … releasing and letting go … Becoming more and more relaxed …..

When you find yourself quiet and fully relaxed — take a moment to enjoy it … Sense the gentle warmth and wellbeing all through your body … If any extraneous thoughts try to interfere simply allow them to pass through and out of you … disregard them and go back to your breathing … inhaling slowly and deeply … exhaling fully and steadily … releasing and letting go with every out breath … and bringing in healing and revitalising oxygen with every in-breath …

Your body has healing power that is already in progress … You can enhance that power by engaging your mind to mobilise your body's healing resources to the fullest … Your determination, will and imagination have a tremendous influence on your capacity to direct and control your own healing process. By imagining the healing process occurring within your body you are using your mind to program your body to heal more effectively … through your images you are sending messages to your body of how you want it to be … and your body responds accordingly … Your body responds to the directives of your mind.

Now, as you continue to relax … inhaling slowly and deeply … exhaling fully and steadily … Imagine this feeling of relaxation and healing energy flowing through your body and to the area you are focused on healing and rehabilitating … washing away any remaining tension and injury … and providing nourishing healing oxygen to every fibre and cell of that area … Feel the blood flow increasing deep within this part of your body providing healing injury … and flushing away any broken down tissues … healing and repairing itself …

Feel the entire area encircled with a warm soothing flow of healing nourishment … see it being enveloped by white light … Now with your mind, go inside your body and imagine the healing and repair work happening smoothly and efficiently … See if healing and getting stronger … See your body healing, mending, and strengthening … mending and strengthening … See this part of your body exactly as you want it to be … becoming healthy and strong … healthy and strong again … Freely use your imagination as you direct your body's healing ... good … Imagine your entire body feeling and functioning efficiently and harmoniously again … Really try to feel and experience these images … imagine your whole body healthy and strong again … Fully recovered … and able to take on any demands that you place on it … It is flexible and it is strong …

Your body is health, strong, and flexible … Ready for any activity you want … You are free and ready to be fully active again … Imagine being able to do all the things you plan to do … all the things you dream of accomplishing and experiencing … Your body is cooperative and ready to support your every move … You are ready to be the best you can be … Knowing you can rely on your body to perform as you direct it … See and feel yourself performing at your best again … moving freely and without hesitation … doing what you most love to do … Feel all the sensations of your movements .. moving freely and confidently … Feeling strong and in control … Freely use your imagination … allow yourself to be fully confident and in control … and enjoying yourself …..

Great! With each moment of every day you are getting better and better …. Stronger and stronger … more and more flexible … You are healing quickly and efficiently … restoring all of your strength, power and mobility … Just continue with your imagery for as long as you like, and when you are finished, remember to take a few seconds to slowly come back to the here and now, and give yourself a mental pat on the back for fully utilising your mind body resources mobilising greater recovery and wellbeing.

And thank your body as well for cooperating with your direction.

And be well.

Personal Best Imagery Guide

The following is a guided imagery exercise for being your personal best.

Before beginning, take a moment to get comfortable and relax ... and then close your eyes and take a few slow, deep abdominal breaths ... inhaling slowly and deeply ... and exhaling fully and steadily ... completely emptying out your lungs before each fresh new breath you take ... Focus your attention on your breathing throughout this entire exercise ... slowly and deeply ... as you focus on your breathing, feel your whole body relaxing ... with every breath, allowing yourself to become more and more relaxed ... inhaling slowly and deeply ... exhaling fully and steadily ... For the next few cleansing breaths as you exhale, imagine any tension or tightness easily flowing out of your body ... releasing and letting go with every out breath ..... and then for next few breaths focus on breathing in soothing and healing oxygen with every in-breath ... and receiving purifying energy with every in-breath ...

Inhaling slowly and deeply ... exhaling fully and steadily ... and with each breath, becoming more and more relaxed ... just continue with your breathing for a moment .. relaxing your body and mind ... inhaling slowly and deeply ... exhaling fully and steadily ... releasing and letting go ... becoming more and more relaxed ...

When you find yourself quiet and fully relaxed, take a moment to enjoy it ... sense the gentle warmth and feeling of well-being all through your body ... if any extraneous thoughts interfere, simply allow them to pass through and out of you ... disregard them and go back to your breathing, inhaling slowly and deeply, exhaling fully and steadily ...

Letting go and releasing with every out breath ... purifying and revitalising with every in-breath ...

Relaxation sets your mind free ... so your imagination may soar ... (remembering that you will never know how far you may soar until you are able to let go and spread your wings ...)

You are letting go of all cares and concerns ... freeing your mind, body and soul of all negativity and tension ... and allowing only positive, glowing feelings to flow ... freeing your imagination (to soar) ... in the spirit of adventure and curiosity ... to go where you've never been before, and would dearly love to go ...

Begin with imagining your fondest hopes and dreams fulfilled ... having achieved your full potential — your all time best future self possible ...

Imagine arriving at your highest destination imaginable ... having achieved your greatest performance possible ... reaching your greatest triumph in your event or pursuit ... finally — all of your efforts and determination are bearing fruit ... and how sweet that is ... immerse yourself in all the possibilities of such a moment ... imagine the emotions ... the jubilation and exhilaration of putting it all together for this triumph ... experience the joy and intense satisfaction ... (and perhaps even the tears?)

Imagine receiving your rewards ... your awards/medal/trophy/bonus/ or other relevant accolades ...

Imagine the congratulations associated with this success or achievement ... from your strongest supporters, coaches, mentors, colleagues and teammates, friends and family ... all those who believed in you even when you had your doubts ... Imagine how grateful you are for all of their support on this journey ... as well as how great it feels to receive their congratulations and to celebrate with you ... How does it feel? Take a moment to congratulate yourself as well ... for having the discipline, perseverance, and determination to go for it! To go after your dreams ... This takes courage and tenacity ... It takes HEART ... you know you have an abundance of courage deep within you from which to draw at any time ... (it takes listening to your heart and soul).

Having fully connected with the image of your ultimate success and fulfilment, see yourself taking all the steps necessary to reach your dream ...

This can mean all the little successes along the way ... putting your energy and strategies in motion ... enjoying the process of working towards a deeply meaningful goal ... remembering that success is a journey and not a destination ... Knowing that success begins the moment you begin moving towards a worthwhile goal ... appreciate the value of having this mission that means so much to you ...

Now think of an upcoming test, event or competition — your next opportunity to achieve the next step on the journey towards your dream goal ... clearly imagine time and place ... the venue and relevant aspects of the environment ... feeling at your best ... fully prepared and ready to be and do your best ... you are performing at your very best ... being highly successful ... executing according to plan ... feeling happy with your experience and result ...

It often helps to think back to a previous best performance where you have successfully met your challenge ... fully recall a recent success ... soak up the feelings and experiences associated with that event ... and flash forward to the upcoming event ... bring those same positive feelings and sense of flow to your upcoming performance or opportunity ... imagine yourself feeling and performing the same way again ... feeling confident and self-assured ... calm and focused ... in great spirits ready for anything ...

Take a moment now, to review all of your strengths in your game, business or activity ... mentally, emotionally, energetically, physically, technically, experience, knowledge, etc. ...

Review what you most enjoy about your chosen endeavour ... what you are best at ... your favourite moves and manoeuvres ... favourite elements of the pursuit before you ... those aspects of your event that you find most fun and satisfying to execute ... that bring you the greatest amount of gratification and fulfilment ...

Feeling strong ... confident ... highly effective and efficient ... moving fluidly or speaking fluently ... total mind/body synchronicity ... doing what you most love to do ... feeling fully ALIVE ... being in the *FLOW* ...

Now take these feelings into your review of all the key elements or critical stages/aspects of your game or pursuit, beginning with your favourite elements ... and gradually covering all elements important to a successful performance ... being open and receptive to what is most relevant, and disregarding the rest ... being fully aware of your options and opportunities ... and ready to make great decisions ... making choices aligned with your best interests ...

Be sure to include even those elements you least enjoy ... bring the good feelings from your favourite elements and infuse them into the less favourite ... to the aspects that you find challenging and keen to overcome ... imagine you are getter better and better at them ...

Practice coping with any distractions and possible setback/s or obstacle/s that may appear in your path ... being able to recover smoothly and efficiently from anything thrown at you ... being able to respond quickly and refocus back into the present moment, and the task at hand ... back to your optimal focus and mood ... Run through the possibilities now, and see yourself successfully and effortlessly overcoming and staying on track ... recognise that these are merely distractions ... they do not have to affect your performance ... you choose to stay on track with your optimal focus ... picture any distraction as a cue to take a couple of deep breaths and return to a positive focus and feeling ... smiling inside as you do so ...

There might be occasions when something unexpected pops up that will require adjusting to ... you can be ready for this too ... imagine yourself taking stock quickly ... reading the situation well and adjusting accordingly ... Imagine doing so with great agility and ease ...

Now, string it all together in a reality sequence ... imagine yourself in a run-through of the entire event from before the start to following a great finish or conclusion ... string it together as it may ideally unfold ... See yourself feeling ready and looking forward to your event ... full of positive anticipation ... feeling well prepared, and ready for anything ... excited for the opportunity, yet calm and focused ... feeling energised and full of enthusiasm ... Imagine yourself off to a great start ... exactly as you wish letting go into the flow ... from moment to moment ... maintaining your positivity and focus ... everything is coming together beautifully and naturally ... you are fluid and strong ... responding well ... feeling free and fully in control ... sharp and focused ... totally immersed in your event ...

Throw in a few possible distractions and picture yourself being completely unaffected by them and recovering instantly ... continuing in ideal fashion ... sticking with your plan ... making best choices ... in the zone ... and thoroughly enjoying yourself ... being in the flow ... fully engaged in what you are doing ... totally connected to the task at hand ... to your performance ... in perfect harmony with the environment ... interacting positively with everyone ... recognising and seising every opportunity (feeling lucky?) and responding optimally to each and every challenge ... totally focused in the moment ... in the here and now ... nothing else matters ... only you and fulfilling your objectives ...

Continue with this imagery for a moment ...

Great!

And now picture a great finish! ... maintaining full focus and intensity as the task requires ... Finishing with a flourish ... feeling happy with having done your best ... fully capitalised on your opportunity ... having given your best chance at achieving your heart's desire ... imagine the aftermath of having fully achieved what you set out to achieve ... experience the satisfaction and joys ... as well as the congratulations and/or positive response from your team, colleagues, supporters, or audience ...

Give yourself a mental pat on the back for fully mobilising your inner resources towards fulfilling your highest potential ...

Enjoy the feelings associated with putting it all together and experiencing the satisfaction and rewards of all your efforts ...

And finally, picture the very next step on your path leading to your desired goal/s ... Remember that your success depends on what you accomplish TODAY ... you do not need to do it all today, but it begins today ... Imagine putting in the time and effort that is immediately before you, and feeling great about it.

Remember that the road to fulfilling your dreams begins with commitment from within and is achieved just one step at a time ... just one foot in front of the other ... one day at a time ...

Use your vision of all-time success, of your dreams being fully realised to inspire and motivate you ... to foster belief in yourself ... and then just turn your focus to the present and what can be achieved and enjoyed TODAY ... Right here and right now ...

And may the power of your imagination be with you! Could we insert a heading:

Guided Imagery Recordings

The following guided imagery recordings from Imagine are available via www.bigskypublishing.com.au

Peak Experience Recall

Peak Performance Recall

Best Future Self

Rewriting History

Inner Healing

Personal Best

Endnotes

1. aka *creative visualisation* — although mental imagery involves multisensory and more visceral processes.

2. This formed the basis for my June 2013 column in *Women's Health and Fitness* magazine.

3. Merton, RK (1968), *Social Theory and Social Structure*, New York: Free Press.

4. Kosslyn, SM,, Thompson, W. L, & Ganis, G, (2006), *The case for mental imagery*. New York: Oxford University Press.

5. See http://www.dosseydossey.com/larry/lecture.html#spiritachieve

6. De Botton, A (2012), *Religion for Atheists,* New York: Penguin.

7. Page 134 in: Vaillant, G (2008), *Spiritual Evolution: A Scientific Defense of Faith,* New York: Broadway Books.

8. Lyubomirsky, S, & Layous, K (2013), 'How do simple positive activities increase well-being?', in *Current Directions in Psychological Science*, 22(1), 47-62.

9. Seligman, M, & Csikszentmihaly, M (2000), 'Positive Psychology: An Introduction', American Psychologist, 55, 5-14.

10. Seligman, M (2002), *Authentic Happiness: Using the New Positive Psychology to Realize Your Potential for Lasting Fulfillment,* New York: Random House.

11. Seligman, M (2011), *Flourish: A Visionary New Understanding of Happiness and Well-being,* New York: Free Press.

12. Page 9 in: Jackson, S & Csikszentmihalyi, M (1999*), Flow in Sports: The keys to optimal experiences and performances,* Champaign, IL: Human Kinetics.

13. Page 3 in: Csikszentmihalyi, M (1990), *Flow: Psychology of Optimal Experience,* New York: Harper Perennial.

14. Peterson, C, & Seligman, M (2004), *Character Strengths and Virtues: A Handbook and Classification.* New York: Oxford University Press.

15. Grant, A, & Leigh, A (2010), *Eight Steps to Happiness: The science of getting happy and how it can work for you.* Melbourne, VIC: Victory Books.

16. Seligman, M (2011), *Flourish: A Visionary New Understanding of Happiness and Well-being,* New York: Free Press.

17. Kabat-Zinn, J (1990), *Full Catastrophe Living,* New York: Bantam Dell.

18. Langer, E (2009), *Counter Clockwise: Mindful Health and the Power of Possibility,* New York: Ballantine Books.

19. Hanson, R, & Mendius, R (2009), *Buddha's Brain: The Practical Neuroscience of Happiness, Love, and Wisdom,* New York: New Harbinger Publications.

20. Emmons, R (2013), *Gratitude Works!: A 21-Day Program for Creating Emotional Prosperity,* New York: Jossey-Bass.
    Emmons, R (2007), *Thanks! How the new science of gratitude can make you happier,* New York: Houghton Mifflin Company.

Endnotes

21. Seligman, M (2011), *Flourish: A Visionary New Understanding of Happiness and Well-being,* New York: Free Press.

22. Seligman, M (2011), *Flourish: A Visionary New Understanding of Happiness and Well-being,* New York: Free Press.

23. Page 127 in: Lyubomirsky, S (2007), *The How of Happiness: A new approach to getting the life you want,* New York: Penguin.

24. Grant, A. M., & Dutton, J. E. (2012), 'Beneficiary or benefactor: The effects of reflecting about receiving versus giving on prosocial behavior'. *Psychological Science,* 23, 1033-1039.

25. Grant, A. M. 2013. Give and Take: *A Revolutionary Approach to Success.* New York: Viking Press.

26. Frederickson, B.L., Cohn, M.A., Coffey, K.A, & Pek, J. (2008). Open Hearts Build Lives: Positive Emotions, Induced Through Loving-Kindness Meditation, Build Consequential Personal Resources. Journal of Personality and Social Psychology, 95(5), 1045-1062.

27. Lopez, S. (2013), *Making Hope Happen: Create the future you want for yourself and others,* New York: Atria Books.

28. Frederickson, B (2009), *Positivity,* New York: Crown Publishers.

29. See www.positivityratio.com which also includes a link to the PEP lab.

30. Bandura, A (1997), *Self-Efficacy: The Exercise of Control,* New York: WH Freeman.

31. Morris, T, Spittle, M & Watt, A (2005), *Imagery in Sport.* Champaign, IL: Human Kinetics.

32. Page 117 in: Vaillant, G (2008), *Spiritual Evolution: A Scientific Defense of Faith,* New York: Broadway Books.

33. Green, E., & Green, A. (1982). *Beyond Biofeedback.* New York: Delacorte Press.

34. From Scientific American interview with Jonah Lehrer, 1 July 2008.

35. Page 41 in: Kosslyn, SM, & Moulton, (2009), 'Mental Imagery and Implicit Memory', in KD Markman, WMP Klein, & J Suhr (Eds), *Handbook of Imagination and Mental Stimulation.* London, UK: Psychology Press of Taylor & Francis.

36. Ganis, G, Thompson, W, Kosslyn, SM (2004), 'Brain areas underlying visual mental imagery and visual perception: an fMRI'. *Cognitive Brain Research,* 20, 226–241.

37. Kosslyn, SM, & Moulton, (2009). 'Mental Imagery and Implicit Memory'. In KD Markman, WMP Klein, & J Suhr (Eds), *Handbook of Imagination and Mental Stimulation.* London, UK: Psychology Press of Taylor & Francis.

38. Page 42 in: Kosslyn, SM, & Moulton, (2009). 'Mental Imagery and Implicit Memory'. In KD Markman, WMP Klein, & J Suhr (Eds), *Handbook of Imagination and Mental Stimulation.* London, UK: Psychology Press of Taylor & Francis.

39. For more on quantum physics and evolution of consciousness, see Thomas Campbell's book My big TOE. Campbell, T (2007), *My Big TOE — the complete trilogy.* Huntsville, Alabama: Lightning Strikes Books.

40. 'Imagery has more powerful emotion consequences then does the verbal representation of equivalent events, and also show that this applies to both negative and positive emotions.' Page 354, in: Holmes, EA, & Mathews, A (2010), 'Mental imagery in emotion and emotional disorders'. *Clinical Psychology Review,* 30, 349–362.

41. RE: I ♥NY -- Lehrer explains how the word was used, but felt inadequate in the designer Glaser's view … until he finally came upon using the symbol instead – which is no doubt far more effective than the words ever would have been. Lehrer, J (2012), *Imagine: How creativity works*, New York: Houghton Mifflin Harcourt.

42. Holmes, EA, & Mathews, A (2010), 'Mental imagery in emotion and emotional disorders'. *Clinical Psychology Review*, 30, 349–362.

43. Remembering the past and imagining the future are parallel processes that are mediated by a core brain system. Therefore, when imagining a future experience, the brain will draw on existing repertoire that will also pick up associated emotional remnants along the way, as they are inextricably linked. All this is then projected to a future scenario. Neuroimaging studies comparing remembering and imagining personal events have demonstrated that both activate same brain regions (pre frontal, medial temporal, and other areas such as in visual cortex). The only difference that occurs is imagining future events tends to trigger greater earlier activation of frontal areas (so-called executive functions of the brain) due to the greater need for creating images (rather than simply recall), i.e. top-down control, From: Holmes, EA, & Mathews, A (2010), 'Mental imagery in emotion and emotional disorders'. *Clinical Psychology Review*, 30, 349–362.

44. According to Holmes and Mathews, such dissociative tendencies regarding 'habitual avoidance of emotional expression' (p. 352) works temporarily to provide relief, but ultimately hinders recovery (i.e. letting go of negative emotional associations with the memory and image). This explains how what you avoid (albeit unconsciously) controls you. From: Holmes, EA, & Mathews, A (2010), 'Mental imagery in emotion and emotional disorders'. *Clinical Psychology Review*, 30, 349–362.

45. Page 358 in: Holmes, EA, & Mathews, A (2010), 'Mental imagery in emotion and emotional disorders'. *Clinical Psychology Review*, 30, 349–362.

46. Page 359 in: Holmes, EA, & Mathews, A (2010), 'Mental imagery in emotion and emotional disorders'. *Clinical Psychology Review*, 30, 349–362.

47. When you sign up for perfect you are signing up for perpetual defeat. Leading writers on perfectionism refer to adjusting focus to satisficing versus maximising… for more about overcoming the tyranny of perfectionism see: Brown, B (2010), *The Gifts of Imperfection: Let Go of Who You Think You're Supposed to Be and Embrace Who You Are,* New York: Hazelden. Shahar, T (2009), *The Pursuit of Perfect: How to Stop Chasing Perfection and Start Living a Richer, Happier Life.* New York: McGraw-Hill.

48. Murphy, M. (2010). *HARD Goals: The secret to getting from where you are to where you want to be.* New York: McGraw-Hill.

49. For an excellent resource for adapting and applying mental imagery for kids see Terry Orlick's work at zoneofexcellence.ca.

50. Holmes and Mathews explain the 'availability heuristic' -- with respect to making choices: 'That is, our intuitive judgements of probability of an event outcome are based in part on the ease of accessing instances consistent with that outcome (e.g. voting research by Libby, et al 2007)' (p. 355). In addition, we are quicker to come up with images of an event that is has greater subjective probability and congruence (i.e. more likely from our perspective and/or experience). 'Dysphoria is associated with a deficit in generating positive imagery of the future, despite an intact ability to experience negative

prospective imagery [italicised emphasis mine]. … [This may then] compromise the ability of people with depression to act on positive goals. From page p. 355 in Holmes, EA, & Mathews, A (2010), 'Mental imagery in emotion and emotional disorders'. *Clinical Psychology Review*, 30, 349–362.). Therefore, cases of anxiety, depression, dysphoria reflect a positive image deficit – and highlights the need to up the ratio of positive images and experiences (beyond 3:1 positivity ratio).

51. Tolle, E (1999), *Power of Now: A guide to spiritual enlightenment,* New World Library.

52. Kabat-Zinn, J (1990), *Full Catastrophe Living,* New York: Bantam Dell.

53. See www.positivityration.com or www.positivityresonance.com for more information.

54. Kabat-Zinn, J (1990), *Full Catastrophe Living,* New York: Bantam Dell.

55. Hanson, R, & Mendius, R (2009), *Buddha's Brain: The Practical Neuroscience of Happiness, Love, and Wisdom.* New York: New Harbinger Publications.

56. For more information see: Karageorghis, C.I., & Terry, P.C. (2010), 'The Power of Sound' [Chapter 8], in *Inside Sport Psychology* (pp. 197-221), Champaign, IL: Human Kinetics.

57. Third person images are recommended only for diffusing (negative) emotions – as has effect of distancing oneself from aversive experience/s (aka dissociation). This is a dissociative strategy that trauma victims report frequently adopting naturally, but which ultimately prolongs the impact. From: Holmes, EA, & Mathews, A (2010), 'Mental imagery in emotion and emotional disorders'. *Clinical Psychology Review*, 30, 349–362.

58. Page 41 in: Kosslyn, SM, & Moulton, (2009), 'Mental Imagery and Implicit Memory', in KD Markman, WMP Klein, & J Suhr (Eds), *Handbook of Imagination and Mental Stimulation.* London, UK: Psychology Press of Taylor & Francis.

59. Page 118 in: Vaillant, G (2008), *Spiritual Evolution: A Scientific Defense of Faith,* New York: Broadway Books.

60. Williamson, M (1992), *A Return to Love: Reflections on the Principles of a Course in Miracles,* New York: Harper Collins Publishers.

61. Gawain, S (2002, 1995, 1978), *Creative Visualization: Use the power of your imagination to create what you want in your life,* Novato, CA: New World Library.

62. While the term 'vision buddy' refers to the visual modality, it is not intended to apply exclusively to visual images. It would be more accurate to use the term 'mental imagery buddy' or just 'imagery buddy'. 'Vision buddy' seems to have a better ring to it.

63. Dossey, L (1995), *Healing Words: The Power of Prayer and the Practice of Medicine,* New York: Harper One.

64. Hitchens, C (2007), *God is not Great: How Religion Poisons Everything,* Twelve / Warner Books.

65. Dawkins, R (2006), *The God Delusion,* Boston: Houghton Mifflin.

66. De Botton, A (2012), *Religion for Atheists,* New York: Penguin.

67. For more information see: Lopez, S. (2013), *Making Hope Happen: Create the future you want for yourself and others,* New York: Atria Books.

68. The term crisitunity was coined by Homer Simpson (from The Simpsons cartoon television program) upon learning of the dual meaning of the word crisis in Chinese = danger and opportunity – highlighting the potential opportunity to be discovered in face of crisis.

69. Vaillant, G (2008), *Spiritual Evolution: A Scientific Defense of Faith,* New York: Broadway Books.

70. See also Chapter 2, which discusses the concept and experience of flow within the positive psychology context/framework, based primarily on the work of Csikszentmihalyi. See: Csikszentmihalyi, M (1990), *Flow: Psychology of Optimal Experience,* New York: Harper Perennial.

71. See http://www.centerforpos.org/the-center/teaching-and-practice-materials/teaching-tools/reflected-best-self-exercise/

72. For research about the wellbeing benefits of imagining your best future self the research, see: Meevissen, Y, Peters, M, & Alberts, H (2011), 'Become more optimistic by imagining best possible self: Effects of a two week intervention', *Journal of Behaviour Therapy and Experimental Psychiatry,* 42, 371–378; Pictet, A, Coughtrey, AE, Mathews, A, & Holmes, EA (2011), 'Fishing for happiness: The effects of generating positive imagery on mood and behaviour', *Behaviour Research and Therapy,* 49, 885–891; Sheldon, K, Lyubomirsky, S (2006), 'How to increase and sustain positive emotion: The effects of expressing gratitude and visualising best possible selves', *Journal of Positive Psychology,* 1, 73–82.

73. For more about premonitions see: Dossey, L (2009), *The power of premonitions: How knowing the future can shape our lives.* New York: Dutton.

74. Lipton, B (2008), *The Biology of Belief: Unleashing the Power of Consciousness, Matter, & Miracles,* New York: Hay House.

75. Recommended viewing: Brene Brown (University of Houston) and her hit presentation on TED – among top 20 most watched on TED.

76. Goleman, D (2005), *Emotional Intelligence: Why it can matter more than IQ,* New York: Bantam Books.

77. Mindfulness practice is recommended as a foundational skill to help shift negative/maladaptive and intrusive images and tendencies.

78. Morris, T., Spittle, M. & Watt, A. (2005*). Imagery in Sport.* Champaign, IL: Human Kinetics.

79. Ievleva, L & Terry, PC (2008), 'Applying sport psychology to business'. *International Coaching Psychology Review,* 3(1), 6–16.

80. Orlick, T (2005), The Wheel of Excellence. http://www.zoneofexcellenceca/free/wheeLhtml Retrieved 30 March 2013.

81. For more about the benefits of 'micromoments of love'; or 'positivity resonance' See: Frederickson, B (2013), *Love 2.0: How our supreme emotion affects everything we feel, think, do, and become,* New York: Penguin.

82. For more information go to www.self-compassion.org or www.positivityresonance.com

83. Page 356 in: Holmes, EA, & Mathews, A (2010), 'Mental imagery in emotion and emotional disorders'. *Clinical Psychology Review,* 30, 349–362.

84. Kahneman, D (2011), *Thinking, Fast and Slow,* New York: Farrar, Straus and Giroux.

85. Kahneman, D (2011), *Thinking, Fast and Slow,* New York: Farrar, Straus and Giroux.

86. Lehrer, J (2012), *Imagine: How creativity works,* New York: Houghton Mifflin Harcourt.

87. Ievleva, L (2012), *Inner Spa: Optimising health and wellbeing Supplement.* Sydney: Soul in Motion.

88. Botterill, C, Flint, F, & Ievleva, L (1996), 'Psychology of the injured athlete', in Zachezewski, Magee, & Quillen (EdS), *Athletic Injuries and Rehabilitation* (pp. 791–805), Sydney, NSW: W.B. Saunders

89. Highly recommended books on mental imagery and health and healing: Achterberg, J (1985), *Imagery in Healing: Shamanism and Modern Medicine*, Boston: Shambhala Publications; Epstein, G (1989), *Healing Visualizations*. New York: Bantam Books; Rossman, ML (2000), *Guided Imagery for Self-Healing*, Tiburon, CA: HJ Kramer and New World Library; Sheikh, AA (Ed) (2002), *Handbook of Therapeutic Imagery Techniques*, Amityville, NY: Baywood Publishing Company; Sheikh, AA. (2003), *Healing Images: The Role of Imagination in Health*, Amityville, NY: Baywood Publishing Company.

90. Ievleva, L (Speaker), Stillwell, L (Composer/Musician) (2012), 'Inner Healing', In *Inner Spa: Optimising health and wellbeing guided imagery*. Sydney: Soul in Motion.

91. Pages 38-39 in: Seligman, M (2011), *Flourish: A Visionary New Understanding of Happiness and Well-being*, New York: Free Press.

92. PERMA model of wellbeing includes the following source elements: P= Positive emotions and pleasure; E=Engagement (aka Flow); R=relationships; M=Meaning & purpose; A=accomplishment. Described in detail in Seligman's (2011) book: Flourish. Excerpt available here: http://www.authentichappiness.sas.upenn.edu/newsletter.aspx?id=1533 Google PERMA and Seligman to find video links.

93. Adapted from: Grant, A., & Leigh, A. (2010). *Eight Steps to Happiness: The science of getting happy and how it can work for you*. Melbourne: Victory Books.

94. Adapted from: Cayoun, B. A. (2011). *Mindfulness-integrated CBT: Principles and practice*. Chichester, UK: Wiley-Blackwell. Frederickson, B. (2009). *Positivity*. New York: Crown Publishers.

95. Ievleva, L. (Script/Speaker), & Stillwell, L. (Composer/Musician). (1997). *Inner Sports: Mental Skills for Peak Performance*. (Double Cassette Recordings). Champaign, IL: Human Kinetics. This is the script for the recorded version that is available on the Inner Spa CD, as well as MP3 track on Amazon.

96. Ievleva, L. (2011). Inner Spa – *Optimising Health and Wellbeing*: Supplement. (Compact Disc/MP3 recording). Sydney, NSW: Soul in Motion. Available on www.amazon.com.au

97. Orlick, T. (2011). *Positive Living Skills*. Renfrew, ON: General Store Publishing House.

IMAGINE

About the Author

Dr Lydia Ievleva is a psychologist with over 25 years of experience in practice and teaching. She is a former president of the APS College of Sport and Exercise Psychologists, and has extensive experience working with clients seeking health, wellbeing, relationship, performance and professional goals, including Olympic and professional athletes, dancers, musicians, artists, writers, corporate clients, and others seeking to fulfil their potential.

Lydia received her training in Canada and the U.S., and holds the following qualifications: BA Hons Psychology, Carleton University; MSc Sport Psychology, University of Ottawa; PhD Counseling Psychology, specialising in health and sport, Florida State University. Lydia currently resides and practices on Sydney's Northern Beaches.

Lydia has previously taught at the University of Technology, Sydney, University of New South Wales, University of Western Sydney, and Florida State University. She is currently coordinator for the Happiness and Positive Psychology course within the Masters of Wellness program at RMIT University; and also Introduction to Happiness and Positive Psychology, a popular elective undergraduate course.

Lydia has been leading the charge for incorporating the application of mental imagery in the newly burgeoning area of Positive Psychology and Coaching, drawing from her extensive experience in Health, Sport and Performance Psychology.